Meeting Expectations in Management Education

Elizabeth Christopher
Editor

Meeting Expectations in Management Education

Social and Environmental Pressures on Managerial Behaviour

palgrave
macmillan

Editor
Elizabeth Christopher
Independent Scholar
Avoca Beach, NSW, Australia

ISBN 978-3-319-76411-5   ISBN 978-3-319-76412-2   (eBook)
https://doi.org/10.1007/978-3-319-76412-2

Library of Congress Control Number: 2018941207

© The Editor(s) (if applicable) and The Author(s), under exclusive licence to Springer International Publishing AG, part of Springer Nature 2018
This work is subject to copyright. All rights are solely and exclusively licensed by the Publisher, whether the whole or part of the material is concerned, specifically the rights of translation, reprinting, reuse of illustrations, recitation, broadcasting, reproduction on microfilms or in any other physical way, and transmission or information storage and retrieval, electronic adaptation, computer software, or by similar or dissimilar methodology now known or hereafter developed.
The use of general descriptive names, registered names, trademarks, service marks, etc. in this publication does not imply, even in the absence of a specific statement, that such names are exempt from the relevant protective laws and regulations and therefore free for general use.
The publisher, the authors, and the editors are safe to assume that the advice and information in this book are believed to be true and accurate at the date of publication. Neither the publisher nor the authors or the editors give a warranty, express or implied, with respect to the material contained herein or for any errors or omissions that may have been made. The publisher remains neutral with regard to jurisdictional claims in published maps and institutional affiliations.

Printed on acid-free paper

This Palgrave Macmillan imprint is published by the registered company Springer International Publishing AG part of Springer Nature.
The registered company address is: Gewerbestrasse 11, 6330 Cham, Switzerland

Foreword

Introducing the Book

It is intended for faculty members, teachers, and designers of university and college curricula to stimulate creative thinking on how to include concepts and practices of social responsibility in management education.

The book is a collection of writings by teaching practitioners from a wide range of national and social backgrounds on the general theme of social responsibility in management education curricula. It is unique in its eclectic range of perspectives on the responsibilities of management educators to include the teaching of ethical, social, and environmental management behaviour. Its content should satisfy the needs of all readers who seek an overview of the historical background and contemporary picture of management education principles in contexts of cultural diversity.

Each chapter is written by an expert in the given field and the overall content is international. It ranges far beyond the relatively narrow confines of traditional western-style business management training to link management to wider social themes. Contributors include academics from Australia, Canada, Europe, Singapore, South Africa, India, the UK, and the USA. One writer cannot be expert in all aspects of any topic, hence this wide range to which many talents have contributed. Between them, the writers convey immediacy, information, interest, and humour, and emphasis is on discussion rather than lecture and on finding practical applications of theoretical principles.

Principles of Responsible Management Education (PRME)

The Principles for Responsible Management Education (PRME) is a United Nations-supported initiative, founded in 2007, as a platform to raise the profile of sustainability in schools around the world and to equip today's business students with the understanding and ability to deliver change tomorrow (PRME, 2018: About us).

Not surprisingly, three chapters in the book are reports of various applications of PRME to management education. Shaun Ruggunan and Dorothy Spiller (Chap. 2) write of the transformation of business education in post-Apartheid South Africa, Carol Pomare (Chap. 11) refers to PRME in her chapter on responsible managers and responsible management education, and Sapna A. Narula, Ambika Zutshi, and Rajiv Seth (Chap. 6) describe the integration of PMRE with a conventional system of management education at TERI University, India.

Developing Economies

Another feature of the book is its focus on management education in developing economies. There are chapters here on South Africa (Shaun Ruggunan and Dorothy Spiller, Chap. 2), the Philippines and Costa Rica (Ronald K. Goodenow, Chap. 3), India (Kay Gillis, Chap. 4; and Shashwat Shukla, Chap. 5), and Singapore (Jiunwen Wang, Chap. 7).

Education and Society

It is interesting to note the preponderance of chapters dealing with experiential teaching methods for management education—methods that empower students to take responsibility for their own and each other's learning, under the guidance of trained and competent instructors.

This new emphasis on collaborative learning is in line with social trends; therefore, this teaching method is particularly likely to appeal to, and be effective for, young students. Botsman (2015) pointed out that in 2015 the *Oxford English Dictionary* included for the first time the phrase 'sharing economy'—proof that the practice is here to stay. It is an economic system based on sharing underused assets or services directly from individuals, for free or for a fee. Similar concepts include 'peer economy' and 'collaborative consumption', and they go hand in hand with 'crowdfunding', 'crowdsourcing,' and 'co-creation'. The common factor is the creation of a sense of belonging, of collective accountability and mutual benefit through membership of a community.

These are exactly the kinds of response that experiential learning seeks to evoke, and the relevant authors in this book do great service to management education by recommending various strategies and tactics to implement it.

Independent Scholar Elizabeth Christopher
Avoca Beach, NSW, Australia

References

Botsman, R. (2015). Defining the sharing economy: What is collaborative consumption—And what isn't? Retrieved May 27, 2015, from www.fastcompany.com

PRME. (2018). *Overview*. Retrieved January 22, 2018, from http://www.unprme.org/about-prme/index.php

Acknowledgements

The editor thanks Madeleine Holder, Gabriel Everington, and all Palgrave Macmillan's UK editorial staff for their help and support and extends her gratitude to all the authors who have contributed so generously to this edition.

Contents

1 Introduction: Playing Devil's Advocate: What is
   the Business of Business?   1
   Elizabeth Christopher

2 The Transformation of Business Education in
   Post-Apartheid South Africa   11
   Shaun Ruggunan and Dorothy Spiller

3 From Occupation to Cultural and Social Responsibility
   in Philippine and Puerto Rican Business Education:
   A First-Stage Historical Research Perspective   27
   Ronald K. Goodenow

4 A Historical Perspective on Social Expectations
   for Management Education: Training for Empire   43
   Kay Gillis

5 Problems in Management Ethics Training: An Indian
   Perspective   49
   Shashwat Shukla

6 Integrating Responsible Education Principles into a Conventional System: The Case Study of TERI School of Advanced Studies, India 65
Sapna A. Narula, Ambika Zutshi, and Rajiv Seth

7 Tri-Sector Leadership and Collaboration in Management Education: The Case of Singapore 73
Jiunwen Wang

8 Demand for and Supply of Responsible Managerial Behaviour 83
Duane Windsor

9 Social and Environmental Pressures in Management Education: How Anticipatory Stress and Social Support Interact to Predict Students' Academic Engagement and Performance 97
Yannick Griep, Timothy G. Wingate, and Melissa A. Boyce

10 Learning in Higher Education: The Role of Sustainability Integration Strategies, Legitimacy, and Teaching Tools 115
Raquel Antolin-Lopez and Nieves Garcia-de-Frutos

11 Responsible Managers and Responsible Management Education 139
Carol Pomare

12 Sustainable Business Ethics Education 149
Meena Chavan and Leanne M. Carter

13 Creating an Organization in the Classroom: Students Living Management Theories in Action 171
Elyssebeth Leigh and Anne Herbert

14	Reflections on the Development and Delivery of an Experiential Learning Capstone Project Course *Dan Murray and Michael Wood*	189
15	Shaping Managerial Values: Incorporating Experiential Learning in Management Education *Pallvi Arora*	201
16	Management Education for Women—and Men? *Elizabeth Christopher*	217

Index   239

Notes on Contributors

Raquel Antolin-Lopez is Assistant Professor of Management at the University of Almeria. She has also been a visiting researcher at the University of Colorado at Boulder, Indiana University, Loyola Marymount University, and CUNY University. Her main research interest lies at the intersection of sustainability and entrepreneurship. Her lines of research also include sustainability management education, corporate sustainability, innovation, public policies, and renewable energy. The quality of her research has been recognized with different awards. Her research has been published in *Academy of Management Learning & Education*, *Technovation*, *Business & Society*, *Organization & Environment*, *Journal of Cleaner Production*, and *PLOS One* among others. On a teaching side, she teaches Entrepreneurship, Managerial skills, Environmental Management, and International Management.

Pallvi Arora is an assistant professor, International Centre for Cross Cultural Research and Human Resource Management (ICccR & HRM), University of Jammu, Jammu (J&K), India.

Melissa A. Boyce, PhD, is a senior instructor in the Department of Psychology at the University of Calgary in Alberta, Canada. She obtained her PhD from the University of Victoria in 2008 and her Master's degree from Queen's University in 2004. She has won multiple teaching awards and is a University of Calgary Teaching Scholar. Her research focuses on memory, perceptual biases, and decision-making, especially in a legal context. She is also interested in collaborative learning, student engagement, and student satisfaction.

Leanne Carter is Senior Lecturer in Marketing at the Faculty of Business and Economics, Macquarie University. Her research focuses on consumer behaviour, internal marketing, market orientation, and employability as a result of the graduate capabilities that are developed as a result of internships and other work integrated learning activities experienced by students. In addition, Leanne has an interest in ethics, learning orientation, business simulations, peer assessment, and social marketing. Her latest textbook, *Social Marketing: Good Intentions* 2nd edition, examines current social, environmental, health and safety issues affecting individuals and their communities. It provides a critical look at the barriers and challenges to behaviour change. Having 15 years of experience in industry before commencing her career as an academic, Leanne's links with industry will ensure strong connections between academia and practice for the future employability of our students.

Meena Chavan is senior lecturer and programme director at Macquarie University, Sydney, Australia. She provides leadership in teaching and research in the disciplinary fields of international business/management, cross-cultural management, organization studies, entrepreneurship and small business management, and experiential education. She has 30 years of experience in industry and academia, having taught undergraduate and postgraduate programmes in India, Singapore, Hong Kong, Dubai, Australia, Germany, and the USA. She is an advocate for, and practitioner of, experiential learning and teaching (ELA) and critical action learning (CAL). She has been a guest speaker at several universities and conducted workshops on developing and teaching through ELA and CAL.

Elizabeth Christopher is British but resident in Australia. Her academic interests are in business communication, communication across cultures, games and interactive exercises for management training, international management, leadership and teamwork, managing cultural diversity, and online teaching and learning. She spent many years in the private sector before returning to a university environment and was awarded a PhD in 1983 by the University of New South Wales, where she began her teaching career.

From 1993 to 1995, she was professor, CSU's overseas study programmes, in Ankara and Istanbul, Turkey, and throughout the 1980s and 1990s was a visiting professor at various US universities and a visiting fellow at the East-West Center, Honolulu, Hawai'i. Until recently, she was a part-time faculty member of the Honolulu-based Japan-American Institute of Management Science (JAIMS) and since 1993 has been a chartered member of the Australian Human

Resources Institute (AHRI) and an academic examiner of PhD theses for Macquarie University and the University of South Australia. In 1997, she was a member of the Business Studies Examination Committee, Board of Studies, NSW Australia, and from 1998 a reviewer of publishing proposals for Harcourt, Australia; McGraw-Hill, Australia; Palgrave Macmillan, UK; and Pearson Educational (Prentice-Hall), Australia. From 1999 to 2005, she was a member of the Editorial Board of *Simulation and Gaming: An International Journal of Theory, Practice, and Research (S&G)*: Sage Periodicals Press, London.

During 2000–2010, she was an adjunct professor at Macquarie University, Sydney, and in 2003–2005, a visiting professor with the International College of Tourism and Hospitality Management (now the International College of Management, Sydney). In 2009, she won the Macquarie University LEAD award for research on the management of cultural differences in learning and teaching. From 2011 to 2014, she was the creator, convenor, and coordinator of communication in business courses, School of Marketing and Management, Charles Sturt University, NSW, Australia. In 2014, she won the annual Management Book of the Year Award (Chartered Institute of Management, UK) for her book *International Management: Explorations across Cultures* (Kogan Page, London UK). During 2016–2017, she was the leading co-editor of a Special Issue of the *Journal of Management Education: New Approaches to Introduction to Management Courses*.

Though now retired from full-time teaching, she continues to write and edit academic books, papers, and reviews, and is Deputy Chair of the Academic Board, Asia Pacific International College, Sydney, Australia. Her recent publications include:

The dark side of organisational leadership in the transformation of Asia. In N. Muenjohn & A. McMurray (Eds.), *The Palgrave handbook of leadership in transforming Asia* (Palgrave Macmillan, UK, 2017).

The geopolitics of immigrant labour: A climate of fear. In B. Christiansen & F. Kasarcı (Eds.), *Corporate espionage, geopolitics, and diplomacy in international business* (IGI Global, 2016).

(Editor) *International management and intercultural communication: A collection of case studies*, Vols. 1 and 2 (Palgrave Macmillan, UK, 2015; 978-1-13-47989-1)

International management: Explorations across cultures (Kogan Page, London, UK, 2012; 978-0-749-46528-5).

(Editor) *Communication across cultures* (Palgrave 2012, paperback, 978-0-230-27567-6).

Nieves Garcia-de-Frutos is Assistant Professor of Marketing at the University of Almeria. Her main research interests lie in the field of consumer behaviour, particularly ethically and environmentally motivated anti-consumption. Her research topics include pro-environmental consumption reduction behaviour, country driven anti-consumption, and sustainability management education. Her research has been published in *Psychology & Marketing*, *Journal of Macromarketing*, and *Journal of Business Ethics* among other referred publications. She teaches Market Research, E-commerce, and Strategic Marketing.

Kay Gillis, PhD, holds Masters in Economic Development from Deakin University, Melbourne, and a doctorate in Politics and History from Murdoch University, Perth, Australia. She worked as an independent researcher for 15 years in Singapore for clients such as the National Archives of Singapore. Her publications include:

Gillis, E. K. (2005). *Singapore civil society and British power*. Singapore: Talisman Publishing.
Gillis, E. K. (2008). Civil society and the Malay Education Council. In M. Barr & C. Trocki (Eds.), *Paths not taken: Political pluralism in post-war Singapore*. Singapore: National University of Singapore Press.
Gillis, K. (2012). The anti-opium movement in Singapore. In E. Christopher (Ed.), *Cross cultural communication*. London: Palgrave.
Gillis, K., & Tan, K. (2006). *Book of Singapore's firsts*. Singapore: Singapore Heritage Society.

Ronald K. Goodenow, PhD, has held academic and research appointments at various US and British universities, including the State University of New York at Buffalo, Clark University, Boston University, the University of New Hampshire, Columbia University, the City University of New York, the University of London, the University of Liverpool, and the Crummer Graduate School of Business, Rollins College, Florida. He has given Fulbright lectures in the UK and Brazil. Four of his books have been published and he has written over 100 book chapters, articles, and reviews in his chosen fields of history, comparative studies, and information technology services in education and healthcare. He has served as a consultant to Dell Computers, Hewlett Packard, CIO Publications, and other corporations. Recent publications include the following:

Service across cultures: A case study of the emerging role of communication technology. In *Rotary International*—a chapter in Christopher, Elizabeth, editor (2015).
International management and intercultural communication; A collection of case studies. London, Palgrave Macmillan.
Paradigms and practice: Perspectives on ever shifting telework sands. In E. Christopher (Ed.), (2012). *Managing communication across cultures: Different voices.* London: Palgrave Macmillan.

Yannick Griep, PhD, is an assistant professor in the Department of Psychology at the University of Calgary, Canada, and an affiliated member of faculty at Stockholm University, Sweden. He holds a PhD from Vrije Universiteit, Brussel, in 2016 and has held visiting positions at the University of Toronto (Department of Management) and Carnegie Mellon University (Heinz College). His primary research interests focus on psychological contract breaches and how such breaches influence employee responses, including counterproductive responses and incivility spirals. He is also interested in the temporal dynamics associated with psychological contract breaches and how these dynamics influence employees' propensity to engage in dysfunctional behaviour. He is a skilled statistician with advanced knowledge of dynamic modelling techniques. Yannick has published his work in the *Journal of Vocational Behavior, Journal of Occupational Health Psychology, PLOS One, International Archives of Occupational and Environmental Health,* and the *European Journal of Work and Organizational Psychology.* He is a guest editor at the *Journal of Organizational Behavior* and *Frontiers in Psychology,* and an editorial board member of the *Journal of Occupational and Organizational Psychology.*

Anne Herbert, PhD, loves exploring how adults learn in all sorts of ways and places. She is Associate Professor in Education (adjunct) at RMIT University, Australia, and Docent in Management at Aalto University, Finland. After a long and varied career in different countries, she currently teaches Management at Aalto University, supervises research students, advises the Australian Aid Programme in Vietnam, and is active in the Melbourne permaculture collective. She has published elsewhere in the areas of higher education management and organization, teaching and learning in higher education, and research methods. Anne holds a PhD in Education from the University of South Australia.

Wang Jiunwen, PhD, holds a PhD in organizational behaviour from the Kellogg School of Management (Northwestern University). She is a lecturer at the Singapore University of Social Sciences, teaching courses on leadership and talent management. Her works have appeared in in top journals such as the *Academy of Management Journal*, *Psychological Science*, and *Annual Review of Psychology*. Her research interests are in cross-cultural leadership and psychology, developmental readiness, and management education.

Elyssebeth Leigh, PhD, at various times, has been a public servant, human Resources manager, and consultant—and always an educator. Her career has traversed the domains of finance, entertainment, administration, and academic research. Her books and articles on simulation in workplace learning and tertiary education, and designs games and simulations for large and small groups have been published. Her abiding interest in education helps her travel the world as an educator and games designer and drives her commitment to making education relevant to the immediate needs of learners, while holding true to traditions of equity and fairness. She enjoys exploring options for learning and challenges her students to undertake learning in modes they had never considered 'educational'. As an academic, she has taught and researched at Australian Universities and is now also teaching and researching in Finland where her focus is on preparing students for employment in the kinds of complex, uncertain, and exhilarating environments created by evolving knowledge, contexts, and relational expectations. As an educator, Elyssebeth considers it vital to address, in all she does, the question of 'How can we improve the quality of our contribution to the life and career options of our students?'

Dan Murray, PhD, is a lecturer in the School of Environment, Enterprise and Development (SEED). He is a co-instructor of the experiential learning capstone course undertaken by final-year students in the Environment and Business programme. He holds a PhD in Environmental Planning and, with a specialization in environmental policy and research design, encourages a rigorous and evidence-based approach to problem-solving and decision-making.

Sapna A. Narula is working as associate professor and head of the Department of Business Sustainability at TERI University, teaching courses on sustainable business strategy, sustainability reporting, corporate social responsibility (CSR), and strategic planning. She holds around 18 years of experience in teaching and research in agribusiness, sustainability, CSR, and technology dissemination and has been very closely involved with rural and farm communities at the grass root level. Her current research interests include exploring sustainability and CSR issues on the Indian corporate landscape, with a focus on oil and gas, hotel, textile, mining, and agribusiness.

Her research work in the use of information and communication technologies (ICTs) for sustainable development has won many accolades, including Prosper.Net Scopus Young Scientist Award for Sustainable Development, 2011, delivered jointly by German Ministry, United Nations University & Elsevier and a Young Scientist Award (2009) from Uttarakhand Council for Science and Technology, Government of Uttarakhand. A gold medalist from Delhi University, her work has been published in leading international journals, including *Journal of Cleaner Production*, *Social Responsibility Journal*, *International Journal of Healthcare management*, and *International Journal of Sustainable Strategic Management*.

Carol Pomare, PhD, is Assistant Professor of Accounting at the Ron Joyce Center for Business Studies of Mount Allison University, Canada. Her research interests include strategies toward a low-carbon economy, the business case for sustainability, market based accounting, and sustainable finance. Her work has been published in leading journals including the *European Journal of Social Psychology* (i.e., A rated on the ABDC list) and the *Journal of Accounting and Organizational Change* (i.e., B rated on the ABDC list). She is a member of the Canadian Academic Accounting Association, the European Accounting Association, and the American Accounting Association.

Shaun Ruggunan, PhD, is Senior Lecturer in Human Resources Management at the University of KwaZulu-Natal, Durban, South Africa. An industrial sociologist by training, his doctoral and published work has examined the transformation of the global labour market for Filipino, South African, and British seafarers. He also has published on the sociology of professions and critical management studies in South Africa. Shaun is especially passionate and interested in how management studies have developed as a scholarly discipline in postcolonial contexts. He advocates for management education that gives primacy to moral economy especially in highly unequal societies such as South Africa.

Rajiv Seth is an aerospace engineer by training. He holds a B.Tech from the Indian Institute of Technology (IIT), Kanpur, an M.Tech from the Indian Institute of Technology (IIT), Madras, and a PhD in Business Administration (Finance) from the Aligarh Muslim University. Having spent 27 years in the Indian Air Force, he has worked on various types of aircraft and aero engines and has been involved in technical evaluation, field testing, and technology transfer.

Over the last 15 years, he has been associated with the conceptualization and growth of the TERI University. He is the Pro-Vice Chancellor of the university and a Professor of Finance in the Department of Business Sustainability. He was primarily responsible for building a niche for this young university, which imparts postgraduate education in sustainable development. With a strong emphasis on gender, and on empowering women, the university boasts of building women leaders in sustainability.

He has been deeply involved in an international consortium of universities in the Asia-Pacific, which is led by the United Nations University, and which focuses on the integration of sustainable development in higher education. He is a board member of this international consortium. His research interests are in the areas of financial derivatives, risk management, and green aviation.

Shashwat Shukla, PhD, is doctorate in behavioural economics, with postgraduate qualifications in applied psychology. He has worked in administrative positions in Bharat Petroleum and Government of India. He takes courses in public policy, organizational behaviour, and strategy. His interests include playing flute and Indian Classical Music.

Dorothy Spiller is an education consultant at the University of the South Pacific, Fiji. She worked for 23 years in the Teaching Development Unit at the University of Waikato New Zealand. Dorothy has written extensively about higher education and has a strong interest in the relationship between higher education and social change.

Duane Windsor, PhD, a Rice alumnus (BA), is Lynette S. Autrey Professor of Management in the Jesse H. Jones Graduate School of Business at Rice University. He was editor (2007–2014) of the Sage journal *Business & Society*, founded in 1960 and sponsored by the International Association for Business and Society (IABS). He served as elected programme chair and head of IABS and of the Social Issues in Management (SIM) Division of Academy of Management. He is an associate editor on the second edition, forthcoming, of Sage's *Encyclopaedia of Business Ethics and Society*. His recent work focuses on corporate social responsibility and stakeholder theory. His articles have appeared in *Business & Society, Business Ethics Quarterly, Cornell International Law Journal, Journal of Business Ethics, Journal of Business Research, Journal of Corporate Citizenship, Journal of International Management, Journal of Management Studies, Journal of Public Affairs,* and *Public Administration Review*.

Timothy G. Wingate is a PhD student in industrial-organizational psychology at the University of Calgary in Alberta, Canada, and working in the Organizational Behaviour and Interpersonal Influence Lab. His organizational research explores selection interview design, interviewer and applicant social cognition and influence behaviours, and the context, motivations, and outcomes of organizational citizenship behaviours. His educational research focuses on the psychosocial experiences of post-secondary students in relation to academic performance and performance consistency. Timothy's work has been published in *Learning and Individual Differences*, and his other works are under review at *Academy of Management: Learning and Education* and the *Journal of Managerial Psychology*.

Michael Wood, PhD, is Assistant Professor of Environment and Business in the School of Environment, Enterprise and Development (SEED) at the University of Waterloo. He holds a PhD in Strategy and Sustainability from the Ivey Business School. His research examines organizational perceptions and responses to sustainability issues through the lens of space, time, scale, and social license to operate within the contexts of the insurance industry, mining, carbon management, Blue Economy, sustainable concerts and venues, and climate change and global security. He is a passionate sustainability management educator whose professional development-related research focuses on pedagogy for training future sustainability management leaders.

Ambika Zutshi is an associate professor who holds a bachelor's degree in Environmental Sciences and a master's degree in Environmental Management and a PhD (Monash University, Australia). Her current research is on corporate social responsibility, business ethics, the role of stakeholders in environmental management systems (EMS), and supply chain management. She has nearly 80 publications in journals and book chapters. Examples include *International Journal of Management Review, Technovation, Journal of Cleaner Production, Supply Chain Management: An International Journal; European Business Review, Business Process Management Journal, Managerial Auditing Journal,* and *Management of Environmental Quality: An International Journal, Australian Accounting Review,* and *the International Journal of Environmental and Sustainable Development.*

Ambika is also on a number of editorial boards, including *European Business Review* Associate Editor, Australasia, Emerald Publisher, UK; *International Journal of E-Entrepreneurship & Innovation* (editorial board member); *PSU Research Review: An International Journal,* Emerald Publisher, UK (editorial advisory board member).

List of Figures

Fig. 6.1	Sustainability at TERI SAS	67
Fig. 6.2	TERI SAS and PRMEs Six Principles	68
Fig. 7.1	Tri-sector approach to management education (SMU, 2017a)	74
Fig. 9.1	Five distinct academic engagement trajectories during the first term of first-year post-secondary education students. The dashed line indicates the start of the first term. Observations on the left side of the dashed line represent anticipated academic engagement, whereas observations on the right side of the dashed line represent the academic engagement once the first term has started until completion	103
Fig. 9.2	GPA for each academic engagement trajectory (on a 4.0 scale). Error bars represent one standard error of the mean. Note: GPA for moderate match (2.99) is significantly higher than the GPA for low match (1.57) and honeymoon hangover (2.60), whereas it is significantly lower than the GPA for high match (3.79) and learning to love (3.82). GPA for low match is significantly lower than the GPA for all other academic engagement trajectories. GPA for honeymoon hangover is significantly higher than the GPA for low match, whereas it is significantly lower than the GPA for moderate match, high match, and learning to love. GPA for high match and learning to love is significantly higher than the GPA for all other academic engagement trajectories	105
Fig. 15.1	Creation of a climate of understanding	209

List of Tables

Table 10.1	Representativeness of the sample according to students' degree	122
Table 10.2	Descriptive statistics of antecedent variables	123
Table 10.3	Correlation tests	128
Table 10.4	Multiple regression models with WTL about sustainability as dependent variable	130
Table 15.1	Application of Kolb's experiential learning theory (ELT)	211

1

Introduction: Playing Devil's Advocate: What is the Business of Business?

Elizabeth Christopher

The US economist Milton Friedman (2002) argued in 1970 that people who claim a social conscience for business are "unwitting puppets of the intellectual forces that have been undermining the basis of a free society these past decades" (Friedman, 1970, p. 1).

He insisted that in a free enterprise, private property system, corporate executives are directly responsible to their employers—the owners of the organization, that is, the shareholders—to make as much money as possible ethically and within the law. Any social responsibilities to which these executives subscribe should be as private individuals, not as business managers. Otherwise, they may act against the interests of their employers (presumably, e.g., should they risk a loss of productivity by supporting workforce diversity and hiring women or members of disadvantaged minorities instead of better qualified candidates). In such cases, Friedman would argue they would be spending stockholders' money without consent in pursuit of wider social aims and would become, in effect, civil

---

E. Christopher (✉)
Independent Scholar, Avoca Beach, NSW, Australia

© The Editor(s) (if applicable) and The Author(s), under exclusive licence to Springer International Publishing AG, part of Springer Nature 2018
E. Christopher (ed.), *Meeting Expectations in Management Education*,
https://doi.org/10.1007/978-3-319-76412-2_1

servants, which would imply that political—not market—mechanisms determine the allocation of company resources.

Friedman went on to claim the great virtues of private competitive enterprise are that it forces people to be responsible for their own actions and makes it difficult for them to exploit others for selfish or unselfish purposes. They can do good but only at their own expense. In an ideal free market, resting on private property, no individual can be coerced because all parties can choose whether to participate or not. Society is a collection of individuals and of the various groups they voluntarily form; there are no social values or responsibilities other than those shared by individuals. Friedman admitted that some government regulation will be always necessary but maintained the concept of corporate social responsibility to be fundamentally subversive in a free society.

He concluded that the only social responsibility of business is to engage in open and free competition without deception or fraud. Levitt (1958) paraphrased this sentiment as "the business of business is profits". It was Denning's (2013) opinion that though no popular notion has a single origin, the idea that the sole purpose of a firm is to make money for its shareholders gained international popularity with Friedman's article in the New York Times on September 13, 1970. Friedman was the leader of the Chicago School of Economics and the winner of the Nobel Prize in Economics in 1976. He was described by *The Economist* (2006) as "the most influential economist of the second half of the 20th century…possibly of all of it".

The success of Friedman's article was not because his arguments were sound but because people desperately wanted to believe them. Businesses are run by those who must reconcile company profitability with personal values (Kearns, 2007), including executives whose shareholders' demands may weigh heavily against any inclination towards social responsibility. At the time of Friedman's writing, private sector firms were starting to feel the first pressures of global competition and executives sought ways to increase their returns. The idea of focusing totally on making money and forgetting any concerns for employees, customers or society, seemed worth exploring, regardless of logic.

Kearns (2007) noted, moreover, that Friedman's views were attractive to conservative political leaders because they were expressed in an era when communism and socialism were still economic and political realities in many parts of the world. Ronald Reagan was elected in the USA in 1980 with his message that "government is the problem", and in the UK, Margaret Thatcher, who became prime minister in 1979, preached economic freedom in common with Reagan and urged a focus on making money for the good not only of individual firms but also for the country.

Not everyone agreed with the shareholder value theory, even in those early years. For example, in 1973, Drucker (2012) argued that organizations can—and should—strengthen society, but the argument was so seductive that six years post-Friedman it was defended in terms of dubious mathematics by Jensen and Meckling (1976). Their article was widely cited, but it rested on the same false assumption as made by Friedman, that an organization is a legal fiction and its money is owned by the stockholders.

Jensen and Meckling proposed that to ensure firms would focus solely on making money, they should turn their executives into major shareholders by affording them generous compensation in the form of stock—thus any tendency to feather their own nests would act in the interests of the shareholders. The notion that "greed is good" ("Wall Street", 1987) became the conventional wisdom and the management dynamic was to make money by whatever means available (Denning, 2013). Self-interest reigned supreme and in time executives came to view their portfolios as an entitlement, independent of performance.

Stalk and Lachenauer (2004) went even further down the path of corporate self-interest. They recommended that firms should be "willing to hurt their rivals", to "enjoy watching their competitors squirm" and to be "ruthless" in the marketplace in pursuit of shareholder value. They argued that firms should go the very edge of illegality or—if they should go over the line—to pay civil penalties that might appear large in absolute terms but meagre in relation to their illicit gains. In this moral environment, corporate senior executives were free to make up their own rules with the tacit approval of governments, legislators and regulators.

It seemed the magic of shareholder value was working, but when its financial sleights-of-hand were exposed, the decline that Friedman himself had sensed in 1970 turned out to be real and persistent. Martin

(2011) wrote that it was hardly surprising that the corporate world should be plagued by continuing scandals, for instance, the options backdating scandals of 2005–2006 and the subprime meltdown of 2007–2008.

On the other hand, there were many signs that companies were becoming more conscious of their social responsibilities. Vidal (2006) reported a Conference Board survey that found two-thirds of the surveyed firms regarded corporate citizenship and sustainability as issues of growing importance. Community and stakeholder involvement, corporate giving, environmental sustainability and dealing with climate change were high on the list of such activities; enhancing corporate reputation was found to be the main internal driver for sustainability programmes, and measuring results the top challenge.

Oldani, Kirton, and Savona (2013) edited a collection of articles in a debate over policy responses to the 2008 global financial crisis and the implications for international cooperation, coordination and institutional change in global economic governance. It included suggestions for reforming and even replacing the corporate architecture created in the mid-twentieth century to meet the global challenges of the twenty-first century. There was clear support for the idea that companies could operate in a way that would strengthen all their various stakeholders, yet still provide solid, sustainable returns for shareholders.

Nevertheless, thanks to globalization, companies are still free to exploit or pollute whole communities and then move on. Unregulated markets and exploitation-friendly tax schemes reward them for acting in their own interests in the name of economic growth and competitiveness. Kearns (2007) wrote hopefully in 2007 that if anything had changed since Friedman's time, it was recognition that profit is a very poor proxy for societal value—only to report regretfully ten years later (Kearns, 2017) such poor examples as the UK government's report on the possibility of expanding London's Heathrow Airport. It recommended a third runway on primarily economic grounds, as though other factors (environmental damage, demolishing homes, etc.) hardly mattered (Topham, Mason, & Elgot, 2016).

Kearns (2017) makes a distinction between "profit" and "value". The former is focused on the company itself, the latter on satisfying societal needs. He argues that Friedman's failure to use "value" as his criterion undoes not only his argument but also that of any CEO today who hides behind profit but says nothing about value, that is, maximization of the business's potential. He cites the lesson of Enron (Bauer, 2009) that profit performance often hides underlying underperformance and, more importantly, the hidden symptoms of corruption in corporate governance.

The debate today still seems to hinge around a conflict between two, apparently opposing, constructs: social responsibility versus profit; however, increasing awareness of the social cost of consumer goods, coupled with governmental difficulties in regulating across global supply chains, may have driven the rise in corporate social responsibility (Bénabou & Tirole, 2009). Nilssen, GmbH, and Robinson (2017) suggest that in the almost half century since Friedman's admonition, business has evolved along a trajectory quite contrary to what he advocated. Socially responsible businesses, whose executives pursue hybrid goals of social good and financial gain, have become commonplace and it is standard practice for businesses to pursue double-bottom-line objectives in new organizational forms that blend profit and stewardship. These frameworks give them advantage over traditional organizations—and their mechanics are as Friedman imagined. Though individual investors are free to make their own trade-off between financial and social output, it makes sense to leave it to those who can do it most efficiently—the private sector corporate executives. Competition for investment dollars requires them to produce a profitable blend of social and financial returns: in other words, to adopt values that make them more marketable.

Taylor (2017) writes that in the USA under President Donald Trump there is a new consumer awakening in which social and political groups are forcing companies to take a moral stand. Friedman argued that society is made up not only of individuals but also of the various—often mutually opposed—groups they form: economic, social and political. Now that corporate values play an increasingly large role in shopping decisions, connecting a commercial brand to certain values and political beliefs is one way to differentiate a company and establish a high moral and ethical tone.

For instance, in 2017, Trump gave an Executive Order temporarily banning immigration to the USA from seven Muslim countries, and the media focused on a cluster of companies that made public statements against it: Netflix called it "un-American", while Ford Motor Company said, "We do not support this policy or any other that goes against our values as a company". Uber was more equivocal and was criticized for not confronting the issue and thus betraying its purported beliefs as a bold game changer. This motivated so many customers to uninstall the Uber app from their phones that the firm had to implement a new automated process to handle all the deletions and later announced in an email to defecting customers that the Executive Order was "wrong" and "unjust", and CEO Travis Kalanick resigned from Trump's business advisory council.

By remaining silent on important societal issues, executives may be harming performance more than they realize. Meyer (2017) reports on a turning point in what is expected from business leaders who traditionally were assumed to be responsible primarily for delivering products. Shareholders now want chief executives to make statements on social justice or moral issues.

Duff McDonald (2017), author of books critical of the ethics of McKinsey, the consulting firm, and J.P. Morgan's chief executive Jamie Dimon wrote *The golden passport*, in which he calls the Harvard Business School to account for betraying its founding doctrine, which was to develop a heightened sense of responsibility among businessmen (and eventually women) who would handle their businesses in socially constructive ways (Stewart, 2017). McDonald accuses Harvard Business School comprehensively of providing the ideological bases for the scandals of the 1980s, the corporate scandals of the 2000s, the immoral increase in the pay gap between chief executives and ordinary employees, the real estate mortgage bubble and ensuing financial crisis, and even the election of Donald Trump.

Be that as it may, at least McDonald deserves credit for raising questions that every business school needs to be asking: how to play a more important role in helping more people in business to rediscover a purpose other than profit. As he puts it, business schools need to graduate more people who are motivated to solve problems, and fewer people who create them. Now that chief executives engage with current ethical and social issues that are the subjects of international conversations, MBA education can no longer afford to restrict itself to finance, marketing, accounting and economics (Gelles & Millerdec, 2017). Business schools around the world are adding social responsibilities to their curricula. Examples include classes on how companies like Amazon respond when attacked by Mr. Trump; the social justice protests by NFL players; sexual harassment; gender-based inequalities of pay in the workplace; free speech; sexism; and "bro" culture.

Gelles and Millerdec (2017) report that some business schools are drawing support from the social sciences, like behavioural economics and psychology. The Stanford Graduate School of Business's ethics class—taught by two political scientists, one an expert in behaviour and the other in game theory—seems to be more like a course in human nature than in finance. And in 2018 Fern Mandelbaum, a venture capitalist (Broadway Angels, 2017), will teach a new class to Stanford MBA candidates, called "Equity by design: Building diverse and inclusive organizations". The Forté Foundation (Imperial College Business School, 2017) finds that gender is an issue that particularly interests students, and previously taboo subjects are now engaging classroom debate, such as gay rights and drug addiction.

Several factors are contributing to these revised syllabuses. Bad behaviour by big companies has thrust ethics back into the news, from Wells Fargo's creation of fake accounts, to sexual harassment at Fox News, to the litany of improprieties at Uber. A new generation of chief executives is speaking out about moral and political issues in the Trump era. Just four months ago, prominent corporate executives came together to dissolve two business councils consulting with President Trump after he blamed "many sides" for an outburst of white supremacist violence in Charlottesville, VA.

So maybe the commercial wheel has come full circle from Friedman and back again. A recent UN report (United Nations, 2017) described how the international business community has accepted corporate responsibility. Through the UN Global Compact, companies embrace ten universal principles, from supporting the protection of human rights to working against corruption. At the 2017 Climate Summit in New York, corporations made commitments to help mitigate climate change. It now seems to be good business for the international business community to partner with the international community to help solve humanity's problems.

The business of business is still business, but "business" is now defined by its corporate values, and management education, as taught in colleges and universities, is evolving accordingly.

References

Bauer, A. (2009). *The Enron scandal and the Sarbanes-Oxley-Act.* GRIN Verlag Individual and Corporate Social Responsibility.

Bénabou, R., & Tirole, J. (2009). Individual and corporate social responsibility. *Economica, 77*(305), 1–19. January 2010, First published: 16 December 2009.

Broadway Angels. (2017). *Fern Mandelbaum.* Retrieved December 27, 2017, from http://www.broadway-angels.com/fern-mandelbaum-bio/

Denning, S. (2013). The origin of 'the world's dumbest idea': Milton Friedman. *Forbes.* Retrieved from https://www.forbes.com/sites/stevedenning/2013/06/26/the-origin-of-the-worlds-dumbest-idea-milton-friedman/#6d293ce6870e

Drucker, P. (2012). *Management.* Routledge.

Economist. (2006, November 23). The legacy of Milton Friedman, a giant among economists. Online extra. Retrieved from http://www.economist.com/node/8313925

Friedman, M. (1970, September 13). The social responsibility of business is to increase its profits. *The New York Times Magazine.* Retrieved from http://www.nytimes.com/1970/09/13/archives/a-friedman-doctrine-the-social-responsibility-of-business-is-to.html?_r=1

Friedman, M. (2002). *Capitalism and freedom.* Fortieth Anniversary Edition. Retrieved from http://www.press.uchicago.edu/ucp/books/book/chicago/C/bo18146821.html

Gelles, D., & Millerdec, C. C. (2017, December 25). Business schools now teaching #MeToo, N.F.L. protests and Trump. *New York Times.*

Imperial College Business School. (2017). *Forté foundation.* Retrieved December 27, 2017, from https://www.imperial.ac.uk/business-school/programmes/ib-women/forte-foundation/

Jensen, M., & Meckling, W. H. (1976). Theory of the firm: Managerial behavior, agency costs and ownership structure. *Journal of Financial Economics, 3*(4), 305–360.

Kearns, P. (2007). *The value motive: The only alternative to the profit motive.* Wiley. ISBN: 978-0-470-05755-1.

Kearns, P. (2017). Is the social responsibility of business to increase its profits? Retrieved September 25, 2017, from https://www.linkedin.com/pulse/social-responsibility-business-increase-its-profits-paul-kearns/

Levitt, T. (1958). The dangers of social responsibility. *Harvard Business Review, 36*, 41–50.

Martin, R. (2011). *Fixing the game: How runaway expectations broke the economy, and how to get back to reality.* Harvard Business Review Press.

McDonald, D. (2017). *The golden passport: Harvard Business School, the limits of capitalism, and the moral failure of the MBA elite.* New York: HarperCollins.

Meyer, L. (2017, December 26). #MeToo, NFL protests, and Trump on the lesson plan at biz schools. *Boston Globe.*

Nilssen, A., GmbH, S., & Robinson, D. (2017). What is the business of business? *Harvard Law School Forum on Corporate Governance and Financial Regulation.* Retrieved from https://corpgov.law.harvard.edu/2017/06/23/what-is-the-business-of-business/

Oldani, C., Kirton, J. J., & Savona, P. (2013). *Global financial crisis: Global impact and solutions.* Ashgate Publishing Ltd.

Stalk, G., Jr., & Lachenauer, R. (2004). Hardball: Five killer strategies for trouncing the competition. *Harvard Business Review.* Retrieved from https://hbr.org/2004/04/hardball-five-killer-strategies-for-trouncing-the-competition

Stewart, J. B. (2017, April 24). How Harvard Business School has reshaped American capitalism. *New York Times.*

Taylor, K. (2017, November 14). People on the right and left are forcing companies to take a stand in the Trump era—And it's leading to a new 'consumer awakening'. *Business Insider.* Retrieved from https://www.businessinsider.com.au/boycotts-common-in-trump-era-2017-11?r=US&IR=T

Topham, G., Mason, R., & Elgot, J. (2016, October 25). Heathrow airport expansion gets government approval. *Guardian*, Tuesday. Retrieved from https://www.theguardian.com/environment/2016/oct/25/heathrow-airport-expansion-gets-government-approval-gatwick

United Nations. (2017). Retrieved from December 27, 2017, from http://www.un.org/en/sections/resources-different-audiences/business/

Vidal, D. J. (2006). Reward trumps risk: How business perspectives on corporate citizenship and sustainability are changing. *The Conference Board.* Retrieved from https://www.conference-board.org/publications/publication-detail.cfm?publicationID=1237&centerID=5

Wall Street. (1987, December 11). Crime film/Drama. Director: Oliver Stone. Initial release (USA).

2

The Transformation of Business Education in Post-Apartheid South Africa

Shaun Ruggunan and Dorothy Spiller

Introduction

Background and Context

South Africa provides a complex and unique context in which to explore how management studies in higher education have developed in tandem with ideologies and value systems over time. This chapter explores how management studies espoused and reinforced a specific set of *values* at historical moments in South Africa from 1949, when the first business school offering MBAs was established (Arnold, 2017). This date also marked the beginning of the Apartheid project that institutionalised racism in all spheres of society and introduced a form of racialised capitalism that permeated all forms of work design and workplaces (Terreblanche, 2002).

S. Ruggunan (✉)
University of KwaZulu-Natal, Durban, South Africa
e-mail: Ruggunans@ukzn.ac.za

D. Spiller
University of the South Pacific, Suva, Fiji

The Apartheid workplace regime was propped up by a set of discriminatory values about workers, work and human beings, and business schools were complicit in reifying these in the workplace.

In 1994, the ending of Apartheid added further complexity to the socio-political-economic contexts of South Africa. The democratic process culminated in what Webster and Adler (1999) termed the *double transition*. The first transition was the shift from Apartheid to post-Apartheid and the second, simultaneous, transition opened an intensely national economy to neo-liberal globalisation. If Apartheid created various forms of inclusions, exclusions, and inequalities, then globalisation—along with an inexperienced democratic state—helped cement these. Inequality in South Africa remains one of the highest in the world, with South Africa and Brazil competing every year for states with the highest levels of inequality (Sisk, 2017). Unemployment levels in the country are also amongst the highest in the world at 27.7% nationally and at over 50% for youth unemployment (Wilkinson et al., 2016). The economy and labour market continued to reflect Apartheid colour-bar and gendered segregationist legacies almost 25 years after democracy (Butler, 2017). The state and public sectors are beset by *cadre deployment* (Ndevu & Muller, 2017) which has resulted in profound collapses in some vital service delivery sectors.

Whilst the public sector receives much criticism for inefficiency, competencies, and ethical lapses, the corporate sector in South Africa is also culpable. Most middle to senior managers have achieved those positions due to Apartheid-informed human resources practices and not because of any competencies or meritocracy (Webster & Von Holdt, 2005). Both the private and public sector employ candidates from universities with managerial and allied qualifications, but questions need to be asked about the appropriateness of current educational preparation and its underlying values for responding to such complex and profound socio-economic, business, and managerial needs.

These questions become even more urgent when it is noted that of those who do make it into university education, students of management, economics, and finance form the second largest cohort of enrolments, but despite the increase of student numbers (especially in management studies), 50% drop out by the end of their first year of studies (Cloete, 2014).

Business School Education During Apartheid

Business education in the context of this chapter refers to both undergraduate and postgraduate commerce qualifications at public universities in commerce subjects such as management, human resources management, accounting, finance, and business administration. These include the professional MBA qualifications offered in South Africa. Typically, these consist of Bachelor of Commerce, Master of Commerce, and PhD in Commerce as well as MBA and DBA qualifications. Currently, there are 23 accredited business schools in South Africa (Arnold, 2017).

The imperative to examine business education in South Africa today stems from recognition of the powerful legacy of racialised values institutionalised in higher education by Apartheid (Bonnin & Ruggunan, 2016). The oldest business schools were established in the former whites-only and Afrikaner universities at the height of the Apartheid regime. These often acted as the "mother" universities for business disciplines such as industrial psychology, business management, and human resources management and would devolve curricula to the former Black and disadvantaged universities.

Concomitant with South Africa's rapid industrialisation from 1948 was the establishment of the country's business schools (Arnold, 2017). All these were situated in former white universities, except for one at the former Indian-only University of Durban-Westville (now UKZN). Management education and its attendant values were therefore the preserve of white South Africans or of a white managerial class. Indian South Africans were situated higher in the racial and eugenic hierarchy than African and Coloured South Africans and were therefore afforded a business school in the 1970s (Arnold, 2017).

In addition to the entrenchment of white privileged status in the business schools, it has been argued by social historians (Bank, 2015; Dubow, 2006; Sharp, 1981) that higher education in South Africa has its roots in particularly Afrikaner philosophical assumptions about the nature of knowledge and human beings. This philosophy is rooted in an Afrikaner tradition of ethnology known as *Volkekunde*. Volkekunde was the value and epistemological system that dominated South African universities from their inception and filtered into a range of natural and social science disciplines, biology, psychology, sociology, and anthropology. These values were transmitted in complex ways to managers through business school education to sustain the apartheid workplace regime and its hierarchies, in which whites were natural managers and blacks were kept in positions of servitude (Bezuidenhout, 2005, p. 82).

Volkekunde had a profound influence on the philosophical underpinnings and values of business education in South Africa. Its philosophical assumptions were interwoven with what Ruggunan (2016) has termed a "colonial double-bind". This means that business education has been both a nationalist Afrikaner male dominated (Volkekunde) project during Apartheid and driven by Anglo-Saxon literature and empirical studies.

The western academic influence on South African business education has resulted in a curriculum that is "for the most part, a replication of that which can be found in any western country" (Nkomo, 2015, p. 253). This has been reinforced by the adoption of traditional methods of business education such as case studies, texts books, and lectures. Ehrensal (2001, 2016) argues that the cumulative effect of these methods on business education internationally is to create "capitalism's foot soldiers". If so, then the values transmitted to South African students have been informed by this colonial double bind.

Post-Apartheid Business School Education

Two different strategies for making business schools more critically responsive to the needs of post-Apartheid South Africa were the introduction of more MBA programmes and the commitment by many business schools to Principles of Responsible Management Education (PRME).

The Expansion of Business Education in South Africa: The Introduction of MBAs

With the dismantling of Apartheid from 1994, there was a proliferation of business schools offering MBAs and a massification of higher education at undergraduate and postgraduate levels in South Africa.

Management education offerings especially proliferated due to the post-Apartheid state's need to professionalise the public sector. As the Council for Higher Education (CHE) 2004 report on MBA programmes in South Africa noted:

> *The opening up not just of higher education but of state enterprises and private business to black people has accentuated the need to prepare new management cadres and has therefore inspired renewed interest in the MBA, creating an opportunity to shape (or reshape) the purposes of business school* (p. 34).

Another reason for the growth in higher education management studies was the post-Apartheid state's emphasis on the need to inculcate entrepreneurship values amongst young, mainly unemployed, black South Africans (CHE, 2004; Arnold, 2017). Thus a twin strategy of professionalising the public sector through MBA and public administration qualifications, as well as trying to ameliorate unemployment of South African youth through entrepreneurship, dominated the management education landscape post-1994. The formal opening of higher education to all South Africans from 1994 contributed to the growth of higher education at public institutes of higher learning. The private higher education sector, sensing a gap in the market (as public universities suffered a human resources and skills deficit of scholars), stepped in and offered a range of business and MBA qualifications. Their quality however was difficult to assess as well as their capacity to respond to pressing economic and social needs (CHE, 2004; Arnold, 2017).

That all was not well became clear when a review was conducted by the CHE which indicated significant shortcomings of these programmes, with some MBA programmes losing their accreditation. However, in relation to the appropriateness of business education for the changed South African context, the review was positive. It indicated that for the most part the MBAs were socially responsive, with modules being offered that addressed the economic concerns of a developing country. Nevertheless, serious concerns were noted about the pedagogical skills of lecturers in most of the business schools covered by the CHE report. These concerns mainly related to assessments and qualification levels of staff (Nkomo, 2015).

For the CHE, the purposes of business education in a developing country are to:

1. Deepen the terms of engagement between business schools and the developmental objectives of the country,
2. Redefine differences between the roles of business and society through MBA programmes,
3. Professionalise the public sector through MBA programmes, thus improving service delivery,
4. Play a development role in terms of skill development, through MBA programmes, of a new managerial cadre in post-Apartheid South Africa.

These are apparently laudable goals, but critical scrutiny leads to some concerns. Points 1 and 2 are so broad that they would be very difficult to translate into curricula or to evaluate. Also, all the goals are phrased from the perspective of the provider rather than the qualities they hope students will develop. They also do not ask questions about *who* needs to be involved in the design of socially responsive curricula. Furthermore, the notion of skills development can also be a linear and mechanical goal which may not incorporate a critical component.

Despite the intentions of the CHE, critical management scholars in South Africa such as Nkomo (2015), Goldman (2016), and Ruggunan (2016) argue that postgraduate business education has not effectively translated into positive managerial behaviours in the public or private sector in a developing country. Recent corporate scandals in South Africa involving KPMG, Bell Potinger, and SAP (Cave, 2017; Bond, 2017; Prinsloo, 2017), as well as increased levels of corruption at the state level, raise questions about the link between a more responsible management education and the actual practice of management in the private and public sectors in South Africa.

There have been significant reforms and changes in curricula since 1994. Part of these reforms is about making management studies more aligned with the context of South Africa. Two significant challenges exist for the MBA, and management studies in general, in fulfilling their developmental role agendas. One is an ideological bias which continues to inform curricula and pedagogy. The second is a lack of genuine interdisciplinarity. By its very nature, management studies presuppose a neo-liberal capitalist system which may not be appropriate in a developing country context. There is little evidence to show that management education in South Africa is interdisciplinary, in the sense that it does not borrow from disciplines outside the traditional management sciences. For example, business schools very rarely employ sociologists, qualitative method specialists, critical theorists, or anthropologists.

This limitation also narrows the range of values and perspectives available to students. For instance, the environment is still represented as a commodity with a quantitative value, and corporate social responsibility (CSR) programmes are conceptualised as one way of preserving this value. The environment cannot therefore have a value outside its identity as a factor of production and growth. Management education and managing, by its nature, is about organising for efficiency and growth. This, especially in a developing world context is cause for concern—given that indefinite growth is not sustainable.

The Impact of PRME

PRME signatories recognise these shortcomings and are developing strategies for business schools to promote responsible management education (which implies that the universal form of management education is irresponsible?) Commitment to PRME is an important recognition in some of South Africa's management education programmes that previously have been largely uncritical and insensitive to the environment and workers. If Volkekunde symbolised the Apartheid era, then PRME is an optimistic symbol of the post-Apartheid era.

Some insight into PRME and its impact on the priorities of business education schools can be ascertained by scrutiny of the language used by South African business schools. The statements of commitment, description of initiatives, and choice of language all express a strengthened focus on social responsibility. Clearly, being a signatory to PRME has pushed business schools to reconsider their offerings, to foreground social, ethical, and environmental responsibilities and to forge new partnerships which help to redefine the relationship between business and society.

For example, the Graduate School of Business at the University of Cape Town (UCT) has introduced social innovation as a "dedicated specialisation stream on the MBA" (Graduate School of Business, University of Cape Town, 2015, p. 3). The language of the report also indicates a commitment to social responsibility in the goals for their students. They aim to promote "a new model of business school—one that is focussed on developing leaders in their local context, grounded in ethical values, and equipped to handle 'complexity, uncertainty and continuous change'" (Graduate School of Business University of Cape Town, 2015, p. 5). The language indicates a shift from linear, outcome-based performance models.

The UCT report describes the development of two lab spaces to promote experiential learning opportunities by acting as:

> *a collaborative living lab for students, social innovators, entrepreneurs, foundations, governments and industry players interested in finding new and creative ways to address complex problems on the continent.* (Graduate School of Business University of Cape Town, 2015, p. 19)

In all the PRME reports, this is the strongest statement about learning experience and environment that business schools should facilitate. It is collaborative, there is input from multiple participants and it is being shaped organically in response to problems. The drawback is that this commitment is not necessarily implemented in the design of curricula and the pedagogy of the rest of the programme.

The language of PRME permeates the report of the Gordon Institute of Business Science (2016, p. 12) at the University of Pretoria. This report states that the curriculum was revised in 2016–2017 and that the revised goals now focus more strongly on "responsible leadership, social responsibility and inclusivity". The report points to courses that reflect this shift in focus and the introduction of a new South African book as a resource, *The Disruptors: Social entrepreneurs reinventing business and society* (Krige & Silber, 2016). It:

> *contains academic sections which have been integrated into the individual stories in order to create layers of knowledge around responsible leadership in the South African context with a specific focus on Social Enterprise (a blended model adapted by considering the best practices in business and the current needs or challenges faced by civil society).* (Gordon Institute Business School, 2016, p. 18)

A text of this kind is an important development in a field that has traditionally been highly reliant on imported texts.

The report of the Business School at the Nelson Mandela Metropolitan School (2016, p. 10) exemplifies the shift in language away from performance outcomes to a broader vision in the aspiration "to create holistic leaders" and contextual responsiveness in the introduction of a specialist leadership programme "that is specifically designed to inculcate African leadership styles". This report also cites the inclusion of dedicated CSR modules and claims it is "embedded in most modules in the MBA" (p. 6). Another trend is the development of modules that involve community engagement and commitment to social responsibility.

At the same time, the PRME progress reports indicate that there remain serious unanswered questions about the interface between business schools and the social context. Using these reports as the litmus test of the current direction of business education, it is argued that there does not appear to be a fundamental re-evaluation of assumptions about the nature of business relationships within the workforce. There is also a question about the impact of international accreditation on thinking about the curriculum and models of learning and teaching. Furthermore, while there are significant changes to curriculum content and some core innovations in the learning experiences offered to students, the reports do not suggest a strong focus on questions of ownership of curriculum design and appropriate pedagogy to facilitate social change.

All the reports suggest a refocusing of business education, but they do not ask explicit questions about the paradigms of capitalism and the role of workers, nor do they draw on other disciplines such as Sociology, Labour Relations, and Psychology to interrogate the validity of ideological premises. While there is a strong expression of commitment to local and regional needs, quality of postgraduate education is still linked to accreditation by international accreditation agencies such as Equis. These bodies do expect evidence of social responsibility, but their perspectives are global.

Bodies like Equis also focus on the curriculum and expect certain formal structures in curriculum design such as evidence of well-aligned programmes, assessments, and rubrics. The question needs to be asked whether these externally developed frameworks can accommodate business education programmes that evolve more organically and use more open-ended pedagogical approaches. This concern about the disproportionate influence of international accreditation bodies is voiced by Nkomo (2015) who argues—in keeping with her concept of an inside-out perspective of business education—that ""chasing global rankings" should not be the main goal" (p. 253).

The Business School at Stellenbosch University seeks to reconcile these different drivers in the phrases "locally rooted" and "globally recognised" (University of Stellenbosch Business School, 2016, p. 6) but there is no developed account of how these claims may compete or be reconciled. In terms of curriculum changes, there is still a strong tendency to put faith in the addition of targeted special modules although, in some cases (such as UCT), integrated and experiential learning opportunities are provided through lab spaces. While the reports suggest that stakeholders are consulted in reshaping the curriculum, the ownership of the curricula remains with the Business Schools.

The choice of language is illuminating in this respect. For example, the report of the Business school at Stellenbosch includes phrases such as "delivering top quality postgraduate education to individuals and organisations" (University of Stellenbosch Business School, 2016, p. 8). The word "delivering" suggests handing over something predesigned by programme providers, as opposed to something co-constructed and developed organically. A similar implication is conveyed by: "The GSB has made significant changes to the scope of its academic offerings" (University of Stellenbosch Business School, 2016, p. 10) and: "we are continually aiming to improve our curriculum content, delivery modes and throughput rate" (p. 10). Not only do these statements indicate limited ownership of the curriculum but also the language reflects a performance model.

By contrast with this traditional model—by which academia designs what it thinks society needs—the UCT Business School shows indications of moving towards alternative curricula. One hopeful indicator is UCT's "hosting of transformation dialogues to tease out key elements of concern in the GSB community" (Graduate School of Business University of Cape Town, p. 27).

The impact of PRME is felt also at the University of Kwazulu-Natal (2017) where the School of Management, IT and Governance (SMIG) has been a signatory to PRME since 2013. One practical example is a self-standing module whose designers state that:

> This module specifically focuses on responsible and sustainable management practices with a view to positively impact on the economy, the environment and communities. It is strongly linked to the PRME principles. For students that are not specialising in management, the module provides a holistic perspective of what should be done to ensure responsible and sustainable management practices entail. (University of Kwazulu-Natal School of Management IT and Governance, 2017, p. 22)

However, this indicates a standard delivery model, based on textbooks and supplemented by other resources and use of case studies. In an open seminar in 2017, students commented that transforming curricula for relevance and values is not only about changing the content of modules; it is also about changing *how* teaching and learning modes, modes of assessment, and inclusion of indigenous languages can be achieved. A shift in values needs to be both ideological (e.g., post-colonial discourses, critiques of capitalism) and pedagogical (via assessment, delivery, linguistics).

There is a compelling argument that South African higher education has already experienced a range and depth of curricula transformation since 1994. However, empirically both the pedagogics and the curricula of management studies have not shifted much—as demonstrated by Ruggunan and Sooryamoorthy (2016), and Goldman (2016). They take the view that transformation of management studies in South Africa is a profoundly political project—a "decolonial" approach to transmit overt and covert values—a view that is supported, for example, by global critical management scholars such as Jammulamadaka (2017).

Rethinking Management Education Pedagogy For Transformation in South Africa

Pedagogical Approaches

There is evidence in PRME reports of progress in South African management education, of changes in learning environments and approaches that are context-driven, that challenge traditional notions of business school learning and redefine the boundaries and character of the classroom. However, what is missing from the reports is evidence of comprehensive rethinking of the appropriate pedagogies for social change.

Examples that indicate a fundamental shift in pedagogy include a component of the Rhodes MBA (Rhodes Business School, 2016), where students prepare a teaching case study by identifying an organisational ethical dilemma. They then analyse how it came about and how the organisation and stakeholders responded; they assess how it was managed and provide suggestions for future learning. Also at Rhodes University, a new module termed "academic skills" incorporates an element of community engagement and service learning, where groups of students serve as consultants to businesses in the local township. These examples have many of the pedagogical dimensions that Weybrecht (2017) describes on the future MBA. Her ideas include interdisciplinary involvement of both students and faculty, responding to current events and articulating how business should respond, and overturning all the traditional boundaries of the classroom.

While the PRME reports of places like Rhodes and UCT indicate shifts in understanding of how teaching and learning need to be transformed, they do not suggest there has been a sustained interrogation of pedagogy for the entire endeavour of management teaching and learning and curriculum design. Ruggunan and Spiller (in Goldman et al., 2016) suggest an inquiry-based learning model, in which the curriculum is designed around key actual South African cases, problems, or scenarios and participants draw on multiple disciplines and sources to posit possible solutions. This model would provide a framework which challenges the traditional learner teacher boundaries in higher education and subverts the mould of conventional academic subject boundaries. Additionally, the problem focus creates cognitive dissonance which helps to push learners out of their traditional frame of reference.

In this model the role of academics is to work with students to identify appropriate resources, meetings, interviewees, collaborators, and strategies and provide feedback at each stage of the inquiry. In these respects, the lecturers' role (or that of a team of lecturers) is very close to that of a supervisor in the research process. The students work in groups and the classroom (including the online classroom) is the space for guided group work.

The importance of collaborative learning is highlighted by Blasco (2012), who draws on moral psychology research to argue that ethical learning is acquired through a process of social interaction. The level of guidance and scaffolding is adjusted accorded to both the academic level and needs of the students as well the complexity of the problem. Sustained collaborative intellectual inquiry into real problems should also be complemented by interventions in communities which Nkomo (2015) suggests need to be mandatory for management students.

Such radical reshaping of *how* learning takes place is necessary to overturn the hidden ways in which learners are conditioned to accept certain views as authoritative. Ehrensal (2001) suggests that in the traditional higher education model of learning and teaching, students will acquire a "managerial habitus", as the power invested in academic teachers conveys the impression of absolute values and principles (p. 104). This model, within and beyond the classroom, continues to confer power and authority on an elite academic group, and intellectual inquiry is bounded by the confines of standard subject divisions, text book content and formats, and traditional teaching and assessment methods.

Practical Examples of Reimaging the Curriculum

C Wright Mills (2000: 108) defines the sociological imagination as "connecting personal troubles to public issues". In practice this means designing more imaginative assessments and learning experiences in management education, such as film reviews, African drumming workshops, and workplace theatres for student role plays where they act as clients and employees. Assessment questions help them to transfer this learning into an applied HRM intervention.

Films and workplace theatre in HRM are powerful ways of activating students' sociological imaginations and encouraging them to discuss concepts like leadership, unemployment, diversity management, performance management, job satisfaction, and motivation. The learning experience is interwoven with students' lives, as it needs to be if it is to have the capacity to be transformative.

Conclusion

This chapter has discussed the importance of a management teaching and learning environment that will motivate learners to grapple with the immediacy of social and economic problems. It is argued that PRME has helped with this recognition but that much more needs to be done to create dynamic socially responsive learning opportunities in management Education. Learning environments need to be sites of active and experiential learning, whether simulated as in theatre workshops or social laboratories; or real, as mandatory internships in communities. Within the model of inquiry-based learning, the learning process needs to begin with problems and dissonant situations and solutions, needs input from multiple stakeholders in the community and the workforce and from theoretical insights from different disciplines outside the traditional management school model, such as Sociology, Psychology, and Labour Studies.

References

Arnold, M. (2017). Higher education in management: The case of South Africa. In S. Dameron & T. Durand (Eds.), *The future of management education: Volume 1: Challenges facing business schools around the world*. Springer.

Bank, A. (2015). Fathering Volkekunde: Race and culture in the ethnological writings of Werner Eiselen, Stellenbosch University, 1926–1936. *Anthropology Southern Africa, 38*(3–4), 163–179.

Bezuidenhout, A. (2005). Post-colonial workplace regimes in the engineering industry in South Africa. In E. Webster & K. von Holdt (Eds.), *Beyond the Apartheid workplace: Studies in transition* (pp. 73–96). Pietermaritzburg: University of KwaZulu-Natal Press.

Blasco, M. (2012). Aligning the hidden curriculum of management education with PRME: An inquiry-based framework. *Journal of Management Education, 36*(3), 364–368.

Bond, P. (2017). South Africa: Elite schism allows consensus to emerge. *Green Left Weekly*, 1156, p. 20.

Bonnin, D., & Ruggunan, S. (2016). Professions and professionalism in emerging economies. In M. Dent, I. Bourgeault, J. Denis, & E. Kuhlmann (Eds.),

The Routledge companion to the professions and professionalism (pp. 251–264). London: Routledge.

Butler, A. (2017). *Contemporary South Africa*. New York: Springer.

Cave, A. (2017). Deal that undid Bell Pottinger: Inside story of the South Africa scandal. *The Guardian*. Retrieved from https://www.theguardian.com/media/2017/sep/05/bell-pottingersouth-africa-pr-firm

CHE (Council on Higher Education). (2004, October). The state of the provision of the MBA in South Africa. In *Higher Education Monitor*. Pretoria: The Council on Higher Education.

Cloete, N. (2014). The South African higher education system: Performance and policy. *Studies in Higher Education, 39*(8), 1355–1368.

Dubow, S. (2006). *A commonwealth of knowledge: Science, sensibility, and White South Africa 1820–2000*. Oxford: Oxford University Press.

Ehrensal, K. (2001). Training capitalism's foot soldiers. In E. Margolis (Ed.), *The hidden curriculum in higher education* (pp. 97–113). New York, NY: Routledge.

Ehrensal, K. (2016). Making managers: Towards an understanding of how textbooks, lectures and management case studies interact to inculcate linguistic and managerial habitus. *Tamara Journal of Critical Organisational Inquiry, 14*(2), 65–73.

Goldman, G. (2016). On the possibility of fostering critical management studies in South Africa. *Acta Commercii, 16*(2), 3–30.

Goldman, G. A., Callaghan, C. W., Lee, G. J., Moraka, N. V., Nienaber, H., Ruggunan, S., et al. (2016). *Critical management studies in the South African context*. AOSIS.

Gordon Institute of Business Science, University of Pretoria. (2016). *UN principles of responsible management education report. Sharing information on progress (SIP)*.

Graduate School of Business, University of Cape Town. (2015). *Report on Progress PRME 2015*.

Jammulamadaka, N. (2017). A postcolonial critique of Indian's management education scene. In *Management education in India* (pp. 23–42). Singapore: Springer.

Krige, K., & Silber, G. (2016). *The disruptors: Social entrepreneurs reinventing business and society*. Bookstorm Pty Limited.

Mills, C. W. (2000). *The sociological imagination*. Oxford: Oxford University Press.

Ndevu, Z., & Muller, K. (2017). A conceptual framework for improving service delivery at local government in South Africa. *African Journal of Public Affairs, 9*(7), 13–24.

Nelson Mandela Metropolitan University Business School. (2016). *UN principles for responsibility management education, sharing information on progress report.*

Nkomo, S. (2015). Challenges for management and business education in a 'developmental' state: The case of South Africa. *Academy of Management Learning & Education, 14*(2), 242–258.

Prinsloo, L. (2017). U.S. authorities probe Germany's SAP as Gupta scandal escalates. Retrieved from https://www.bloomberg.com/news/articles/2017-10-26/sap-finds-indications-of-misconduct-in-s-africa-on-gupta-links-j9887hnz

Rhodes Business School. (2016). *Principles for responsible management education; Sharing information on progress report.*

Ruggunan, S. (2016). Decolonising management studies: A love story. *Acta Commercii, 16*(2), 103–138.

Ruggunan, S., & Sooryamoorthy, R. (2016). Human resource management research in South Africa: A bibliometric study of authors and their collaboration patterns. *Journal of Contemporary Management, 13*(1), 1394–1427.

Sharp, J. (1981). The roots and development of Volkekunde in South Africa. *Journal of Southern African Studies, 8*(1), 16–36.

Sisk, T. (2017). *Democratization in South Africa: The elusive social contract.* Princeton University Press.

Terreblanche, S. (2002). *A history of inequality in South Africa, 1652–2002.* University of KwaZulu-Natal Press.

University of Kwazulu-Natal. (2017) *Sharing information on progress report.*

University of Stellenbosch Business School. (2016). *Sharing information on progress (SIP) on the implementation of principles of responsible management.*

Webster, E., & Adler, G. (1999). Toward a class compromise in South Africa's "double transition": Bargained liberalization and the consolidation of democracy. *Politics & Society, 27*(3), 347–385.

Webster, E., & Von Holdt, K. (Eds.). (2005). *Beyond the apartheid workplace: Studies in transition.* University of KwaZulu-Natal Press.

Weybrecht, G. (2017). *The future MBA: 100 ideas for making sustainability the business of business education.* Abingdon, UK: Routledge.

Wilkinson, A., Pettifor, A., Rosenberg, M., Halpern, C. T., Thirumurthy, H., Collinson, M. A., et al. (2016). *The future MBA: 100 ideas for making sustainability the business of business education.* Greenleaf: Routledge.

3

From Occupation to Cultural and Social Responsibility in Philippine and Puerto Rican Business Education: A First-Stage Historical Research Perspective

Ronald K. Goodenow

Introduction

MBA programs, where many corporate social responsibility (CSR) programs are located, pose interpretive challenges because of their growth and popularity in many nations (Byrne, 2014).

In 2008, there were over 100,000 MBA degrees awarded yearly. By 2014 the number had doubled and since then has been growing rapidly and globally (Economist, 2015).

Educational transfer and international educational relations include the development and use by dominant external powers of international educational networks to serve their interests and those of local elites. These include concepts of Americanization and citizenship, encouraged both by immigration at home and imperialism abroad. However, newer strategies (Eisemon, 1977) have emerged to develop institutions from the bottom up to meet challenges of economic growth (or decline). They aim to improve leadership in corporations and government agencies

R. K. Goodenow (✉)
Northborough, MA, USA

© The Editor(s) (if applicable) and The Author(s), under exclusive licence to Springer International Publishing AG, part of Springer Nature 2018
E. Christopher (ed.), *Meeting Expectations in Management Education*,
https://doi.org/10.1007/978-3-319-76412-2_3

through robust university-based programs that introduce important moral and ethical components to management education (Augier & March, 2011).

CSR: Cultural Identification and Protection Issues

CSR is a component of many MBA and other business programs that claim increasingly to address cultural identification and protection issues (McWilliams, 2015). There is research (Wanderley, Lucian, Farache, & de Sousa Filho, 2008) which shows that many programs are impacted by local conditions and attitudes, and political considerations may or may not favor capitalistic approaches for embedding students into corporate environments. CSR can be a 'trojan horse' which gives universities greater access to companies, and companies greater access to universities in a symbiotic relationship. It may be argued that CSR is still in an incubation phase and that local conditions may affect its overall development. National setting is important, as are such factors as class, ethnicity, gender, and the respect and trust the business school enjoys in its university.

Two main curricular thrusts encourage management students to identify and address social problems and issues in their future areas of influence, and to deal responsibly with specific problems associated with civic, environmental, inter-agency, and similar organizations. Importantly, as justification for programs, and to attract students and funding, there is generally a focus on ethics and moral values. Many universities require or provide international exchange travel opportunities through which students are exposed to the complexities of global business in a series of engagements with leaders worldwide. Immersions in Asia, Latin America, and Europe provide opportunities to experience other cultures first-hand (Tucker, 2014).

There are many critics of CSR programs (Dudovskiy, 2012). They are viewed either as strengthening the legitimacy and role of capitalism or as weakening business outcomes and perhaps capitalism itself. Cultural issues range from protecting national monuments, recognizing issues-related community history, and expressing concern that dominant cultures pay too little attention to the values of those whom they dominate.

The Philippines: American Occupation and Its Americanization of Local Values

The Spanish–American War, which began with the sinking of the *USS Maine* in Havana harbor in 1898, led to a brief war, after which the Treaty of Paris provided US control of Cuba. Spain ceded Puerto Rico, Guam, and the Philippine islands (Klose & Lader, 2001).

The Philippines is now an independent Asian nation with a population of approximately 103 million people, spread out over 7000 islands. It gained independence from the United States in 1946 under a long-standing agreement and years of virtual independence, save during the World War II Japanese occupation. Prior to colonization by the United States its educational system was subjected to massive amounts of educational transfer and institution building by Spain. Its history has been complicated by geography, religious diversity, corruption, and dictatorial regimes (Abinales & Amoroso, 2017).

After Spain turned the Philippines over to the United States, cultural change became a hallmark of American colonial policy, as in many conquered lands. Because of its emphasis on education, and good citizenship, many Filipinos were supportive, and in any case US policy was reinforced by its position of strategic power, including a powerful navy and expansionist commercial interests (Bello, 1998; Hincks, 2016). Nevertheless, there was local opposition. In 1899 war broke out between the US and Filipino nationalists, led by Emilio Aguinaldo (Turot, 1981), who had fought the Spanish and wanted full independence. The result was huge military and collateral damage, and the deaths of perhaps 200,000 Filipinos.

Despite Filipino anger about American brutality, Americans argued that defeating 'insurgency' would lead to American success as conqueror and nation builder, much as using force at home would turn native Americans into good Christian citizens. The United States established the Insular Government of the Philippine Islands (under the US Bureau of Insular Affairs) in 1901, which ruled the Philippines until Commonwealth status was granted in 1935. The first Philippine Assembly was convened in 1907, and in 1916 the Jones Act promised full independence (Jones, 2012).

Educational Transfer and Relations: American Ideals and Training in the United States

American ideas on preparing Filipinos to be responsible citizens of a newly built nation required that education should serve very important goals of social control. This entailed patiently embedding American moral and political values, setting aside local religious and gender-separated education, 'practical' training and, as time went on, institution building. It was not coincidental that the US military was given responsibilities for building and staffing new schools. Clark (2015) noted that the hallmark of American influence on the Philippine education system has been a relatively inclusive system of higher education.

A major goal of American occupation was to encourage self-rule, building expectations for commonwealth status and ultimate independence. The 1903 Pensionado Act (Baldoz, 2011) legalized a massive educational transfer of the morality of dominant American colonial objectives and behaviors. It provided for students to be sent to the United States to further their education. These students were called *pensionados* since they were scholars studying at the expense of the colonial government and were expected to come home and become civil servants and constitute new elites wrapped in the trappings of de facto Americans (Maramba & Bonus, 2012). Americans ruled that English was to be spoken in the schools because it was cosmopolitan and would open more doors than the many languages spoken in the Philippines. Required religious instruction was ended and the US occupiers built teacher education institutions based on US models (Thompson, 2003).

The prominent Yale educationist, George S. Counts (Counts, 1978), who became a leading 'social reconstructionist', called for schools to reform to meet the challenges facing American education and society. His report strengthened efforts to create teacher education colleges and send Filipinos to the United States for training. It legitimized American policy and created the resources for new higher education efforts, including business schools.

The evolution of business education in the Philippines began with the formation of the Manila Business College (2017), which was created in 1904 to help area businesses to employ trained secretaries and clerks. This was the true 'practical education' goal of many Philippine and American colonial business schools over the years. The name Manila Business College was changed to the Philippine School of Commerce in 1908, and again in the 1970s to the Polytechnic University of the Philippines. Its stated objectives are to develop individuals not only technically but also morally, who will play significant roles in nation building.

A recent British Council study (Darko & Quijano, 2015) projected the Philippines to have one of the fastest growth rates in higher education participation among emerging markets this decade. There is considerable competition for educational resources, which the government has increased, even as much of the economy languishes.

The Founding and Growth of the Asian Institute of Management—United States Influence Personified

Asian Institute of Management (AIM) (2017) was formed in 1968 in partnership with Ateneo De Manila University, De La Salle University, Harvard Business School (HBS), the Ford Foundation, and visionaries of the Asian academic and business communities. It took up the HBS case study teaching methodology and now has over 40,000 graduates and maintains relations with many international organizations and institutions, achieving international distinction. It has the only Philippine CSR program that is recognized in global rankings, though not yet highly so (Financial Times, 2017). It provides a good example of educational transfer through relations with preeminent and powerful US educational forces. Though not on most major rankings of CSR providers (Strauss, 2017), it does offer students opportunities to engage in CSR programs in cooperation with many companies and agencies. Its Policy Center looks at socially marginalized populations and aims to build inclusive democracy in the Philippines.

AIM's Customized Development Education Programs addresses CSR directly. Its web site focuses on Asian companies and agencies with CSR units, and customized courses built in cooperation with companies, students, and potential participants. Programs are in several countries, including the Philippines, Cambodia, India, Hong Kong, Dubai, Indonesia, and the Asia Pacific. Many 'partners' are large multinationals, including the World Bank and government agricultural agencies.

A recent study (Sharma, 2013) suggests that the Philippines lags seriously in CSR application, but on the positive side, large businesses and CEOs are in support of social responsibility and are promoting CSR from the top down, and the government doubled spending on health, education, and social protection between 2010 and 2014. The nation is at high risk for the kind of natural disasters that climate change is making worse, encouraging environmental awareness and support for reducing greenhouse gas emissions. However:

- Corruption is still a part of Philippine business.
- Poverty levels are high, as is unemployment and unofficial employment.
- The current population must be better educated to fill the jobs that will be created in coming years.
- The general definition of 'social responsibility' is still closer to philanthropy or charity than an effort for responsible and sustainable living across all systems.
- There are rebel uprisings, natural disasters, and infrastructure issues that often compete with achieving greater social responsibility (Lorenzo-Molo, 2009).

Added to this list must be the current international outcry over extrajudicial killings ordered by the Philippine president, and this may impact individual international programs which value morality and civic responsibility as part of robust CSR programs. There is also evidence of change in pedagogy, including a growing online presence for business education and management training which expands the reach of institutions in many directions. One university which offers courses online is the AMA Computer University (AMA). Its major instructional goal is to teach an appreciation of cultural, ethical, and global issues and their impact on business theory and practices. It offers a course on Social Responsibility and Good Governance. The AMA also offers programs which stress the knowledge needed to use information technologies effectively, a subject that recently seems to have entered business school curricula.

A Distributed and Cooperative Learning Environment

The Asian Institute for Distance Education offers a bachelor of science in business administration which includes courses in marketing management. It has agreements with several universities to provide 'learning centers' for enrolled students. It addresses quality improvement, good governance, and the relationship between organizations and various environmental forces which are key components of the global economy (Vallado, 2017). A general review of business school websites and management programs by this writer reveals a heavy emphasis on creating leaders to provide nation building and finding a place in the regional political economy, with associated goals. These include conducting research and managing for national development, cultural/heritage preservation and protection, addressing topical climate issues, joining regional networks and programs, and applying religious values to business practices.

Continued American Ties

An example of collaborative relations with an American business school, the Harvard Business School Club of the Philippines (2017) is available to graduates of the HBS or have spent a year in a Harvard program leading to a degree, as well as HBS faculty and staff. Its goals are to:

- Be one of the premier HBS clubs in the world,
- Engage the majority of HBS alumni on a regular basis,
- Showcase HBS' thought leadership,
- Develop future leaders,
- Help build the Philippines.

The American Chamber of Commerce of the Philippines (AMCHAM Philippines), founded in 1920, has a wide ranging and powerful group of sponsors, including Ford, Pfizer, and P&G, and a long list of corporate members committed to developing and looking after the welfare of American businesses in the Philippines. Though most members are companies, it encourages students to join. Its programs discuss a wide range of subjects, including technology, business development in poor urban areas, leadership and organizational development issues. From its curriculum it can be argued that AMCHAM plays a major business education role in the Philippines (Negron de Montilla, 1975).

Puerto Rico

The American occupation of Puerto Rico, officially now a Commonwealth and Unincorporated Territory of the United States, resembled that of other territories gained at the turn of the twentieth century (Van Middeldyk, 1903). The first Puerto Rican governor was elected popularly roughly 50 years later, in 1949.

Previously, under the Foraker Act of 1900 (Sanabria, 2017), a US appointed governor oversaw a House of Representatives limited in nature, and in 1917 The Jones–Shafroth Act—also known as the Jones Act of Puerto Rico—established a Senate, and restricted trade to the island to favor US shipping companies and industries (Rivera-Negrón, 2017). As in the Philippines, Americans, as an imperial power, struggled to recast 'passive and plastic' natives in their own 'civilized' image (Maunier, 2013), eventually using native Puerto Ricans who incorporated American behaviors and ideas to administer the system and its values. Unlike the Philippines, Puerto Rico has endured long-standing cycles of economic decline, affected deeply by recent hurricanes which are driving out migrations of up to 2000 individuals a day (Platt, 2017).

In 2017, there were 203 accredited post-secondary institutions on the island (US Department of Education, 2017). Approximately 250,000 students were enrolled in the 155 Puerto Rican institutions that received federal financial aid in the fall of 2015.

Commissioners of Education, virtually all of whom were Americans, appointed by the president of the United States from 1900 until 1949, focused on Americanization, system centralization, and language requirements for Americanization (Negrón de Montilla, 1975). In the Philippines, American history was introduced to the schools, and steps in the direction of independence were taken and honored. In the case of

Puerto Rico, Americanization was a given, but there have been numerous Presidential, Congressional and commission recommendations which pointed to political solutions, all clouded by indecision on the part of Puerto Ricans themselves (Newkirk II, 2016).

English was used in non-public education and higher grades, and Spanish in most elementary education, with steps to bilingualism taken over time (Soong, 2000). To the degree possible, Americanization was assumed totally to replace Puerto Rican culture, and Puerto Ricans were selected to study in the United States, to be immersed in American history and culture. In the early years Booker T. Washington and his Tuskegee Institute (Bailey, 2016) welcomed students to study his form of industrial education, and programs for Native Americas were emulated in Puerto Rico. Historically, major changes in the economy and society have posed significant challenges to the education sector, including higher education, with 'modernization' coming to an island of approximately 3.7 million but late in the twentieth century, 100 years after occupation.

Angulo (2012) writes that US political and corporate interests overwhelmed Puerto Rico's political economy during the first decades of the US occupation. The Foraker Act (Burnett & Marshall, 2001)—as much an economic instrument as a political one—denied the island the ability to negotiate treaties with other countries, gave the United States control over the island's tariff rates, and required partial distribution of tariff revenues to the United States. The wealth extraction from Puerto Rico removed a vital revenue source for internal developments, particularly those having to do with the Puerto Rican educational system.

Significant changes took place between 1947 and 1952 when Commonwealth status was awarded, and the late 1960s when Puerto Rico saw major industrialization (Dietz, 1986). With an emergent urban industrial society, issues of social class, modern capitalism, and economic consumption transformed the island's culture and contributed to the rise of violence and the use of drugs. At the same time, an educated work force was needed. This in turn led to growth in higher and business education which, however, has neither stemmed the tide of emigration nor reduced poverty, which, along with employment, will doubtlessly be made worse by recent hurricanes.

There are now three business schools in Puerto Rico, all of which offer MBA degrees (Wintergreen Orchard House, 2010): the University of Puerto Rico (UPR)—Río Piedras Campus, the University of Turabo, and the Pontificia Universidad Catolica de Puerto Rico. Prior to the 1960s large numbers of Puerto Rican students studied at universities in the United States and returned home, where it was hard to apply what they had learned, in part because their mainland training contained virtually no emphasis on cultural issues, whether those issues applied to Puerto Rico or the United States itself, where there were large number of Puerto Ricans. Clearly, it appears that knowledge transfer was blocked by conditions on the ground and in the halls of policy formation.

Puerto Ricans have responded with business programs that resemble those in the domain of CRS, though not called such, and have applied communications technologies to build distance and online learning in an environment of economic decline and, now, hurricane devastation.

Distance Learning for the Diaspora—A Culturally Sensitive Initiative

The Carlos Albizu University (CAU) was founded in 1966 in San Juan Puerto Rico (Albizu, 2017). It is now a relatively small non-profit school (c. 2000 students) with an offshore campus and business school which has highly diverse goals. The Miami campus is the only institution in the United States named after a Hispanic, in this case a distinguished psychologist, professor, and prolific author who specialized in the study of cross-cultural issues in mental health training and service delivery and helped found the institution (Gotay, Santana, & Vazquez, 2016).

The founding of the Miami school in the 1980s corresponded to a growing interest in Puerto Rican culture and mental health, heretofore dominated by US interests that showed little concern for Puerto Rican life and culture, let alone a growing diaspora. The university's small business program is not on its Puerto Rico campus. It is in Miami and graduates about 30 business students per year. Its orientation is toward multicultural, psychological, and ethical issues sensitive to community needs. 'Cultural sensitivity' is a commonly used descriptor as part of its claim to be the first business school to focus on multicultural issues. Clearly, this fits into a broad definition of CSR.

Pedagogically, the MBA program at CAU uses a non-traditional 'fast-track' delivery format and focuses on non-profit organizations. MBA students complete one cluster of three courses per academic session. Its format is designed for attending classes once a week and completing one intensive course at a time. In contrast to Philippine business offerings, there is no mention of a need for national leaders and nation building, focusing instead on the 'multicultural' character of Miami and its student body.

The Status of Puerto Rico's National Universities—Steps Forward

The UPR provides the most academic choices with 472 academic programs, including 32 which can lead to a doctorate. The UPR is also the only institution with a business school, an engineering school, a law school, a nursing school, a school of architecture, and a school of medicine. Almost all its schools and programs rank first on the island, although competition has increased in the last decades, with private universities gaining traction at a fast pace. It has undergraduate and graduate programs in business education, some of which offer online courses.

Current data (UPR, 2017) suggest that of the 16,454 students currently enrolled at the UPR—Río Piedras, the site of business programs, only about 0.1% (20) participate in some form of distance or online learning, and but 20 students take classes exclusively because students enrolled in online programs live in a variety of places. Eighteen live in Puerto Rico, 20 live in the United States and none live outside of the United States.

Generally, efforts at the university to establish distance learning programs have not been successful. The Río Piedras campus is the flagship institution of the UPR. It has made several attempts, throughout its history, to establish a distance education environment. None have succeeded. A new grassroots movement is developing, which is conscious of history. It is growing in a conscious process of organizational culture change (Meléndez, 2001).

The Inter American University of Puerto Rico, founded in 1912 as an elementary and secondary school, is now a large ecumenical Christian university, with campuses throughout the country and a population of around 40,000 students (San Juan, PR, 2017). It is the largest private university in Puerto Rico and offers several business degrees, including an Associate in Applied Science (AAS) and Bachelor in Business Administration (BBA) and MBA programs in Accounting, Finance, Human Resources, Marketing, and Managerial Information Systems. Its Ponce campus houses a Small Business Development Center, through a cooperative agreement with the US Small Business Administration. Training, seminars, workshops, advising of new and existing small businesses, and assistance to minorities (women, veterans, and handicap) are among its services, and it offers online distance education courses in business. It is now marketing online learning internationally, focusing on Florida, which has a growing number of Puerto Ricans, and where it has established a Cyber Study Center. The Ponce campus of the university offers ten online bachelors degrees, including Business Administration and Management, from which 103 students graduated in 2016.

A Partial Conclusion: Needs and Opportunities for Further Research

It is apparent that though the Philippines and Puerto Rico (now virtually destroyed by a hurricane) have lagged behind much of the rest of the world in terms of both business school development and attention to CSR and indigenous culture, steps are now being taken—though limited in scope—to catch up, partly with the help of new communications technologies.

The Philippines, which has a long history of focusing on such cultural elements as historic artifacts, tradition, and its Spanish past, continues its focus on those views of native culture and is slowly implementing CSR in relatively new business school programs in its most highly ranked universities. This is partly in light of its rapid economic growth in a geographic region which has many leading programs and new opportunities for corporate, agency, and inter-agency relationships. In part, as a door to a very prosperous region, it has had extensive international educational relations with the HBS, the Ford Foundation, MIT, and many American agencies and corporations. Beyond this, there are enormous defense relations, and the United States has been aiding in dealing with conflicts with a new generation of radical Muslims.

Puerto Rico is a much smaller entity, ravaged by decades of failed economic policy and political indecision, and now hurricanes. In terms of this chapter, it has a more 'mixed' approach to management education that links its nearby diaspora to its homeland and builds creative uses of communications technologies to do so, albeit limited in nature. The power of outside economic interests—which have dominated the island's overall development through investment and federal aid policies—has introduced instability and created local pressures for more indigenous training. Signs of high prestige business school and corporate involvement are less apparent than grassroots efforts.

The individuals responsible for developing business schools in both the Philippines and Puerto Rico were mostly from educationally elite backgrounds, aware that the creation of such institutions was a critically important task for the maintenance of social order—and American acceptance (Morsing & Rovira, 2011). In choosing the professionalization of management as a path to the institutionalization of university business schools, these organizational entrepreneurs doubtlessly sought to yoke their enterprise to those of other institutional builders in late nineteenth and early twentieth century America. Their efforts were part of what the historian Robert H. Wiebe called the 'search for order' (Wiebe, 1967). This search has included highly professionalized university programs and highly professionalized business management that legitimize emerging industrial and managerial orders, a tradeoff to gain American acceptance and support.

This chapter has not probed the scale or level of detail of courses, textbooks, individual relationships, and other factors—such as national culture and its interplay with cosmopolitan and other external pressures—that might influence managerial behavior in the Philippines and Puerto Rico. Doubtlessly business school faculties attempt to apply concepts and standards of professionalism which would meet corporate approval and at the same time lead companies to more socially responsible behavior. The degree to which relationships, individual backgrounds, and university and corporate cultures can overcome the many historical constraints of colonial and post-colonial influence needs further study.

References

Abinales, P. N., & Amoroso, D. J. (2017). *State and society in the Philippines*. Rowman & Littlefield.

AIM. (2017). Asian Institute of Management. Retrieved December 8, 2017, from http://www.mastersportal.eu/universities/11314/asian-institute-of-management.html

Albizu. (2017). Albizu University. Retrieved December 8, 2017, from http://www.albizu.edu/

Angulo, A. J. (2012). *Empire and education, A history of greed and goodwill from the war of 1898 to the War on Terror* (Kindle ed.pp. 34–35). Basingstoke: Palgrave Macmillan US.

Augier, M., & March, J. G. (2011). *Rituals, and theoretics of change: North American business schools after the Second World War*. Palo Alto: Stanford University Press.

Bailey, B. (2016). *Booker T. Washington and the Tuskegee Institute*. Cavendish Square, 15 July 2016—African American educators.

Baldoz, R. (2011). *The third Asiatic invasion: Migration and empire in Filipino America, 1898–1946*. New York: NYU Press.

Bello, W. (1998). U.S. imperialism in the Asia-Pacific. *Peace Review, 10*(3), 367–373.

Burnett, C. D., & Marshall, B. (2001). *Foreign in a domestic sense: Puerto Rico, American expansion, and the constitution*. Durham: Duke University Press.

Byrne, J. A. (2014, May 31). Why the MBA has become the most popular master's degree in the U.S. *Fortune*.

Clark, N. (2015, June 7). Education in the Philippines. *World Education News and Reviews*, 16–17.

Counts, G. S. (1978). *Dare the school build a new social order?* SIU Press.

Darko, E., & Quijano, T. (2015, August). A review of social enterprise activity in the Philippines. *British Council*.

Dietz, J. L. (1986). *Economic history of Puerto Rico: Institutional change and capitalist development*. Princeton University Press.

Dudovskiy, J. (2012). Criticism associated with corporate social responsibility (CSR). Retrieved from https://research-methodology.net/criticism-associated-with-corporate-social-responsibility-csr/

Economist. (2015, October 17). Still a must-have; MBAs remain surprisingly popular, despite the headwinds.

Eisemon, T. (1977, February). Educational transfer: The social 'ecology' of educational change. *Teachers College Record, 78*, 359–369.

Financial Times. (2017). Business education. Retrieved December 8, 2017, from http://rankings.ft.com/businessschoolrankings/asian-institute-of-management

Gotay, S. S., Santana, R. M., & Vazquez, N. A. (Eds.) (2016). *Love reaches beyond knowledge: Dr. Carlos Albizu Miranda, architect of modern multicultural psychology*. Universidad Carlos Albizu.

Harvard Business School Club of the Philippines. (2017). Retrieved December 8, 2017, from http://www.hbsph.com/s/1738/cc/index.aspx?gid=38&pgid=61

Hincks, J. (2016, October 25). A brief history of U.S. Philippine relations. *Time Magazine*.

Jones, G. (2012). *Honor in the dust: Theodore Roosevelt, war in the Philippines, and the rise and fall of America's imperial dream*. New American Library.

Klose, N., & Lader, C. (2001). *United States history since 1865*. Barron's Educational Series.

Lorenzo-Molo, M. C. F. (2009, June). Why corporate social responsibility (CSR) remains a myth: The case of the Philippines. *Asian Business and Management, 8*(2), 149–168.

Manila Business College. (2017). Retrieved December 8, 2017, from http://www.mbc.edu.ph/

Maramba, D. C., & Bonus, R. (2012). *The 'other' students: Filipino Americans, education, and power*. IAP.

Maunier, R. (2013). *The Sociology of colonies [Part 2]: An introduction to the study of race contact*. Routledge.

McWilliams, A. (2015). Corporate social responsibility. In *Strategic Management* (Vol. 12). Wiley Encyclopedia of Management (published online January 22, 2015).

Meléndez, J. (2001). Distance education: The experience of the University of Puerto Rico/Río Piedras campus. *Journal of Higher Education in Europe, 26*(4), 537–540. Published online July 14, 2010.

Morsing, M., & Rovira, A. S. (2011). *Business schools and their contribution to society*. London: SAGE.

Negron de Montilla, A. (1975). *Americanization in Puerto Rico and the public-school system, 1900–1930* (pp. 18–20). Rio Piedras: Editorial Universitaria.

Newkirk II, V. R. (2016, April 27). A commonwealth in crisis: As Puerto Rico reaches another debt cliff, political dysfunction on the mainland spells disaster. *Atlantic*.

Platt, E. (2017, October 9). Puerto Rico after the storm: An island on the edge. *Financial Times*.

Rivera-Negrón, V. (2017). Through a Puerto Rican lens: The legacy of the Jones Act. Smithsonian Institute; American History. Retrieved February 28, 2017, from http://americanhistory.si.edu/blog/through-puerto-rican-lens-legacy-jones-act

San Juan, PR. (2017). Inter American University of Puerto Rico: Metropolitan campus. Retrieved December 8, 2017, from https://bigfuture.collegeboard.org/college-university-search/inter-american-university-of-puerto-rico-metropolitan-campus

Sanabria, C. (2017). *Puerto Rican labor history 1898–1934: Revolutionary ideals and reformist politics.* Lexington Books.

Sharma, B. (2013). *Contextualising CSR in Asia: Corporate social responsibility in Asian economies and the drivers that influence its practice.* Lien Centre for Social Innovation, Singapore Management University.

Soong, R. (2000). Bilingualism among Puerto Ricans. Retrieved March 25, 2000, from http://www.zonalatina.com/Zldata106.htm

Strauss, K. (2017, September 13). The 10 companies with the best CSR reputations in 2017. *Forbes*.

Thompson, R. M. (2003). *Filipino English and Taglish: Language switching from multiple perspectives* (p. 20). Amsterdam/Philadelphia.

Tucker, L. (2014). 25 reasons to study abroad. Retrieved from https://www.topuniversities.com/blog/25-reasons-study-abroad

Turot, H. (1981). *Emilio Aguinaldo, first Filipino president, 1898–1901.* Philippines: Foreign Service Institute.

UPR. (2017). University of Puerto Rico—Rio Piedras; Online distance learning & online degrees. Retrieved December 8, 2017, from https://www.college-factual.com/colleges/university-of-puerto-rico-rio-piedras/academic-life/distance-learning/

U.S. Department of Education. (2017). Data base of post-secondary institutions and programs. Retrieved December 8, 2017, from https://ope.ed.gov/accreditation/GetDownLoadFile.aspx

Vallado, M. (2017). AIDE…the first distance learning institution for higher education. *AIDE INFO Board, 1*(4), 2. Asian Institute for Distance Education.

Van Middeldyk, R. A. (1903). *The history of Puerto Rico: From the Spanish discovery to the American occupation.* Puerto Rico: Library of Alexandria.

Wanderley, L. S. O., Lucien, R., Farache, F., & de Sousa Filho, J. M. (2008, October). CSR information disclosure on the Web: A context-based approach analysing the influence of country of origin and industry sector. *Journal of Business Ethics, 82*, 369.

Wiebe, R. H. (1967). *The search for order, 1877–1920.* New York: Farrar, Straus and Giroux.

Wintergreen Orchard House. (2010). *Postsecondary sourcebook for community colleges, technical, trade, and business schools; northeast/southeast edition.* Wintergreen Orchard House.

4

A Historical Perspective on Social Expectations for Management Education: Training for Empire

Kay Gillis

Introduction

In 1600, Queen Elizabeth granted a charter to the East India Company (Roy, 2016) and gave it a monopoly of all trade in the Asian region. The company developed into a large trading joint-stock company with factories or trading depots in many parts of India.

In the mid-eighteenth century, however, the role of the company began to change. In 1857, the company's military forces, under Clive (Henty, 2012), defeated the ruler of Bengal and expanded control over the richest state in India (Chowdhury, 2004). By 1800, the company had already gained control over Mysore and Delhi. In less than 50 years, the company had transformed itself from a trading enterprise into an imperial power.

K. Gillis (✉)
Singapore, Singapore

Training for Empire

Low-Level Bureaucrats

These rapid changes led to a demand for improved training and selection criteria for young entry-level employees of the East India Company, who would better meet new expectations for colonial conquest and administration.

For the first 150 years, these employees had been selected by patronage to become 'writers' or low-level bureaucrats (Farazmand, 2001) and were dispatched to India without any training. The shareholders of the East India Company had the right to nominate young lads to these posts, and the number of each shareholder's nominations depended on the size of their shareholding. In 1600, the first 21 shareholders were amongst the wealthiest men in England (Chatterjee, 1998), and this ensured that the nominees came from upper middle-class families.

Many of these boys retired home in later life with extensive private funds of their own and invested in the company to become shareholders with rights to patronage. This formed a closed circle of Anglo-Indian families who dominated the posts within the company. The funds also allowed them to buy seats in Parliament through the purchase of a *rotten borough*, (McGilvary, 2006) and in time they formed an Indian Interest voting bloc within the Parliament which ensured that the rights of patronage were continued. This bloc was often referred to as the Bengal Squad (Keay, 2010).

The 16-year-old boys were dispatched off to India with no training. With some notable exceptions, the system worked well for the company for 150 years. The young servants, as East India Company employees were called (Banerjee, 1943), came from a similar background and education and shared similar values. The company required only that they be 'gentlemen', although this term was not defined. They had survived many years in a harsh boarding school environment, where they developed survival skills, resilience and independence, and were well prepared for the hardships they could expect to find in India. These young lads were chosen by patronage, and a large percentage of these writers came from long-established Anglo-Indian families. This was an advantage as the close-knit community provided the boys with a vital support mechanism when they first arrived in India. The new arrivals learned their trade from experience and guidance rather than training.

Need for Formal Training

With the huge changes taking place in India in the late eighteenth century (Bayly, 1987), it became evident that the admissions criteria and lack of formal training were no longer meeting expectations. What had worked well in a closed trading environment was no longer appropriate for imperial administration.

The first to realise this was Lord Wellesley (Prakash, 2004), the newly appointed Governor General of India. In 1800, he proposed to the directors of the East India Company that a training college be set up at Fort William in India, to provide training for newly arrived writers. Due to communication delays between London and India, Lord Wellesley went ahead with plans for the college without approval from company headquarters in London. The plan never gained any support or backing in London, and the college remained a small shadow of Lord Wellesley's ambitious plans and was only used for language training.

Although Lord Wellesley's suggestion was rejected by the company directors, London finally realised that there was a need to provide suitable training for 'writers' who could assist the company in their new role as colonial administrators and set up the East India College at Haileybury in 1806 (Buettner, 2004). The curriculum was a mixture of traditional English education, such as Latin and Greek, as well as more practical subjects such as Indian law, culture and languages. The students were not subjected to examinations in any subjects and were generally taught by members of the Anglo-Indian group.

Despite some antagonism towards the college at its inception, there is evidence to show that the college graduates were well prepared for their new roles (Vasunia, 2013). They also formed a useful yearly cohort that worked well together during their time in India. To a certain degree, the new training scheme did go some way to professionalise the Indian civil service and to meet the growing demands of Empire.

However, there was no serious attempt to replace patronage with open competition for entry into Haileybury. There was an understanding that any attempt to remove patronage as the entry criteria to the college would bring the weight of the Anglo-Indian lobby down against the idea of a training college. The candidates continued to come from the same background as before. Indeed, until universal education was introduced later in the nineteenth century (Wilson, 2013), there would have been a shortage of well-educated boys outside of these social parameters, and the company did not attempt to search further afield for candidates.

The nineteenth century in England was a period of reform (Cannadine, 2017), and there was a strong push to make changes to the entry criteria to both the Indian Civil Service and the Home Civil Service. It was felt that the use of patronage for entry into both services was outmoded and needed to be replaced by open competition. There were two early attempts to bring the topic of civil service reform to Parliament, in 1813 and again in 1833, but both were defeated by the Indian interest (Neild, 2002). In 1853, a committee was set up to investigate selection and training of candidates for the Indian Civil Service. The objective of the report was to end the use of patronage as the main criteria for entry-level selection.

The committee was dominated by the work of Lord Macaulay, who had long lobbied for the end of patronage and the introduction of open competition (Masani, 2013). He was heavily influenced by Charles Trevelyan, Macaulay's brother-in-law, and by Bernard Jowett, Master of Balliol College. The report was steadily transformed, from an investigation of the need for open competition for entry to Haileybury, into one in which entry to the Indian Civil Service was closed to all but products of universities such as Oxford and Cambridge. Due to the influence of Jowett, there was a strong emphasis on the merits of Balliol College as a training ground for India. In later years, more than 60% of Indian civil servants came from Balliol College (Jones, 1997)

Macaulay's Report emphasised the need for candidates for admission to the service to be 'gentlemen graduates' with intellectual maturity and connections within society, developed within universities. The report was accepted and passed in 1854 and his guidelines for entry into the Indian Civil Service became the blueprint for training and entry criteria for the next 50 years. Haileybury was rapidly bypassed and was closed several years after the report. The report had successfully eliminated patronage and had opened entry requirements to a wider field but remained extremely restrictive.

Summary

Training for Empire passed rapidly through several stages since its inception in 1600. The first stage was the traditional means of patronage and training on the job. This seemed to meet expectations at a time when the East India Company was primarily a vast worldwide trading concern. However, it failed to accommodate the role of imperial administration. The next step was the short-lived college in Fort William. Lord Wellesley had recognised the need for a well-regulated course of training for young writers, but patronage remained in place, and Fort William was replaced by Haileybury in 1806. This college offered training to the young students and provided them with some limited skills in Indian languages, culture and law to meet changing expectations of the task ahead. Entry, however, was still by patronage. The final step was to demand tougher entry criteria by accepting only graduates, 'gentleman graduates', preferably from Balliol College in Oxford. Shortly after Macaulay's report was accepted, the era of the East India Company came to an end, and India instead became the Jewel in the Crown of the British government. However, Macaulay's recommendations for *training for Empire* met the expectations of the new regime and survived the handover. It has been argued (Whitehead, 2003) that education in 'training for Empire' was not entirely a form of cultural imperialism but became effectively a vital preparation for independence and nationhood.

References

Banerjee, D. N. (1943). *Early administrative system of the East India Company in Bengal*. Bengal, India: Longman's Green & Company, Limited.

Bayly, C. A. (1987). *Indian society and the making of the British Empire*. Cambridge University Press.

Buettner, E. (2004). *Empire families: Britons and late Imperial India*. Oxford: OUP.

Cannadine, D. (2017). *Victorious century: The United Kingdom, 1800–1906*. Penguin UK.

Chatterjee, A. (1998). *Representations of India, 1740–1840: The creation of India in the colonial imagination*. Springer.

Chowdhury, M. R. (2004). *Economic exploitation of Bangladesh*. iUniverse.

Farazmand, A. (2001). *Handbook of comparative and development public administration*. CRC Press.

Henty, G. A. (2012). *With Clive in India: Or, the beginnings of an empire*. The Floating Press.

Jones, J. (1997). *Balliol college: A history, second edition: Reissue, with revisions*. Oxford: OUP.

Keay, J. (2010). *The honourable company*. HarperCollins UK.

Masani, Z. (2013). *Macaulay: Britain's liberal imperialist*. Random House.

McGilvary, G. K. (2006). *Guardian of the East India Company: The life of Laurence Sulivan*. I.B.Tauris.

Neild, R. (2002). *Public corruption: The dark side of social evolution*. Anthem Press.

Prakash, O. (2004). *Lord Wellesley and policy of expansion*. India: Anmol Publications.

Roy, T. (2016). *The East India Company: The world's most powerful corporation*. Penguin UK.

Vasunia, P. (2013). *The classics and colonial India*. Oxford: OUP.

Whitehead, C. (2003). *Colonial educators: The British Indian and Colonial education service 1858–1983*. I.B.Tauris.

Wilson, J. P. (2013). *The Routledge encyclopaedia of UK education, training and employment: From the earliest statutes to the present day*. Routledge.

5

Problems in Management Ethics Training: An Indian Perspective

Shashwat Shukla

Introduction

India gained independence from British colonial rule in 1947, led by Mahatma Gandhi, the father of the new nation. The Freedom Movement he created (Kibriya, 1999) was unique in several ways and became a template for other self-rights struggles across the world (Lelyveld, 2011). It was based on principles of ethics and social responsibility, designed to assert the moral authority of the indigenous people and to appeal to the higher conscience of the British.

From the birth of the nation state, these principles constituted a significant part of the Indian psyche, and it might be assumed that, post-independence, India would continue down her chosen ethical path. Indeed, the nation did adopt a forward-looking socialist policy of economic nation building. However, then ended the straight ethical trajectory and there was a twist in the path. As of 2016 the Corruption Perceptions Index of Transparency International ranked India at 79th

---

S. Shukla (✉)
Department of Management, University of Allahabad,
Allahabad, India

place out of 176 countries (Kiran, 2017). The question arises, how did a country, that became independent on the basis of an ethical movement, become so corrupt? This chapter seeks answers and focuses on the importance of educating socially responsible and ethically competent mangers in business and economy—with consequent far-reaching implications for India's developing economy.

The Indian View

Gandhi called himself a practical idealist and was aware of the challenges facing the new nation. His 'talisman' for political and business leaders (Singh & Sundaram, 1996) was that when in doubt or when the self becomes too much, recall the face of the poorest and weakest person you have seen and ask yourself if the step you contemplate will lead to *swaraj* (freedom) for the hungry and spiritually starving millions.

Despite this profound and practical message from Gandhi to managers, the nation has become beset with endemic corruption, and the key players are organizational leaders who represent the sum of individual decisions taken at various levels in the hierarchy. Any action on behalf of an organization is the result of a chain of events wherein the output of one decision maker becomes the input of another, and the power and importance of that final action is immense. This makes a strong case for the inclusion of an ethical and social dimension in the curricula for management education and training.

Currently such education remains mostly on a theoretical, descriptive level that leads to formalism (Dameron & Durand, 2011), that is, excessive adherence to prescribed forms. Formalism is widely prevalent in India, where managerial procedures are very complex and consist of multiple checks and balances. They require concurrence of several authorities, which makes the process dilatory and convoluted. In consequence, efficiency is sacrificed on the altars of probity and transparency, but this is not the worst result. The impression is given that all procedures are being properly followed, but in reality managerial actions are all too often based on greed, nepotism, and prejudice (Vaidya, 2017).

Most Indians have become socialized to accept this as the norm (Dhamija, 2016), so when students receive management training on ethics and social responsibility, they view these concepts from a laissez-faire attitude. This makes the challenge of ethical and social training in the Indian context even more demanding. Students must learn to reject formalism in favour of guidelines on how to work constructively to change a system which rewards unethical and punishes ethical behaviour.

To gain an experiential sense of the ethical challenges faced by Indian managers, the plot lines of two Indian feature fiction films are offered as examples.

Corporate (Bhandarkar, 2006)

The plot of the motion picture *Corporate* centres round the power games of two corporate rivals in the food and beverages business, the Sehgal family group (SGI) and the Marwah Group. The senior vice president of SGI, Ashwani, befriends the Union Finance Minister, and he helps his firm to gain a major competitive advantage over Marwah. However, a public-sector company goes up for sale and each company uses every trick in the book to outsmart the other, with Marwah emerging the victor. Then a member of SGI steals critical information from a Marwah manager's laptop and SGI discovers Marwah has misled the media with a false announcement they would manufacture mineral water in the new plant, whereas in fact they are planning to launch a soft drink. Sehgal promptly announces a launch of their own soft drink, thus pre-empting Marwah.

Ten days before the launch, SGI learns that the Food and Drug Administration (FDA), the food quality regulator, has found a large amount of pesticide in the drink—but Sehgal, the head of the business, decides to go ahead by bribing the FDA agents, though the SGI's chief executive officer resigns in protest. The drink is a great success, but a SGI whistle-blower—furious that he has been overlooked to replace the outgoing CEO—tells Marwah about the pesticide. Marwah blows up the issue in the media, leading to a raid on the SGI plants and a lawsuit against the firm.

Sehgal decides that some SGI employee, who is not a member of the Sehgal family, will have to take the blame. A woman called Nishi is chosen and agrees on the promise she will soon be released by the Enquiry Commission. Foreign investors urge the Union Finance Minister (the SGI executive, Ashwani) to settle the dispute, as it would lead to flight of capital and loss of overseas investment, causing serious havoc in the economy. After mediation, Marwah agrees to withdraw all the allegations and lawsuits and in return gets an equity stake in SGI's soft drink company.

However, the head of the Enquiry Commission refuses to release Nishi, as to do so might damage his chances of being appointed chief minister in the forthcoming state elections. Nishi is pregnant by one of the Sehgal family members, Ritesh, who threatens, when he discovers Nishi is still under arrest, to expose Sehgal's concealment of the pesticide in the soft drink if Nishi is not released within 48 hours. The next day he is found dead, having fallen from the terrace of his apartment building. It is assumed to be suicide, but the movie ends with the narrator concluding that Marwah and Sehgal are living happily in their world, while Nishi has become the victim of corporate tactics. The final scene shows Nishi, alone with her child in a court room, still fighting the legal case two years after it began.

The movie fictionalizes the realities of corruption and inefficiency in the upper echelons of Indian industry. The characters indulge in the kind of malpractices engaged in by senior managers in real life who, ironically, are expected to be custodians of organizational moral and ethical values. Research by Bloom, Mahajan, McKenzie, and Roberts (2011) indicates that, as in the movie, market share of Indian firms is restricted by span-of-control constraints so that all senior managerial positions are held by members of owning families. If these functionaries engage in immoral activities, corruption spreads through the entire organization via the chain of command (Ghoshal, 2005). Employees who resist such actions are shunted out of their positions, as happened in the movie when the CEO of SGI refused to agree to the market launch of a pesticide-infested soft drink. In the movie, whistle-blowers are made scapegoats with the connivance of state agencies, and innocent victims are left to suffer—as can happen in India in real life (Bhatnagar, 2016).

The movie is fiction, but the plot reflects a real situation: that Indian business schools need to address these problems at a much deeper level than at present (Pathak, 2015). If business school campuses are gladiator arenas where the 'winner takes all', then management students are likely to cross ethical boundaries at some point in their careers. More sober and tranquil approaches and reward systems on campuses should go a long way towards mitigating dark practices (Dalal, 2017).

The fundamental issue revealed by the movie *Corporate* is that managers increasingly face pressures of performance to further their careers, and some actively pursue unethical and socially irresponsible behaviour to do so, while others choose to be silent spectators. This suggests that in real life business schools need to discuss extensively with students the concept that instead of striving to win at all costs, ethical action should be evaluated as success.

Rocket Singh: Salesman of the Year (Amin, 2009)

In this movie an average student, Harpreet, decides to make sales and marketing his career. He finds a job at a company called At Your Service (AYS) but fails in his first assignment by refusing a request for a bribe from a potential customer and complaining about it to the customer's firm. AYS loses the contract and Harpreet's boss calls him a fool for not understanding the tricks of the trade. Harpreet finds that his company sells computers to clients at inflated prices, refusing to provide after-sales service even though promising to do so at the time of sale. He is disgusted and plans to start his own company to sell computers at a reasonable price and provide robust after-sales service and support. Four other AYS employees join him as equal partners in a democratic new company called Rocket Sales.

Rocket targets dissatisfied AYS clients and soon builds a strong reputation for customer service. AYS's sales start decreasing and the managing director (MD) becomes aware of the small company's success and decides to buy it. His enquiries lead him to discover that Harpreet and his partners have been secretly running Rocket from AYS premises while still in AYS employment. The MD fires them all and forces Harpreet to hand over ownership of Rocket as compensation.

However, AYS is unable to maintain Rocket's commitment to customer satisfaction because of its greed for profit. The MD returns the contract to Harpreet, telling him his success was due to lack of 'normal' business practices such as kickbacks, false advertisements, and low wages—and therefore Rocket would eventually become bankrupt. However, the movie ending shows the new Rocket Sales office building, implying the firm's success, and closes with Harpreet smiling genially at a desk—thus the moral is that, in the long run, honesty and hard work are sound business practices.

This movie illustrates the real-life challenges faced by individuals in India when they join an organization at a junior level. On the one hand, they are vulnerable and dependent on seniors for promotion and appraisal; on the other hand, they may become aware that those same seniors are engaged in corrupt and unethical practices and may have to pay a high price for speaking out against them.

Another topic is that of competing alliances. Organizational cultures are in a dynamic equilibrium whose balance keeps shifting with differences in the views of various groups and individuals within the organization. If people who share an ethical point of view begin to network, they may force changes to a corrupt system and resist any vindictive action to silence them.

Another fundamental management issue that the film explores is resource constraints (Weiss, 2014). The hero puts himself under constraint by pursing an ethical policy. However, at least one real-life study of strategic management (Keupp & Gassmann, 2013) shows that such constraints can be a source of great dynamism and innovation for the organization. They may constitute an incentive for the organization to improve its processes and structures, while unethical practices may lead to stagnancy and complacency that erode competitive advantage—as in the film the corrupt AYS corporation proves unable to provide prompt and efficient customer service and loses market share to the more competitive Rocket.

The movie deals also with the relationship between ethics and human resource policies. A corrupt organizational culture is one of secrecy, suspicion, and intrigue, and the quality of work life suffers accordingly. In the movie, Rocket's ethical culture values all employees' contributions equally, no matter what their position in the hierarchy—in contrast to the disrespect with which AYS treats its employees.

Finally, the issue is raised of individual choice of behaviour. The hero, in the closing moments of the movie, is shown as having moved on successfully to a new organization. He was not seen as a helpless victim when faced with an ethical challenge; he exercised his option to find better opportunities outside the old organization rather than compromising his core values.

Framework for Ethical Teaching in Management Education

Four important implications emerge from these fictional examples of managerial behaviour, in terms of ethical issues that need to be addressed in management education curricula:

1. *Ethical challenges are linked to organizational hierarchies*

   In organizational contexts, ethical challenges change with career development. At junior levels, individuals tend to absorb the organizational culture and to follow its norms, even if these are sometimes at odds with their personal values. This is partly in fear of being criticized for insubordination and partly to avoid any threat to career, but there may be collateral damage in the form of psychological stress and mental and physical fatigue (Rossy, 2011). Cooper and Cartwright (1997) have devised a three-pronged intervention strategy for managing pressures at work that provides an example of how management education might deal with this issue.

   At senior levels, challenges arise from the need to make decisions on behalf of the organization. Temptations may arise to compromise company interests for personal benefit or to misuse authority by bullying or harassing juniors, and management education should deal with these (Heyneman, 2004).

2. *Ethics as a set of simple rules*

   The literature on strategic management (e.g. Eisenhardt & Sull, 2001) suggests that a set of strategic objectives can be converted into a series of processes or rules. If this argument is applied to management education, it may be that ethics should be introduced to students as a set of work-related statements or processes that can be applied easily to corporate situations (Baggini & Fosl, 2007). For example, the University of California in San Diego (Blink, 2014) elaborates on a seven-step path before making ethical decisions:

- Stop and think
- Clarify goals
- Determine facts
- Develop options
- Consider consequences
- Choose
- Monitor and Modify

3. *Ethics as a resource constraint*

Ethical training for management students might include discussion of the resource constraint theory of strategy management (Ronen, 2005) and include ethics as a behavioural constraint (Sims & Quatro, 2008) that can be a vital source of innovation, creativity, and efficiency (Gibbert & Scranton, 2009).

4. *Ethics as a core professional attribute of management*

All professional disciplines subscribe to defining codes of conduct and values that give meaning to members' roles, work, and careers (Guttmann, 1996). Management education should include discussion of the psychological importance of professional values: if abandoned—even for pecuniary or other material gain—the loss must lead eventually to personal dissatisfaction and spiritual emptiness.

Current Ethical Training and Education of Managers in Indian Universities

In terms of the above, these can be discussed on three levels: curriculum, textbooks, and teaching methodology.

Curriculum

The University Grants Commission of India (UGC) is a statutory body set up by the Indian Union government (UGC ACT, 1956) under the Ministry of Human Resource Development, charged with coordination, determination, and maintenance of standards of higher education. It provides recognition to universities in India and disburses funds to recognized universities and colleges. Under the UGC, the National Educational Testing Bureau of University Grants Commission conducts the National Eligibility Test (NET) to ensure minimum standards for teaching and research. Its syllabus is the model followed by most Indian universities, and for ethics in management training is as follows:

- *Ethical issues and analysis in management;*
- *Value-based organizations;*
- *Personal framework of ethical choices;*
- *Ethical pressures on individuals in organizations;*
- *Gender issues;*
- *Ecological consciousness;*
- *Social responsibilities of business;*
- *Corporate governance and ethics.*

This general curriculum aims to give teachers pedagogical flexibility, but the NET for teachers does not require candidates to demonstrate more than a superficial understanding of business ethics, and the relative importance of ethics in the question paper is less than that given to other topics in the syllabus.

Textbooks

Another important factor in ethics and social responsibility education for prospective managers is the quality of the prescribed text books for students. There are of two kinds: international books by foreign authors, and those written by Indian authors. Both are inadequate in some ways. While the international editions are of high academic quality, the examples and case studies are not of Indian origin and this constitutes cross-cultural barriers to understanding nuanced topics like ethics in management. As for Indian textbooks, they tend to be mostly theoretical, with a focus on student examination material rather than guidelines for real-life management situations.

For example, a popular and respected international text book in India, on organizational behaviour, is Robbins and Judge (2012). It illustrates the relationship between organizational culture and ethics as follows:

> *If the (organizational) culture is strong and supports high ethical standards, it should have a very powerful and positive influence on employee behavior When Tylenol (a Johnson & Johnson product) was found poisoned on store shelves, employees… across the United States independently pulled the product from (their) stores…they knew what Johnson & Johnson leadership would expect them to do. On the other hand…Enron's aggressive culture, with unrelenting pressure on executives to rapidly expand earnings, encouraged ethical corner cutting and eventually contributed to the company's collapse and the ultimate conviction of leaders Ken Lay and Jeff Skilling…(p. 288).*

Though Indian students can relate to these examples, identification would be much stronger had they been of Indian companies—for instance, the telecommunication industry scam (Yardley & Timmons, 2010) that plunged India into political crisis. Since the background would be known to students, they would be more likely to acquire emotional and experiential understanding of the importance of managerial ethical and social responsibility rather than from American examples.

Another case from the same book (Robbins & Judge, 2012) deals with ethical standards of political behaviour:

> *Major league baseball player Al Martin claimed he played football at the University of Southern California when in fact he never did…Outright lies … may be a rather extreme example of impression management, but many of us have distorted information to make a favorable impression…* (p. 237)

The example is of a United States sport star and related to a sport which is not followed much in India. It is not likely to evoke the same interest as, say, accusations of match fixing by the Indian Premier League of cricket (Bhatia, 2017). Cricket is a very popular sport in India and this controversy was a topic of considerable public debate.

As for Indian text books on management, the authors write from an examination point of view. They do not focus on practical application of management concepts, but concentrate on theoretical material, and in any case, are often merely simplified versions of international texts. The following quotation is from a widely studied Indian text (Aswathappa, 1991), on ethics and political behaviour:

> A person's behavior must satisfy three criteria if it were to be ethical. These are...of utilitarian outcomes...of individual rights...of distributive justice... (p. 354).

While this would be useful for management students in answering examination questions in 30–50 words, they do not equip them to deal with the kinds of ethical issues discussed above.

Teaching Methodology

Since business ethics is paid less attention than is given to other topics in management education curricula, students remain ill-equipped to deal with ethical issues they will face in their careers. They are taught largely to perceive ethics in formalistic terms, and there is a great need for more experiential methods such as case studies and films to provide some real-life management scenarios. Choice theory of psychotherapy (Glasser, 2010) may be used to identify ethical alternatives to the kinds of unethical behaviour seen in movies *Corporate* and *Rocket*, and may lead to deeper understanding by students of ethical values as well as skills to apply them.

The Way Forward

Granted a demand–supply gap between the needs of the management students and the training they receive, it is imperative to fill it by developing a fresh model for ethics education. The model needs to incorporate the following four key concepts:

Concept #1
Managers' ethical challenges are linked with their position in the organizational hierarchy. At the lower level the challenges are more about choosing between insubordination or compliance with an unethical practice, while at the senior level the issues tend to be related to greed and personal grandiosity.

Concept #2
Ethics comprises a set of simple and connected rules for problem-solving, such as a seven-step path to making ethical decisions (Blink, 2014). In brief, the basic tenets of choice therapy (Glasser, 2010) are as follows:

1. Identify the relevant behaviour
2. Identify the fundamental need it fulfils
3. Create an alternative behaviour that will fill the need.

Concept #3
Ethics is a form of resource constraint (Keupp & Gassmann, 2013) that can be a vital source of innovation, creativity, and efficiency.

Concept #4
Ethics is the core of management education, and students need to make the link between ethics and strategic management. In the present system, ethics is seen largely as a voluntary responsibility and has been accorded little importance in the curriculum and the examination system. If ethics were to be taught as a critical extension of strategic management and a core principle of the management profession, concepts 2 and 3 would be incorporated in the new model, and would offer students the philosophical background against which to create their own meanings and find their jobs more fulfilling and enriching (Glasser, 2010).

Conclusion

The indigenous base of ethics in India is very strong, with its roots in the Freedom Movement led by Mahatma Gandhi. Paradoxically, the present status of Indian industry and government is one of the rampant corruption and unethical practices (Berger & Herstein, 2014) due to many factors including lack of management education and training in ethics. Education in this discipline consists mostly of theoretical knowledge without application to real-life management.

Moreover, as business ethics is given less attention than other management issues, so students emerge ill-equipped to deal with ethical problems as they build their business careers. Students largely perceive ethics from a formalistic view, to be followed in theory while in reality ethical behaviour often is compromised and rules are bent for unethical purposes, with severe and damaging consequences for a developing country like India where the regulatory mechanism is already poor. There is great need to rethink the ways in which ethics is taught to students, for example, to use experiential teaching methods with real-life management scenarios. Another learning strategy may be based on a choice theory of psychotherapy to reveal alternatives to unethical actions such as those of the characters in the film stories summarized above. Education on the power of personal choice should lead students to deeper understanding of ethical values as well as promoting the skills to apply them as managers in real life.

References

Amin, S. (Director). (2009). *Rocket Singh: Salesman of the year* (motion picture). India.
Aswathappa, K. (1991). *Organisational behaviour.* Himalaya Publishing House.
Baggini, J., & Fosl, P. S. (2007). *The ethics toolkit: A compendium of ethical concepts and methods.* Blackwell.
Berger, R., & Herstein, R. (2014). The evolution of business ethics in India. *International Journal of Social Economics, 41*(11), 1073–1086.
Bhandarkar, M. (Director). (2006, July 7). *Film corporate* (motion picture). India.
Bhatia, G. (2017, September 27). The richest sport in India just keeps getting richer. *CNBC.*
Bhatnagar, G. V. (2016, October 18). Murder of Mumbai activist highlights how India is failing its whistleblowers. *The Wire.*
Blink. (2014, April 1). Making ethical decisions: A 7-step path. *UC San Diego.*

Bloom, N., Mahajan, A., McKenzie, D., & Roberts, J. (2011, April 13). 'The Office' goes to India: Why bad management is keeping India poor. Retrieved from http://voxeu.org

Cooper, C. L., & Cartwright, S. (1997, July). An intervention strategy for workplace stress. *Journal of Psychosomatic Research, 43*(1), 7–16.

Dalal, B. (2017, August 22). Responsibility of improving MBA education in India lies with corporate leaders. *Forbes India*.

Dameron, S., & Durand, T. (2011). *Redesigning management education and research: Challenging proposals from European scholars*. Edward Elgar Publishing.

Dhamija, B. (2016, July 15). There is reason for India's corruption (and it's not us or even the politicians). *Huffington Post India blog*.

Eisenhardt, K. M., & Sull, D. N. (2001). Strategy as simple rules. *Harvard Business Review, 79*(1), 106–119.

Ghoshal, S. (2005). Bad management theories are destroying good management practices. *Academy of Management Learning & Education, 4*(1), 75–91.

Gibbert, M., & Scranton, P. (2009). Constraints as sources of radical innovation? Insights from jet propulsion development. *Management & Organizational History, 4*(4), 385–399.

Glasser, W. (2010). *Choice theory: A new psychology of personal freedom*. Harper Collins.

Guttmann, D. (1996). *Logotherapy for the helping professional: Meaningful social work*. Springer Publishing Co.

Heyneman, S. P. (2004, November). Education and corruption. *International Journal of Educational Development, 24*(6), 637–648.

Keupp, M. M., & Gassmann, O. (2013). Resource constraints as triggers of radical innovation: Longitudinal evidence from the manufacturing sector. *Research Policy, 42*(8), 1457–1468.

Kibriya, M. (1999). *Gandhi and Indian freedom struggle*. APH Publishing.

Kiran, N. (2017, January 27). India ranked 79th in the Corruption Perception Index 2016. *Business Today*.

Lelyveld, J. (2011). *Great soul*. Knopf Doubleday Publishing Group.

Pathak, K. (2015, February 19). Business schools face a crisis of confidence. *Business Standard*.

Robbins, S. P., & Judge, T. A. (2012). *Essentials of organizational behavior* (11th ed.). Upper Saddle River, NJ: Pearson Education.

Ronen, B. (2005). *The theory of constraints: Practice and research*. IOS Press.

Rossy, G. L. (2011). Five questions for addressing ethical dilemmas. *Strategy & Leadership, 39*(6), 35–42.

Sims, R. R., & Quatro, S. A. (2008). *Executive ethics: Ethical dilemmas and challenges for the CSuite.* Charlotte, NC: IAP—Information Age Publishing, Inc.

Singh, R., & Sundaram, S. (1996). *Gandhi and the world order.* APH Publishing.

UGC ACT. (1956). *The University Grants Commission Act and rules & regulations under the Act, 1956*; as modified December 20, 1985. Retrieved from https://www.ugc.ac.in/oldpdf/ugc_act.pdf

Vaidya, A. (2017, September 26). Nepotism is not just a Bollywood problem. *HuffPost Blog.*

Weiss, J. W. (2014). Business ethics: *A stakeholder and issues management approach.* Berrett-Koehler Publishers.

Yardley, J., & Timmons, H. (2010, December 13). Telecom scandal plunges India into political crisis. *New York Times.*

6

Integrating Responsible Education Principles into a Conventional System: The Case Study of TERI School of Advanced Studies, India

Sapna A. Narula, Ambika Zutshi, and Rajiv Seth

Introduction

The purpose of this chapter is to showcase the study of The Energy and Resources Institute School of Advanced Studies (TERI SAS) in India which has experimented with integrating sustainability in its academic and research programmes. The chapter discusses the evolution of the sustainability paradigm within a conventional education system, describes the challenges faced and strategies adopted by the institute, and offers lessons for upcoming similar institutions in India and other countries.

The need for responsible education has been felt globally by all the stakeholders, demanding future generations be made aware of to the needs of planet and society. The education system trains learners to

---

S. A. Narula (✉) • R. Seth
TERI School of Advanced Studies, New Delhi, India
e-mail: sapna.narula@terisas.ac.in; rseth@terisas.ac.in

A. Zutshi
Deakin University, Melbourne, VIC, Australia
e-mail: ambika.zutshi@deakin.edu.au

understand and value the norms of changing social paradigms amidst rising environmental concerns. On one hand, education in sustainability creates a new generation of future managers who will keep abreast of sustainability associated challenges, and on the other hand, education provides new opportunities for the current and future generations. The United Nations (UN), through its Sustainable Developmental Goals (SDGs) has acknowledged the importance of educational institutions and educators, and accordingly given responsible education a significant and deserving place in its new agenda. Integrating education and sustainability nevertheless is not an easy task to be implemented through an otherwise conventional education system. The latter can create hindrance in modernising education curricula especially in developing countries with financially constrained and academically rigid educational and, at times, political systems.

The Case: TERI SAS

The TERI SAS, in India offers world-class teaching and research facilities to students with its state-of-the-art infrastructure and well-equipped laboratories. Spread over two acres, the university campus comprises an administrative block, an office block, and a convergence and hostel block. The TERI SAS campus has been planned to provide a setting that enhances student learning and showcases the concept of modern green buildings. Well-equipped classrooms and laboratories enable students and faculty alike to access the latest information and to encourage research. The aesthetic design incorporates several features of passive solar design, energy-efficiency, and water and waste management systems.

The thought process behind TERI SAS—in addition to building capacity around various themes of sustainable development—was to develop an infrastructure aligned with the different teaching programmes, so students could study real and practical aspects of sustainable development (Jain & Pant, 2010; Jain, Aggarwal, Sharma, & Sharma, 2013; Jain et al., 2017). Figure 6.1 shows the overall sustainable practices followed by TERI SAS. The details of each sustainable practice are detailed in subsequent paragraphs.

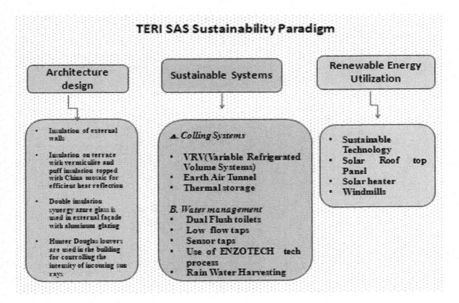

Fig. 6.1 Sustainability at TERI SAS

Integrating PRME into Educational System

Principles for Responsible Management Education's (PRME's) six principles, which each member institution is expected to abide by, are also followed by TERI SAS as shown in Fig. 6.2.

Beyond Physical Infrastructure

The programmes at the TERI University are focused around the needs of society and efforts to build capacity towards a sustainable future. To this end, the effort is on building capacities for meeting the Sustainable Development Goals (SDGs) of the UN.

A typical example is the MBA (Business Sustainability) programme at the TERI University. In today's tumultuous times, business leaders are being challenged to take new roles in modern societies. Government and civil organisations are encouraged to work efficiently to achieve social objectives.

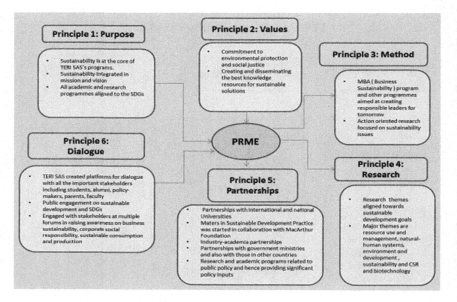

Fig. 6.2 TERI SAS and PRMEs Six Principles

For industry, now more than ever, there is a demand for sustainable and ethical practices, and accountability to consumers and the public at large. The MBA (Business Sustainability) programme tries to create a fresh cadre of sustainability managers who, within the current management education framework, develop a high level of social consciousness and ethical behaviour. The programme tries to enhance the scope and knowledge levels of management education in India by providing its students with unique skill sets to deal with sustainability issues. As part of the programme, students engage with sustainability experts, international faculty, and global issues to develop a broader outlook towards sustainability issues.

They engage with industry to take up sustainability challenge and participate in analysis and problem solving. Each internship culminates with a cross-disciplinary seminar in which students present their problem-solving ability along with learning from the experts and bring out cross-disciplinary linkages, the importance of context in identifying sustainable development challenges, and key management issues.

Case studies drawn from real-world sustainability challenges are designed and integrated into the curriculum. Ultimately, graduands are instilled with a core value system and an understanding of the larger issues and environmental responsibilities that would make them stand out as business leaders. Beyond the physical infrastructure, the institute comprises various committees which ensure that sustainability initiatives beyond the classrooms integrate both teaching curriculum and real-world practices. For instance, the Green Committee encourages the use of environmental friendly practices such as use of no paper cups on Wednesday, an off day for elevator use to encourage students to take the staircases, shared transport facilities, energy saving practices, and so on. Regular seminars, open houses, and internal forums encourage new ideas for innovative practices.

In 2014, a unique initiative, Building Learning in Sustainability (BLISS) was adopted to engage youth and other public stakeholders in building learning in sustainability, which later attracted support from United Nations Environment Programme (UNEP) and other international organisations. A five-day summer school received commendable response from school children and college students. This public engagement programme is also being used to enhance awareness of school students about sustainability. Interdisciplinary learning encourages students to employ creative learning for solving everyday sustainability problems. The unique curriculum and pedagogy ensure that students and faculty of all programmes learn from each other. There is an active engagement of students across programmes in group learning by means of industry talks, study tours, and university festivals.

The TERI University is a founder member of a network of Universities of the Asia-Pacific which focus on the promotion of sustainability in postgraduate education and research. Called ProSPER. Net, this is a United Nation University network, supported by the Government of Japan. As part of this network, the university organised a Young Research School where the primary goal was to offer a differentiated experience to enhance doctoral students' understanding of sustainable development and foster a network of researchers in the region.

Critical Enablers, Challenges and Way Forward

1. A critical success factor which enabled these initiatives to be adopted at TERI SAS was the small size of the targeted group of faculty and students, who already had a bent towards sustainability. It is comparatively easy to experiment with such a group but challenging to implement in large universities with diverse curricula.
2. Another factor was the autonomy, academic freedom, and consultative approach which encouraged faculty and students to make joint decisions and put together various proposals. The expertise of faculty members with expertise in sustainability teaching, and a strong research base, also ensures right initiatives and practices.
3. One of the challenges which TERI SAS faces, in implementing and integrating sustainability, is financial support. Being a privately funded university, it is difficult to sustain such initiatives at a large level, and without much national interest in the subject, few funds are available.
4. Another challenge is the absence of a platform of all stakeholders, including the regulator, external stakeholders, and peer institutes, who could help spread the word and voice their opinions.
5. Some other challenges involve convincing stakeholders to donate time and finances. Training human resources is a giant task, especially when delivering the same message to different target groups. Government support to endorse and fund these initiatives would help to overcome some of these hurdles.

Summary

TERI SAS is a unique institute which has very innovatively adopted diverse approaches in integrating sustainability across its curriculum. The institute provides a best practice example for other universities, and many other institutes have started replicating many of the initiatives. TERI SAS has provided leadership, direction, and hands-on experience and training support. The institute is currently working towards establishing an inter-university think tank that can assist other institutions across the nation whilst simultaneously enhancing awareness of the importance of sustainability. This will also assist towards attracting additional funding to undertake more research and teaching in this area

Bibliography of Works Consulted

Jain, S., & Pant, P. (2010). An environmental management system for educational institute: A case study of TERI University, New Delhi. *International Journal of Sustainability and Higher Education, 11*(3), 236–249.

Jain, S., Aggarwal, P., Sharma, N., & Sharma, P. (2013). Fostering sustainability through education, research and practice: A case study of TERI University. *Journal of Cleaner Production, 61*, 20–24.

Jain, S., Agarwal, A., Jani, V., Singhal, S., Sharma, P., & Jalan, R. (2017). Assessment of carbon neutrality and sustainability in educational campuses (CaNSEC): A general framework, New Delhi. *Ecological Indicators, 76*, 131–143.

7

Tri-Sector Leadership and Collaboration in Management Education: The Case of Singapore

Jiunwen Wang

Introduction

Nation Building in Singapore: Transformation from Third to First World

Knowledge of the Singaporean context is helpful in discussing applications of the tri-sector model of business and public policy (as described, for instance, by Warhurst, 2001) to management education, because Singapore is unique in terms of its rapid economic and societal growth over the past 50 years (see Fig. 7.1).

Singapore became independent in 1965, a sovereign city state rife with economic and social problems. The population was generally young and unskilled, and one in four people lived below the poverty line. A rapidly growing population either lived as many as six to a room in city

---

J. Wang (✉)
Singapore University of Social Sciences, Singapore, Singapore
e-mail: jwwang@suss.edu.sg

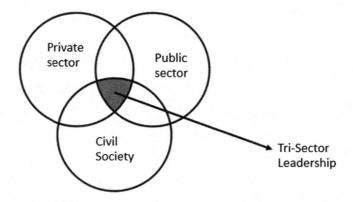

Fig. 7.1 Tri-sector approach to management education (SMU, 2017a)

dwellings or spilled over into illegal squatter colonies. Public hygiene was poor and diseases such as malaria and tuberculosis were public health issues (Richardson & Lee, 2012).

Within 50 years, Singapore's development trajectory catapulted it into one of the world's most competitive economies (Fuchs & Jacobs, 2014). In 2016, PwC's Cities of Opportunity report (PwC, 2016) ranked Singapore second after London in terms of social and economic health. In 2016, it ranked second among global cities for green buildings (Azmi, 2016). The state's gross domestic product per capita, US$52,888, ranks among the top 10 in the world (Koh, 2016; Tasch, 2017). In 2016, *Monocle* (Connelly, 2016) named Singapore the 20th most liveable city in the world in 2016, and in the same year it was ranked second in the Sustainable Cities Index (Arcadis, 2016).

Leadership in Nation Building

The success of Singapore hinged on an effective government, the People's Action Party (PAP), and the leadership of the late Prime Minister Lee Kuan Yew—whose management style was mostly top-down and tended to be authoritarian. Many have referred to him as a 'benevolent dictator' (Huff, 1997; Miller, 2012). However, given the changing landscape and complex problems, new forms of leadership were needed to deal with pressing challenges such as an aging population, healthcare, and digital and technological advances. Lee's leadership and governance style worked for Singapore when housing and economic problems had to be solved quickly and effectively in a state with a few natural resources (Cao, 2016), but new challenges face Singapore over the next 50 years (Liang, 2016).

New Forms of Leadership and the VUCA World

The trendy managerial acronym VUCA (Bennett & Lemoine, 2014; Inam, 2017) stands for 'volatility, uncertainty, complexity, and ambiguity' and refers to four distinct types of challenges—such as those faced by Singapore today—that demand four distinct types of leadership response (Joiner & Josephs, 2007). Against the backdrop of a VUCA world, the call for tri-sector leadership in Singapore has never been stronger (Lovegrove & Thomas, 2013). Management education in the private business, government, and civil sectors is needed to train leaders to navigate different cultures, align incentives, and draw on the individual strengths of a wide range of actors to solve large-scale problems.

Singapore Management University's Post-Graduate Management Education Programme

Singapore Management University (SMU) has created a Masters' Degree in Tri-Sector Collaboration, MTSC (SMU, 2016), to help overcome the handicap that public policy and business training traditionally remain segregated. The rationale for the programme is the need for self-regulated business enterprises to monitor and manage the social and environmental impacts of their activities, to create new business models to supplement government initiatives (OECD, 2011), and to face the VUCA challenges of volatile, uncertain, complex, and ambiguous economic, social, and political environments.

The post-graduate MTSC (SMU, 2017b) enrols mid-career managers from government, business, and civil society in a programme of 11 intensive weeks over 18 months. Participants stay in their jobs throughout, thus allowing them to apply their new skills and knowledge to their places of employment. Students are from one of three employment groups: they are managers in the private business sector, the governmental sector, or they are citizens involved in community work leadership. The reasons for this diversity are to initiate cross-boundary conversations and cross-fertilization of ideas across sectors. The programme is aligned to an Asian context in terms of business, culture, management, and values. A broad scan of the courses in the programme reveals three key themes.

Key Theme 1: Developing Partnership Mindsets

One objective of the tri-sector MTSC is that students shall develop partnership mindsets—a concept described, for example, by Howieson and Hodges (2014)—across boundaries between sectors, because government, business, and civil society managers differ in how they pursue common goals, mobilize, and deploy resources. The relevant module provides students with concepts, cases, and experiential learning activities to help them develop and combine conceptual insights, tools, and personal capabilities to better understand, communicate, and practice collaboration—as recommended, for example, by IGI Global (2011); Roschelle (1992).

Another module was designed to help public officers and policy makers shift their perspectives on the delivery of public services—a shift suggested, for instance, by Middleton (2010). Students are encouraged to think about designing and delivering public services *with*, rather than *for* citizens and community. Business leaders need to work with public servants and the government to co-create public services and engage in problem solving for the community. Historically, Singapore politicians and citizens have tended to harbour pragmatic and economic mindsets (Lim & Lee, 2016) that led to a modern capitalist focus on preserving and accounting for financial capital. A shift towards consideration of natural and social capital (Bofota, 2012) would hold business leaders more responsible in their decision making. More importantly, it might allow business and government to partner each other to solve more complex problems to ensure sustainability.

Key Theme 2: Decision Making

On the assumption that business leaders should be equipped to make decisions that are ethical, socially responsible, and sustainable (SMU, 2017b), the MTSC aims to equip managers with knowledge of global trends, such as increasing climate change, and the influence of technology on future jobs and the economy—as discussed, for instance, by Manyika (2017)—and to enable them to identify reliable sources of information. MTSC also aims to train business leaders to make decisions that are non-linear, because social, economic, and ecological factors need to be studied with a different lens by policy makers and decision makers respectively. Decision-making skills are part of a complex and dynamic system of training in sense-making, learning, and thinking about the future.

Scenario Planning

The Singapore Minister for Home Affairs and Law, K Shanmugam, spoke in 2016 at the Nanyang Technological University's Annual Ministerial Forum, on 'Progressing Towards SG100' (Hui, 2016). He referred to Singapore's ageing population and low fertility rate and how they would contribute to rising healthcare costs and a lower tax base. He warned that Singaporeans in some sectors will contend with competition from global counterparts for jobs and that the threat of terrorism in Singapore was as high as it had ever been.

Thus, organizational leaders now operate in a VUCA world. They need not only to gauge the future but also to be prepared to respond to different scenarios and changes. MTSC teaching methods in these areas include requiring students to construct multiple possible scenarios and to make hypothetical decisions in those contexts. Problem-based learning (PBL) is not without its critics (Hoffman & Ritchie, 1997). Adult learners may not be ready to engage in PBL; they may be used to more passive methods of instruction and may struggle to grasp the concept of an open problem, since they cannot rely on their instructors for 'the one right answer'. However, as an instructional tool for the management of change, it is extremely useful.

Key Theme 3: Application of Tri-Sector Collaboration

Academic knowledge and learning are applied in this module on tri-sector collaboration through case studies (mostly drawn from Asia) to illustrate how public policy can make the private sector a constructive force for economic growth and development. An important tactic is to veer away from treating policy making as if it were a science with discrete skills and clear optimal solutions. Instead, teaching highlights the importance of recognizing multiple realities and constraints, ranging from economic, financial, political, to cultural (Castells, 2010).

The final module, Policy Task Force, requires students to work together to analyse in depth and develop solutions for one or more real-world issues. Students start preparing for this module at the start of the programme. Along the way, they apply the knowledge and skills they have acquired in the different modules to propose recommendations on how to solve real-world problems that require tri-sector collaboration and leadership. Examples of student projects include 'engaging citizens in the design of future public service experiences'—as discussed, for instance, by Nambisan and Nambisan (2013); 'enabling the disabled through a tri-sector approach' (SMU, 2017c); and 'a better life for Singapore's foreign construction workers' (whose plight was reported in 2015 by TodayOnline).

These projects on tri-sector collaboration steer away from the traditional top-down approach to decision making that the Singapore government has taken over the years (Kraar, 2015). Rather, they emphasize a ground-up approach, whereby citizens and business owners collaborate to generate solutions to pressing problems.

Summary

To achieve sustainability and not only to survive but also to thrive in a VUCA world, management and business education needs to expand knowledge and skills sets for business leaders. These include the ability to navigate different organizational cultures and contexts, in interaction with multiple stakeholders from the private, public, and civic sectors.

Such expansion requires a change of mindset from one based on linear, logical cause-and-effect reasoning to a more holistic apprehension that issues are not clear cut. Organizational leaders need to move away from a sole focus on financial matters, to consider the social, political, and cultural impacts of their activities.

Management education can expose future business and public-sector leaders to the importance of sustainable and ethical decisions, and how to achieve better business and social outcomes. If they fail to learn the importance of accountability, their management education will be of little relevance to the organizations over which they will one day preside. Beyond the re-design of management education to expand managers' repertoire of skills and knowledge, there is a resounding call to redefine organizational performance—not just based on financial outcomes, but also on social impact. Only then will there be a better chance of achieving sustainable business outcomes.

Conclusion

The central thesis of this chapter is that in a VUCA world (characterized by volatility, uncertainty, complexity, and ambiguity) business leadership, to be both effective and ethical, should be a matter of tri-sector collaboration between private business, public, and community sectors of society.

Disclaimer The views expressed in this chapter are the author's, and do not represent the views of the Singapore Management University or the Singapore University of Social Sciences.

References

Arcadis. (2016). *Sustainable Cities Index*. Retrieved from https://www.arcadis.com/en/global/our-perspectives/sustainable-cities-index-2016/

Azmi, S. (2016, June 15). Singapore ranks 2nd among global cities for green buildings. *Business Times*.

Bennett, N. G., & Lemoine, J. (2014, January–February). What VUCA really means for you. *Harvard Business Review*. Issue.

Bofota, Y. B. (2012). *Social capital, human capital and economic development: Theoretical model and empirical analyses*. Presses univ. de Louvain.

Cao, L. (2016). *Culture in law and development: Nurturing positive change*. Oxford University Press.

Castells, M. (2010). *End of millennium: The information age: Economy, society, and culture* (Vol. 3). John Wiley & Sons.

Connelly, M. A. (2016, June 21). Monocle names Hong Kong and Singapore among world's most liveable cities. *Living*. Retrieved from http://www.lifestyleasia.com/471908/monocle-names-hong-kong-singapore-among-worlds-livable-cities/

Fuchs, E., & Jacobs, H. (2014, May 26). The 11 cities with the most opportunity right now. *Business Insider Australia*.

Hoffman, B., & Ritchie, D. (1997, March). Using multimedia to overcome the problems with problem based learning. *Instructional Science, 25*(2), 97–115.

Howieson, B., & Hodges, J. (2014). *Public and third sector leadership: Experience speaks*. Emerald Group Publishing.

Huff, W. G. (1997). *The economic growth of Singapore: Trade and development in the twentieth century*. Cambridge University Press.

Hui, C. (2016, March 28). Ageing population, global competition among challenges Singapore must contend with. *Channel NewsAsia*.

IGI Global. (2011). *Organizational learning and knowledge: Concepts, methodologies, tools and applications* (Vols. 1–4). IGI Global.

Inam, H. (2017, October 18). To lead in a VUCA world, practice leadership agility. *Forbes*.

Joiner, W. B., & Josephs, S. A. (2007). *Leadership agility: Five levels of mastery for anticipating and initiating change*. John Wiley & Sons.

Koh, T. (2016, October 15). Small and successful. *The Straits Times*.

Kraar, L. (2015, March 23). Singapore, the country run like a corporation. *Fortune*. (This Fortune article first ran in July 1974 and again in 2015 to mark the passing of Lee Kuan Yew, Singapore's first and longest-serving prime minister, and the architect of the nation's remarkable transformation).

Liang, L. Y. (2016, March 29). Four key challenges for Singapore in next 50 years. *Straits Times*.

Lim, J., & Lee, T. (2016). *Singapore: Negotiating state and society, 1965–2015*. Routledge.

Lovegrove, N., & Thomas, M. (2013, February 13). Why the world needs tri-sector leaders. *Harvard Business Review*.

Manyika, J. (2017, May 2017). Technology, jobs and the future of work. *McKinsey Global Institute*.

Middleton, P. (2010). *Delivering public services that work*. Triarchy Press Limited.
Miller, M. (2012, May 12). What Singapore can teach us. *Washington Post*.
Nambisan, S., & Nambisan, P. (2013, January). Engaging citizens in co-creation in public services: Lessons learned and best practices. *IBM Center for the Business of Government*.
OECD. (2011, September 29). *Guidelines for multinational enterprises* (2011 edition). OECD Publishing.
PwC. (2016, September 7). London ranks top in PwC Cities of Opportunity Index, followed by Singapore and Toronto. *PWC News Release*.
Richardson, J., & Lee, E. O. L. (2012, September). The improbable resilience of Singapore. *The Solutions Journal, 3*(5), 63–71.
Roschelle, J. (1992). Learning by collaborating: Convergent conceptual change. *The Journal of the Learning Sciences, 2*(3), 235–276. Taylor & Francis, Ltd.
SMU. (2016, May 12). Tri-sector forum 2016—Understanding the power of cross-sector partnership for solving complex problems in finance, food, sustainability, and society. Singapore Management University.
SMU. (2017a). Master of tri-sector collaboration; Creating thought leaders to bridge business, government and civil society. Singapore Management University; SMU Tri-Sector Publication 2017.pdf; Retrieved December 22, 2017.
SMU. (2017b). Tri-sector partnerships for sustainable development. *Singapore Management University School of Social Sciences*. Retrieved December 23, 2017.
SMU. (2017c). Master of Tri-Sector Collaboration (MTSC). Singapore Management University. Retrieved December 20, 2017, from https://www.smu.edu.sg/programmes/postgraduate/master-tri-sector-collaboration
Tasch, B. (2017, March 6). Ranked: The 30 richest countries in the world. *Business Insider*.
TodayOnline. (2015, December 12). The big read: Making Singapore a better place for workers who come from afar. *TodayOnline*.
Warhurst, A. (2001). *Corporate citizenship and corporate social investment drivers of tri-sector partnerships*. Greenleaf Publishing Ltd. JCC 1 Spring.

8

Demand for and Supply of Responsible Managerial Behaviour

Duane Windsor

Introduction

Business education influences the attitudes, beliefs, and values of managers and would-be managers and presumably should pressure them in a socially desirable direction, which here is defined in general terms of reducing irresponsibility and increasing responsibility. The alternative to this presumption is a strictly market approach to management education, by which students are taught that rational self-interest should govern business behaviour. In this approach, evidence of social responsibility—other than wealth creation—is disputable.

Increased knowledge of demand and supply should affect significantly how educators influence students towards social responsibility. The chapter is based on two working assumptions. The first one is that the level of social irresponsibility in business management is

---

D. Windsor (✉)
Rice University, Houston, TX, USA
e-mail: odw@rice.edu

substantial; therefore, educational tactics are needed to shift managerial behaviour towards greater social responsibility—which is not the same as decreasing irresponsible behaviour. The second working assumption is that need and demand for responsibility exceed the supply of responsibility in business management—hence the importance of management education to increase the supply. The related issue is the interaction of demand and supply in the context of corporate social responsibility (CSR).

The chapter discusses four key considerations. Section 1 explains a theoretical framing in terms of a demand and supply perspective. Section 2 concerns the normatively defined difference between irresponsibility and responsibility. Section 3 concerns the supply of managerial responsibility as shaped by the attitudes, beliefs, and values of business managers, who are the individuals to be influenced in their official roles in profit-seeking enterprises. Section 4 discusses the implications of the above for management education.

1: Theoretical Framing

The Analogy of Demand and Supply

Theoretical demand-and-supply framing (Coombs, 1998) illustrates that social and environmental pressures reflect increasing community demand for responsible management of private- and public-sector organizations—involving simultaneously a shift away from irresponsible behaviour and towards increasingly high standards of corporate responsibility. By this argument, irresponsibility and responsibility are assumed to be different forms of organizational behaviour. Therefore, these two concepts need to be handled differently in management education curricula.

Responsible and Irresponsible Behaviour

Irresponsible management behaviour involves violations of law and ethical norms damaging to stakeholders and the natural environment, and reducing such behaviour should greatly improve economic and social conditions. Responsible behaviour undertakes improvements for stakeholders and the natural environment (Windsor, 2013b).

In management literature, there is a core set of anti-responsibility beliefs and arguments (Ebenstein, 2015; Friedman, 1970) that needs to be refuted with post-graduate management students who would otherwise absorb rational self-interest from most existing MBA programmes equating to a proposition that wealth-seeking is good, based on an assumption of the wealth-creating capacity of the market economy (Jensen, 2001). Supporters of this assumption are interested in their share of this wealth, as distinct from the wealth effects for customers and employees. Most traditional MBA programmes take the following precepts for granted and base their educational content on them:

- Value independence—which is a variant of individual subjectivism—in which ethics has no objective basis and cannot be imposed (Baporikar, 2016);
- A culturally relativistic stance that national ethical values (such as anti-corruption) should not be imposed on other countries (Blunt, 1995);
- A belief in the principal-agent theory of fiduciary responsibility as a moral duty rather than simply a voluntary legal contract under which managers would not benefit (Marens & Wicks, 1999);
- A belief that markets are self-correcting and thus will eliminate bad actors without formal ethics and regulations (Tsang, Kazeroony, & Ellis, 2013);
- A belief that lobbying exerts a corrupt influence on legislation, in keeping with an anti-government and anti-regulation attitude (Cullen, 2013);
- Rejection of the idea that business managers should be professionals, in the sense that a professional is subject to a code of ethics including the possibility of self-sacrifice in accord with that code (Donaldson, 2000). Reasons for this belief may include a preference for self-interested egoism, confined to the marketplace and defined by managers as not violating law sufficiently to be prosecuted (Luyendijk, 2015).

2: Defining Irresponsibility and Responsibility

Irresponsibility can involve either failure to comply with laws or the imposition of negative consequences for others even if there is no violation of law. Irresponsible behaviour is unethical, regardless of legal status, and reducing irresponsibility is arguably more important because it benefits human welfare by reducing harm (Armstrong, 1977; Chatterji & Listokin, 2007).

Managerial responsibility comes in two forms. One is altruism or philanthropy; the other involves political CSR—under which, according to some literature (Keig, Brouthers, & Marshall, 2015; Putrevu, McGuire, Siegel, & Smith, 2012; Scherer, Rasche, Palazzo, & Spicer, 2016), firms have moral duties to provide public goods under given conditions, but defining responsibility depends on perspective. An instance is definition of the social responsibility status of corporate tax liability, especially for multinational firms operating across tax jurisdictions. Christensen and Murphy (2004) argue that firms should adopt voluntary CSR standards in taxation, because tax avoidance, in their view, is irresponsible when not founded in a substantial economic purpose. This view ignores the issue that tax liability minimization is profitable for the firm. Tax evasion is illegal and unethical; tax avoidance is not illegal, and the ethics of tax avoidance is debatable.

Firms may engage in CSR only to offset irresponsible acts, in expectation that stakeholders may forget about them (Mena, Rintamäki, Fleming, & Spicer, 2016). That is, irresponsibility tends to drive responsibility initiatives as a kind of compensation that helps to protect corporate reputation and legitimacy. A study by Kotchen and Moon (2011) suggests that concerns about irresponsibility in corporate governance tend to result in CSR actions rather than corporate governance reforms. Kang, Germann, and Grewal (2016) identify four mechanisms potentially linking CSR to firms' (financial) performance:

- "Slack resources" for CSR activities.
- CSR directly improves firm performance, and thus can be characterized as good management.
- "Penance" expressed as current compensation for past irresponsibility.

- Insurance as a form of protection or hedge against the reputational effects of future irresponsibility.

Research by Sarre, Doig, and Fiedler (2001) tested for these four mechanisms and rejected the slack resources and insurance mechanisms. They reported that CSR investments are profitable and that though CSR measures may be put in place following discovery of corporate irresponsibility, the penance mechanism will not offset the negative performance effects of that irresponsibility.

3: Supply of Managerial Responsibility

Demand and Supply

When applied to management, the demand and supply analogy (Angelidis & Ibrahim, 1993; McWilliams & Siegel, 2001) suggests that social and environmental pressures reflect increasing demand by stakeholders for responsible managerial behaviour. Supply is how corporations respond to stakeholder demands, as well as to their own personal values.

Behavioural ethics research (Agle, Hart, Thompson, & Hendricks, 2014) suggests the supply of responsible management behaviour is not very elastic in response to increases in external pressures. There are internal anti-responsibility pressures operating (Crane, Matten, McWilliams, Moon, & Siegel, 2008); for example, CSR reports tend to withhold negative information concerning industry association misbehaviour (Aras & Crowther, 2009; Holder-Webb, Cohen, Nath, & Wood, 2009; Petticrew, Hessari, Knai, & Weiderpass, 2018).

The supply of managerial responsibility responds to three key factors:

- The economic market defines the costs and benefits of corporate responsibility to stakeholders and the environment,
- The political market exercises pressure from external and internal stakeholders,
- Managers have personal values for or against responsible behaviour that will determine whether they react favourably to conditions of low costs and high benefits and strong external and internal pressures.

Managerial Attitudes, Beliefs, and Values

One of the factors affecting supply of managerially responsible behaviour is managers' attitudes, beliefs, and values. Some managers emphasize profit-seeking (Strine, 2012) in adherence to the market-oriented economic perspective, as articulated by Friedman (1970) and McWilliams and Siegel (2001). Jensen (2001) argues that managers can handle only one goal, not dual or multiple goals, and that goal must therefore be profit-seeking. Some managers presumably adhere to some combination of the CSR and stakeholder-oriented perspectives. Murdock (2017) criticized the CEO of Unilever for being too CSR-oriented, to the neglect of the corporate bottom line. In contrast, Windsor (2013a) proposed a typology of moral exemplars in business as a framework for thinking about different kinds of cases and conditions.

Linking managerial behaviour (responsible or irresponsible) to managerial attitudes, beliefs, and values is subject to external influence, on the one hand, and to concealment, on the other. There is a growing literature on "whitewashing" or "greenwashing" as misleading marketing of CSR (Prasad & Holzinger, 2013) and on corporate hypocrisy with respect to responsibility (Christian Aid, 2004; Fassin & Buelens, 2011). Euphemism is arguably at work in corporate and activist communications (la Cour & Kromann, 2011).

Ultimately, business ethics operates as a constraint on irresponsible profit-seeking, and citizenship operates through responsibility as a tax on profit (Windsor, 2016), and managers develop their own operational philosophy through education and experience (Windsor, 2015).

Bartling and Özdemir (2017) have demonstrated the important role of social norms, and that in their absence, competitive markets will drive behaviour and erode ethics. It is possible that competition might encourage responsible corporate behaviour (Kemper, Schilke, Reimann, Wang, & Brettel, 2013); alternatively, competition might squeeze it out as proving too costly, but ultimately, governments determine social norms through laws and regulations (Sjåfjell, 2011), and strong social norms encourage voluntary self-regulation (Sheehy, 2012).

4: Implications for Management Education

Management education should be directed at cultivating more responsible managers over time, and the following is a summary of the likely implications for business (and by extension professional) schools.

There is some evidence that firms and individuals within those firms can learn from examples of irresponsibility such as DuPont's environmental disasters and subsequent lawsuits (Shapira & Zingales, 2017). They might learn rather to model themselves on the responsible behaviour of Unilever, which is by far considered to be the most lauded company in terms of sustainability by a 2014 survey (Whan, 2014). As another example, Zadek (2004) studied the CSR evolution at Nike that occurred through changes in the views and behaviours of key stakeholders, including managers (Newell, 2015). Moreover, the new generation of "millennials" appears to support more sustainable and thus more responsible initiatives (Berr, 2017; Chong, 2017; Landrum, 2017; Morgan Stanley, 2017).

Education can reinforce this evolution, but ethics education is difficult (Soltes, 2017). Part of the difficulty is that managers must develop independent moral judgement on business issues, but corporate managers and would-be managers tend to be wealth-seeking individuals in wealth-seeking enterprises (Strine, 2012). They are not likely readily to accept normatively based constraints on this pursuit. Moreover, traditional MBAs prepare students for their management roles in a curriculum setting that emphasizes wealth accumulation, market opportunities, and reputation, rather than helping them to make value judgements about controversial issues of irresponsibility and responsibility.

There are three important considerations affecting management education:

- Demand for and supply of responsibility behaviour,
- The difference between irresponsibility (to be reduced) and citizenship (to be increased),
- The role of managerial attitudes, beliefs, and values.

The strength of demand depends on the power of stakeholders to convince managers that calculation of benefits and costs favours responsiveness (Martin, 2002). The stronger the net benefits, the greater the likelihood of managerial responsiveness, with a resulting increase in the supply of responsible behaviour. A practical consideration in gauging demand is that stakeholders may have conflicting interests (Wagner, Lutz, & Weitz, 2009; Welford, Chan, & Man, 2008), and management education includes stakeholder relationship management, which is normative in orientation (Freeman, 2016). Successful managers must find ways to satisfy (or improve the welfare) all stakeholders (Peloza & Shang, 2011). This imperative is ethical, rather than power oriented. Freeman (2016) explicates a "responsible capitalism" built around this stakeholder approach.

While managers should understand something about formal theories of business ethics, it is equally important for them to learn to differentiate between irresponsibility (i.e. behaviour that results in social harm) and responsibility (citizenship behaviour). As an illustration of irresponsible behaviour, what is wrong with DuPont calculating the net benefit to the firm of emissions harming stakeholders (Shapira & Zingales, 2017)? As an illustration of responsible (citizenship) behaviour, what is right with Unilever's approach (Confino, 2011)? How does the manager individually, and as part of a profit-oriented enterprise, judge the difference between irresponsibility and responsibility in any situation?

Managers need to learn who they are, ethically, philosophically, and spiritually. Ethical identity is about what individuals voluntarily accept as constraints, duties, and goals. Philosophical identity is self-conception as a business person and member of a profit-oriented organization. Spiritual identity is understanding of conscience, guilt, and shame (Antonetti & Maklan, 2016). One educational approach to offsetting personal preferences is to inculcate strong social norms for management students, which are not necessarily legal requirements. Social norms are increasingly being defined by proposed or adopted international standards (Baur & Umlas, 2017; de Colle, Henriques, & Saravathy, 2014; Jutterström, 2006). They include ISO 26000 (Corporate Social Responsibility), ISO 37001 (Anti-Bribery Management Systems), Global Reporting Initiative (GRI), the UN Global Compact, the UN Convention against Corruption (UNCAC), and similar arrangements.

Summary This chapter has examined management education and other influences that might move managers away from irresponsibility and towards responsibility. The enquiry proceeded in three steps, after defining some basic terms and ideas: first, a demand and supply analogy for influencing business managers; second, discussion of the normative basis for distinguishing irresponsibility and responsibility; and third, the role of managerial attitudes, beliefs, and values in education and operational philosophy, as developed by managers themselves in their daily work lives.

References

Agle, B. R., Hart, D. W., Thompson, J., & Hendricks, H. M. (2014). *Research companion to ethical behavior in organizations: Constructs and measures*. Edward Elgar Publishing.

Angelidis, J. P., & Ibrahim, N. A. (1993). Social demand and corporate supply: A corporate social responsibility model. *Review of Business, 15*(1), 7–10.

Antonetti, P., & Maklan, S. (2016). An extended model of moral outrage at corporate social irresponsibility. *Journal of Business Ethics, 135*(3), 429–444.

Aras, G., & Crowther, D. (2009). Corporate sustainability reporting: A study in disingenuity? *Journal of Business Ethics, 87*(1), 279–288.

Armstrong, J. S. (1977). Social irresponsibility in management. *Journal of Business Research, 5*(3), 185–213.

Baporikar, N. (2016). *Management education for global leadership*. IGI Global.

Bartling, B., & Özdemir, Y. (2017). The limits to moral erosion in markets: Social norms and the replacement excuse. *CESifo Working Paper Series No. 6696*, October 18. Available at SSRN: https://ssrn.com/abstract=3074338

Baur, J., & Umlas, E. (2017). Making corporations responsible: The parallel tracks of the B Corp movement and the business and human rights movement. *Business and Society Review, 122*(3), 285–325.

Berr, J. (2017, June 1). Millennials and the demand for socially responsible investments. Retrieved from https://advisorhub.com/millennials-demand-socially-responsible-investments/

Blunt, P. (1995). Cultural relativism, 'good' governance and sustainable human development. *Public Administration and Development, 15*, 1–9.

Chatterji, A., & Listokin, S. (2007, Winter). Corporate social irresponsibility: Progressives need to end their fixation with corporate social responsibility— And focus on reform that actually works. *Democracy Journal, 3*, 52–63.

Retrieved from https://democracyjournal.org/magazine/3/corporate-social-irresponsibility/

Chong, K. (2017, January 20). Millennials and the rising demand for corporate social responsibility. Retrieved from https://cmr.berkeley.edu/blog/2017/1/millennials-and-csr/

Christensen, J., & Murphy, R. (2004). The social irresponsibility of corporate tax avoidance: Taking CSR to the bottom line. *Development, 47*(3), 37–44.

Christian Aid. (2004). Behind the mask: The real face of corporate social responsibility. Retrieved from https://www.st-andrews.ac.uk/media/csear/app2practice-docs/CSEAR_behind-the-mask.pdf

de Colle, S., Henriques, A., & Saravathy, S. (2014). The paradox of corporate social responsibility standards. *Journal of Business Ethics, 125*(2), 177–191.

Confino, J. (2011, November 22). Paul Polman: 'The power is in the hands of the consumers'. *Guardian Professional Network*. Retrieved from https://www.theguardian.com/sustainable-business/unilever-ceo-paul-polman-interview

Coombs, W. T. (1998). The Internet as potential equalizer: New leverage for confronting social irresponsibility. *Public Relations Review, 24*(3), 289–303.

la Cour, A., & Kromann, J. (2011). Euphemisms and hypocrisy in corporate philanthropy. *Business Ethics: A European Review, 20*(3), 267–279.

Crane, A., Matten, D., McWilliams, A., Moon, J., & Siegel, D. S. (Eds.). (2008). *The Oxford handbook of corporate social responsibility*. Oxford University Press.

Cullen, P. (2013, May 6). Education lobbying in Australia? *Treehornexpress*. Retrieved from https://treehornexpress.wordpress.com/2013/05/06/education-lobbying-in-australia/

Donaldson, T. (2000). Are business managers "professionals"? *Business Ethics Quarterly, 10*(1), 83–94.

Ebenstein, L. (2015). *Chicagonomics: The evolution of Chicago free market economics*. St. Martin's Press.

Fassin, Y., & Buelens, M. (2011). The hypocrisy-sincerity continuum in corporate communication and decision making: A model of corporate social responsibility and business ethics practices. *Management Decision, 49*(4), 586–600.

Freeman, R. E. (2016, November 1). The new story of business: Towards a more responsible capitalism. *Bentley University*. Waltham, MA: W. Michael Hoffman Center for Business Ethics.

Friedman, M. (1970, September 13). The social responsibility of business is to increase its profits. *The New York Times Magazine*. Retrieved from http://www.umich.edu/~thecore/doc/Friedman.pdf

Holder-Webb, L., Cohen, J. R., Nath, L., & Wood, D. (2009). The supply of corporate social responsibility disclosures among US firms. *Journal of Business Ethics, 84*(4), 497–527.

Jensen, M. C. (2001). Value maximization, stakeholder theory, and the corporate objective function. *Journal of Applied Corporate Finance, 14*(3), 8–21.

Jutterström, M. (2006). Corporate social responsibility—The supply side of CSR-standards. *Working Paper 2006-2*, Stockholm Centre for Organizational Research (SCORE), Stockholm. Retrieved from http://www.score.su.se/polopoly_fs/1.26586.1320939799!/20062.pdf

Kang, C., Germann, F., & Grewal, R. (2016). Washing away your sins? Corporate social responsibility, corporate social irresponsibility, and firm performance. *Journal of Marketing, 80*(2), 59–79.

Keig, D. L., Brouthers, L. E., & Marshall, V. B. (2015). Formal and informal corruption environments and multinational enterprise social irresponsibility. *Journal of Management Studies, 52*(1), 89–116.

Kemper, J., Schilke, O., Reimann, M., Wang, X., & Brettel, M. (2013). Competition-motivated corporate social responsibility. *Journal of Business Research, 66*(10), 1954–1963.

Kotchen, M. J., & Moon, J. J. (2011). Corporate social responsibility for irresponsibility. *NBER Working Paper No. 17254*, July 2011. Retrieved from http://www.nber.org/papers/w17254

Landrum, S. (2017, March 17). Millennials driving brands to practice socially responsible marketing. *Forbes*.

Luyendijk, J. (2015). *Swimming with sharks: My journey into the world of the bankers*. Guardian Faber.

Marens, R., & Wicks, A. (1999). Getting real: Stakeholder theory, managerial practice, and the general irrelevance of fiduciary duties owed to shareholders. *Business Ethics Quarterly, 9*(2), 273–293.

Martin, R. L. (2002). The virtue matrix: Calculating the return on corporate responsibility. *Harvard Business Review, 80*(3), 68–75.

McWilliams, A., & Siegel, D. (2001). Corporate social responsibility: A theory of the firm perspective. *Academy of Management Review, 26*(1), 117–127.

Mena, S., Rintamäki, J., Fleming, P., & Spicer, A. (2016). On the forgetting of corporate irresponsibility. *Academy of Management Review, 41*(4), 720–738.

Morgan Stanley Institute for Sustainable Investing. (2017, August 9). Millennials drive growth in sustainable investing. Retrieved from http://www.morganstanley.com/ideas/sustainable-socially-responsible-investing-millennials-drive-growth.html

Murdock, D. (2017, April 1). For corporate social hypocrisy, see Unilever's CEO. *National Review*. http://www.nationalreview.com/article/446342/corporate-social-responsibility-unilever-ceo-exemplifies-its-hypocrisy

Newell, A. (2015, June 19). How Nike embraced CSR and went from villain to hero. *TriplePundit*. Retrieved from www.triplepundit.com

Peloza, J., & Shang, J. (2011). How can corporate social responsibility activities create value for stakeholders? A systematic review. *Journal of the Academy of Marketing Science, 39*(1), 117–135.

Petticrew, M., Hessari, N. M., Knai, C., & Weiderpass, E. (2018). How alcohol industry organisations mislead the public about alcohol and cancer. *Drug and Alcohol Review, 37*(3), 293–303.

Prasad, A., & Holzinger, I. (2013). Seeing through smoke and mirrors: A critical analysis of marketing CSR. *Journal of Business Research, 66*(10), 1915–1921.

Putrevu, S., McGuire, J., Siegel, D. S., & Smith, D. M. (2012). Corporate social responsibility, irresponsibility, and corruption: Introduction to the special section. *Journal of Business Research, 65*(11), 1618–1621.

Sarre, R., Doig, M., & Fiedler, B. (2001). Reducing the risk of corporate irresponsibility: The trend to corporate social responsibility. *Accounting Forum, 25*(3), 300–317.

Scherer, A. G., Rasche, A., Palazzo, G., & Spicer, A. (2016). Managing for political corporate social responsibility—New challenges and directions for PCSR 2.0. *Journal of Management Studies, 53*(3), 273–298.

Shapira, R., & Zingales, L. (2017). Is pollution value-maximizing? The DuPont case. Stigler Center for the Study of the Economy and the State, University of Chicago Booth School of Business, *New Working Paper Series No. 13*, September 2017.

Sheehy, B. (2012). Understanding CSR: An empirical study of private self-regulation. *Monash University Law Review, 38*(2), 103–127.

Sjåfjell, B. (2011). Why law matters: corporate social irresponsibility and the futility of voluntary climate change mitigation. *European Company Law, 8*(2–3), 56–64.

Soltes, E. (2017, January 11). Why it's so hard to train someone to make an ethical decision. *Harvard Business Review*. Retrived from https://hbr.org/2017/01/why-its-so-hard-to-train-someone-to-make-an-ethical-decision

Strine, L. E. (2012). Our continuing struggle with the idea that for-profit corporations seek profit. *Wake Forest Law Review, 47*, 135–172.

Tsang, D., Kazeroony, H. H., & Ellis, G. (2013). *The Routledge companion to international management education*. Routledge.

Wagner, T., Lutz, R. J., & Weitz, B. A. (2009). Corporate hypocrisy: Overcoming the threat of inconsistent corporate social responsibility perceptions. *Journal of Marketing, 73*, 77–91.

Welford, R., Chan, C., & Man, M. (2008). Priorities for corporate social responsibility: A survey of businesses and their stakeholders. *Corporate Social Responsibility and Environmental Management, 15*(1), 52–62.

Whan, E. (2014, May 26). Unilever maintains sustainability leadership amid change. *GlobeScan blog*. Retrieved from https://globescan.com/unilever-maintains-sustainability-leadership-amid-change/

Windsor, D. (2013a). A typology of moral exemplars in business. In M. Schwartz & H. Harris (Eds.), *Moral saints and moral exemplars* (pp. 63–95). Emerald Group Publishing.

Windsor, D. (2013b). Corporate social responsibility and irresponsibility: A positive theory approach. *Journal of Business Research, 66*(10), 1937–1944.

Windsor, D. (2015). Philosophy for managers and philosophy of managers: Turf, reputation, coalition. *Philosophy of Management, 14*(2), 17–28.

Windsor, D. (2016). Economic rationality and a moral science of business ethics. *Philosophy of Management, 15*(2), 135–149.

Zadek, S. (2004). The path to corporate responsibility. *Harvard Business Review, 82*(12), 125–132.

9

Social and Environmental Pressures in Management Education: How Anticipatory Stress and Social Support Interact to Predict Students' Academic Engagement and Performance

Yannick Griep, Timothy G. Wingate, and Melissa A. Boyce

Introduction

Students in higher education face a formidable challenge when acclimatizing to their new learning community. They must integrate with a new social and academic culture, with different standards for work and behavior from those they experienced in secondary school. The term *learning shock* (Griffiths, Winstanley, & Gabriel, 2005) draws attention to an emotional jolt, but successful adjustment will result in academic

---

Y. Griep (✉)
University of Calgary, Calgary, AB, Canada

Stockholm University, Stockholm, Sweden
e-mail: yannick.griep@ucalgary.ca

T. G. Wingate • M. A. Boyce
University of Calgary, Calgary, AB, Canada
timothy.wingate@ucalgary.ca; mboyce@ucalgary.ca

engagement and can strongly increase students' potential to perform academically (Pascarella & Terenzini, 2005).

Academic engagement is traditionally characterized by three components (Fredricks, Blumenfeld, & Paris, 2004): cognition (rationality), emotion (subjectivity), and conation (intention). Highly engaged students tend to *think* positively about their education, *feel* deeply connected to it, and *act* to achieve their academic goals.

In practice, however (Guthrie & Klauda, 2014; Wang & Holcombe, 2010), most students seem to engage either increasingly or decreasingly with their learning context, which leads them respectively to academic achievement or idleness. How students *become* engaged and remain so has been researched, for example, by Solinger, van Olffen, Roe, and Hofmans (2013); the present study found three indicators of students' likely strength of engagement with their studies and hence the level of their academic performance: (1) degree of anticipatory stress, (2) quality and extent of early social support from instructors, (3) extent of early involvement in social activities (i.e., orientation activities).

The following sections provide a brief overview of the above described three factors and then a discussion of the research context, including the methodological approach and findings. Finally, interpretation and discussion of the findings suggest practical steps that might be taken to improve and enhance the learning potential of management education.

Precursors to the Development of Students' Academic Engagement

Anticipatory Stress

In general, students' stress and anxiety seem to have detrimental effects on their academic performance (Richardson, Abraham, & Bond, 2012) and consistency (Wingate & Tomes, 2017). However, some research (e.g., Keeley, Zayac, & Correia, 2008) has found that sometimes students with moderate stress levels performed better than those who reported high or low stress. Moreover, Wingate and Tomes (2017) found that the most anxious students were characterized as having either exceptionally high or exceptionally low levels of motivation and conscientiousness, both of which are excellent precursors to academic achievement (high for the former group; low for the latter).

These studies seem to suggest that the effects of stress and anxiety on academic performance are more complex than a simple linear relationship; different people respond differently to the same stressors, and a certain level of stress might be adaptive instead of detrimental to academic performance. Though students' anticipatory stress may have an important impact on their subsequent academic performance, such impact might be different for different students, and therefore might lead them to different paths of engagement or disengagement, leading in turn to higher or lower academic performance, respectively.

Social Support from Instructors

Gerdes and Mallinckrodt (1994) suggest that new post-secondary students tend to overestimate the challenge of academic adjustment and tend to underestimate its more personal and emotional aspects, but emotional support is critical (Friedlander, Reid, Shupak, & Cribbie, 2007), as is informational and instrumental support from other students and academic staff (Wilcox, Winn, & Fyvie-Gauld, 2005). Although a great deal of research on student social support emphasizes the role of friendships, a growing body of research has acknowledged the importance of social support from instructors and parents when successfully predicting student outcomes (Wentzel, Baker, & Russell, 2012).

The current generation of post-secondary students is considered especially reliant on parental support, but when this is lacking, students might need extra consideration from university officials (Elam, Stratton, & Gibson, 2007). Given the difficulties, complexities, and stressors of adjusting to a new learning environment, it is to be expected that early social support from instructors is instrumental to students' successful development.

Involvement in Orientation and Other On-campus Activities

Students' level of involvement with their studies is a fundamental predictor of academic performance (Schaufeli et al., 2002; Ullah & Wilson, 2007), hence orientation programs to help new students adjust (Keup, & Barefoot, 2005). A study of more than 20,000 students across 365 four-year post-secondary schools (Zhao & Kuh, 2004) found that those who were members of learning communities—that is, groups with common academic goals who collaborate on classwork (DuFour, 2004)—integrated better, gained more skills and knowledge, and achieved higher grades. However, first-year students with lower academic performance were more likely to engage in these learning communities than were their higher performing peers.

These results suggest that most students benefit by participating in social groups and activities, but that some students, and especially those new to post-secondary education, might use these activities as a distraction from schoolwork. It seems likely that some forms of socialization are more helpful than others, especially to first-year students.

Academic Engagement Trajectories

Research in organizational psychology (Solinger et al., 2013) suggests that students' academic engagement develops along five distinct pathways over their first semester. Three of these represent comparisons between students' expectations and those of their academic institution. These are:

1. *High match* (a high and stable level of academic engagement, consistent with the university's academic expectations),
2. *Medium match* (a moderately stable level), and
3. *Low match* (a low but stable level).

The remaining two trajectories are dynamic and represent changing levels of students' academic engagement throughout their first term. The first change may be informally described as *Honeymoon hangover*. It is experienced by students who begin their academic journey with an optimistic outlook, but whose high levels of initial engagement steadily decrease as the term progresses. The second change may be called *Learning to love*, and is experienced by students who start with moderate levels of engagement that increase steadily throughout the first term.

It was anticipated that the sampled students' experience of anticipatory stress, early social support by instructors, and involvement in orientation activities would predispose them toward any of these five trajectories of engagement, which in turn would affect their academic performance.

Research Context

Data were collected from 180 students, average age 18 years, enrolled in the first year of post-secondary education in management at a large European university. Sixty-nine percent were female, 98.6% had a high school diploma, and 1.4% had a higher educational degree. The sample was random, and the selected students were contacted via e-mail. They were asked to complete weekly surveys, beginning two weeks prior to the start of the academic year and throughout the entire first term (18 weeks in total).

At the start of the first term, information was gathered on (1) the extent to which students reported receiving social support from their instructors (e.g., help, care for their well-being, and recognition of their academic performance; Rhoades & Eisenberger, 2002), (2) the extent to which they participated in early orientation activities organized by the university, and (3) the extent to which they experienced anticipatory stress about starting their post-secondary education (e.g., feeling nervous, anxious, lacking control, irritated, and overwhelmed; Stanton, Balzer, Smith, Parra, & Ironson, 2001).

Within each survey, information was collected on the extent to which students felt academically engaged (e.g., feeling a sense of pride, belonging, and engagement in their education, Solinger et al., 2013). Finally, at the end of the first term, the students were asked to consent to the university disclosing their grades. Focus was on grade point average (GPA) over the five courses they studied in the first term, as an indicator of academic performance. In total, 2778 observations by these 180 students were recorded.

Because the intention of the research was to examine how social and environmental factors might influence the development of the students' academic engagement, data were analyzed by latent-class growth modeling (Andruff,

Carraro, Thompson, & Gaudreau, 2009; Nagin & Tremblay, 2005). This technique allowed division of students into five groups in which (1) individuals' academic engagement developed in similar ways, (2) social and environmental factors had a similar influence on all members in developing engagement with their studies, and (3) members' levels of academic engagement had a similar influence on their academic performance.

Results

Preliminary Findings

The results supported the findings by Solinger et al. (2013), that academic engagement does develop in five distinct ways among first-year post-secondary students. The following description is of (1) the exact developmental path of academic engagement in these five groups, (2) how social and environmental factors affected the development of academic engagement, and (3) how the developmental nature of academic engagement affected academic performance.

1. The development of academic engagement

Based on the growth parameter estimates of the five different latent classes of academic engagement, a graphical representation was created of the development of academic engagement over the course of the first term (see Fig. 9.1).

The first group consisted of 20 students (11.00% of the sample) who displayed moderate and stable academic engagement throughout the first term (i.e., a 'moderate match' between student and university expectations). The second group contained 13 students (7.20%) characterized by low and stable academic engagement (i.e., a 'low match'). The third group contained 60 students (33.30% of the sample), characterized by high levels of academic engagement throughout the first term (i.e., 'high match' students).

The fourth group contained 66 students (36.70%), characterized by moderate levels of academic engagement two weeks prior to the start of

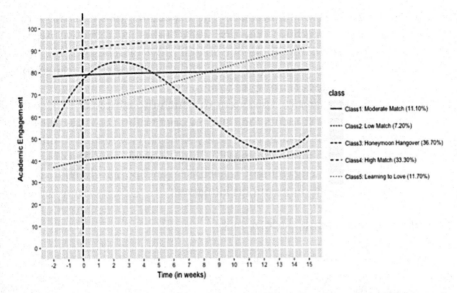

Fig. 9.1 Five distinct academic engagement trajectories during the first term of first-year post-secondary education students. The dashed line indicates the start of the first term. Observations on the left side of the dashed line represent anticipated academic engagement, whereas observations on the right side of the dashed line represent the academic engagement once the first term has started until completion

the first term, who became increasingly engaged in the first weeks but later disengaged and only partially re-engaged as the term ended. These students appeared to follow a 'honeymoon hangover' trajectory.

The fifth group contained 21 students (11.70%), characterized by moderate levels of academic engagement two weeks prior to the start of the first term, which gradually increased as the term progressed, following a 'learning to love' trajectory.

2. Social and environmental factors affecting academic engagement

> 2a. *Anticipatory stress.* In the two weeks prior to the start of the first term, anticipatory stress was negatively related to the 'moderate match' and 'learning to love' academic engagement trajectories, and positively related to 'low match', 'high match', and 'honeymoon hangover'.

2b. *Social support from instructors.* The experience of social support from instructors during the first week of the first term was negatively related to the 'moderate match', low match, and 'honeymoon hangover' engagement trajectories, and positively related to 'high match' and 'learning to love'.

2c. *Orientation activities.* The extent to which the sample of first-year post-secondary students took part in orientation activities during the first week of the academic year was negatively related to membership in the 'moderate match', 'high match', and 'learning to love' academic engagement trajectories, and positively related to 'low match' and 'honeymoon hangover'.

3. Influence on academic performance

Figure 9.2 illustrates the differences in academic performance, as indicated by average GPA, across the five different groupings of academic engagement. The average GPA was highest among students characterized by 'high match' or 'learning to love'. Notably, these respondents did not differ significantly from each other in terms of average GPA. Moreover, the average GPA was lowest among students characterized by 'low match'. The average GPA for students characterized by 'moderate match' or 'honeymoon hangover' was higher than the average GPA for 'low match' students but lower than for students characterized by 'high match' or 'learning to love'.

There was a direct positive relationship between receiving social support from instructors and students' average GPA, but no similar statistically significant relationships between taking part in orientation activities and average GPA or between anticipatory stress and average GPA.

Discussion

The findings underscore the importance of social (i.e., instructor support and orientation activities) and environmental (i.e., anticipatory stress) factors on the development of students' academic engagement and performance.

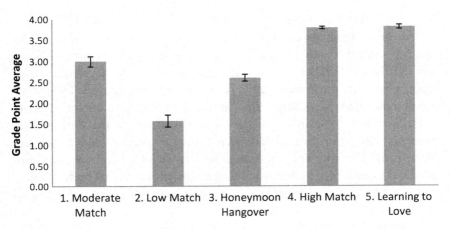

Fig. 9.2 GPA for each academic engagement trajectory (on a 4.0 scale). Error bars represent one standard error of the mean. Note: GPA for moderate match (2.99) is significantly higher than the GPA for low match (1.57) and honeymoon hangover (2.60), whereas it is significantly lower than the GPA for high match (3.79) and learning to love (3.82). GPA for low match is significantly lower than the GPA for all other academic engagement trajectories. GPA for honeymoon hangover is significantly higher than the GPA for low match, whereas it is significantly lower than the GPA for moderate match, high match, and learning to love. GPA for high match and learning to love is significantly higher than the GPA for all other academic engagement trajectories

Stable Trajectories: Low Match, Moderate Match, and High Match Low Match

Students in the 'low match' trajectory exhibited high levels of anticipatory stress prior to their post-secondary education. Although they might have benefitted from instructor support to help them, these students were more likely to take part in orientation activities, which helped them engage informally with other students. They might have been unaware or uncomfortable with the formal resources available to them, or afraid to approach their instructors. Unfortunately, rather than helping them to feel integrated within their campus community, engaging with other students during orientation may have distracted them from their studies. If so, it is not surprising that these students attained the lowest levels of academic performance of all the trajectories at the end of the term.

The importance of providing support for students who fit this trajectory is evident, given that first-year academic performance has been found to predict whether students continue into their second year of post-secondary education (Szafran, 2017). Because these students are less likely to seek out formal support from their instructors, it is crucial that instructors explicitly encourage all their students to contact them and to clarify the protocol for doing so.

It might help to set up an online course discussion board. Posing questions via discussion boards has been found to reduce student anxiety when compared to posing questions in a face-to-face context (Sullivan, 2002). Furthermore, an overwhelming majority of students prefer courses that include such discussion boards because they find them to be helpful for their learning (Badawy, 2012).

These students may also benefit by learning that anticipatory stress can be helpful and that increase of tension in the face of novel challenges may actually help the sufferers to deal more effectively with stressful events (Jamieson & Mendes, 2013; Roelofs, Bakvis, Hermans, van Pelt, & van Honk, 2007). Jamieson and Mendes (2013) found that students who were taught to think about stress as an adaptive, rather than a maladaptive response, reported lower subjective levels of stress and exerted more effort during the completion of a stressful task. Similarly, Roelofs et al. (2007) found that students could adapt more healthily to stressful events if they were trained to think about them as helpful.

Thus educators would be well advised to help students to reframe their anticipatory stress as helpful, to enable them to show greater resilience in the face of early academic stressors, and to achieve stronger academic performance as a result.

Moderate Match

Students who conformed to a 'moderate match' trajectory reported that they experienced low levels of anticipatory stress in the two weeks before their post-secondary education. As a result, they may have been less motivated to seek out instructor support or to participate in early orientation activities—they reported little of either activity. These students demonstrated a moderately stable level of engagement throughout the term, with moderate academic performance.

It may be that it is these students, rather than those on the 'low match' trajectory, who are most apathetic about their university experiences. The consistency between these students' academic engagement and performance implies that, should their engagement improve, they might enter a 'high match' trajectory and achieve a significant increase in academic performance as a result. To do so, the research results suggest that early intervention by instructors is pivotal.

These students may become increasingly engaged when they perceive that their post-secondary education has important implications for their ability to achieve their short- and long-term goals. One way to manage this might be for academic advisers to emphasize professional and career development for first-year university students; for example, universities could build these into program recruitment efforts.

Additionally, many introductory level courses provide a broad coverage of the foundational areas within a discipline, which may make it difficult for some students to connect the material they are learning to their career and professional plans. In such cases, instructors might explain how each topic is relevant to a professional setting and, when possible, include signature pedagogies, where students' learning is tied to the activities they will engage in as future professionals (Shulman, 2005). These approaches may help to further promote these students' academic engagement, and consequently their academic performance.

High Match

The 'high match' trajectory seems to be followed by 'high flyers'. Although they report heightened levels of anticipatory stress, this is not inherently negative (Jamieson & Mendes, 2013). It appeared that these students were more likely to channel their stress into effective academic habits, including seeking out instructor support when needed. Students on a 'high match' trajectory are likely to exhibit a growth mindset (Dweck, 1999), to be invigorated by new challenges (Yeager & Dweck, 2012), and to show resilience from disappointment or failure (Zeng, Hou, & Peng, 2016).

Although it may seem that these students are not in need of support—given their consistent high levels of academic engagement, performance, and ability to seek out formal supports as needed (Berzonsky & Kuk, 2005)—they may be further encouraged through academic enrichment opportunities. Given their tendency to reframe challenges as opportunities, they might be especially likely to benefit from academic experiences that enhance their personal and professional growth (Jones, 2009), including participation in honor, co-op, or international exchange programs.

Dynamic Trajectories: 'Honeymoon Hangover' or 'Learning to Love'

These appear to be more heavily influenced by social factors, or interaction between social and dispositional factor. Identifying the social factors that predict membership in these trajectories leads to suggestions for improving academic engagement and achievement.

'Honeymoon Hangover'

Students who followed this trajectory were like those in the 'low match' category, in reporting high levels of anticipatory stress. They took part in early orientation activities, and perceived little support from instructors. However, this group differed from the 'low match' group in one important way: they began the term with moderate levels of academic engagement, but approximately one month into the term, experienced a downtown in engagement that continued until the term neared its close. This group subsequently achieved relatively low GPAs (second only to the 'low match' group).

The timing of this group's shift from growing engagement to growing disengagement reveals the effects of contrasting expectations. While these students might feel initially that stress and anxiety over transition to university were not warranted, unexpected challenges (e.g., their first set of midterm scores) might be extremely disappointing. These students would benefit from a review of their exams, to learn from their mistakes and adopt more active techniques to improve their performance (Freeman et al., 2014). Instructors should provide assistance at this time, but unfortunately this group may be less likely to approach their instructors, because of feeling unsupported by them. As a result, these students may be more likely to consider high levels of academic performance an unattainable goal, which may result in learned helplessness, further academic disengagement, worse academic performance, and even less support-seeking from their instructors (Klem & Connell, 2004).

There are ways instructors can support students who follow this trajectory. Arguably the best option is to prevent students doing so in the first place, by building rapport to ensure they feel secure in consulting their instructors if they are struggling academically. Some examples of activities instructors can engage in to build rapport with students include 'ice breaker' games; using students' first names, offering personal examples in class, using humor, and explicitly stating and repeating invitations to contact their instructor if they have any questions about the course and/or their learning (Gorham & Christophel, 1990). Research has found that students who develop a rapport with their instructors are more likely to pay attention in class, exhibit resilience in the face of academic challenges, and engage in more effective study strategies (Benson, Cohen, & Buskist, 2005).

Another way in which these students' academic engagement, and ultimately their academic performance, can be supported is by instructors' fostering a growth mindset (Dweck, 1999) by providing feedback that emphasizes the value of effort over intelligence (Mueller & Dweck, 1998). Mueller and Dweck (1998) found that when instructors adopted this approach, students were more likely to believe their skills were improvable, expressed greater enjoyment of their work, demonstrated greater resilience after experiencing failure, and were more persistent and achieved better performance on subsequent tasks.

'Learning to Love'

Students on this academic engagement trajectory experienced low anticipatory stress as they approached their post-secondary education. Although they tended to take part in fewer orientation activities, they reported more social support from their instructors. Once again, the benefits of instructor support over orientation activities was apparent, as these students finished their first term with the highest GPAs overall (although not statistically different from the GPAs of students in the 'high match' trajectory).

It is for this group that the benefits of instructor support emerge most clearly. These students began their post-secondary education with early experiences (low anticipatory stress, high involvement in orientation activities) that could have set them on the path to a 'low match' academic engagement trajectory. However, the support they received from their instructors differentiates them from those who fit a 'low match' trajectory and may have helped them to become increasingly engaged as the term progressed.

These students seem to benefit substantially from receiving early and consistent support from their instructors—engaging in casual conversation, touching base throughout the term to see if they have any queries or concerns, letting them know they believe in them and their capacity to learn. Behavior such as this by instructors can constitute a transformative experience for students. This is evidenced by the fact that students who set out with early experiences that could have set them on the path of a 'low match' academic engagement trajectory, overcame these obstacles and thrived academically when they received sufficient support from their instructors.

Conclusions

The research revealed negative effects, on students' academic engagement, of taking part in orientation activities. This suggests that universities might benefit from spending fewer resources on organizing these activities and more on teacher supply and teacher training—because the social support that students get from their instructors appears to be far more effective for their academic success. Anticipatory stress is not inherently negative: when it is accompanied by high levels of social support from instructors, it may lead to high levels of academic engagement and academic performance.

References

Andruff, H., Carraro, N., Thompson, A., & Gaudreau, P. (2009). Latent class growth modelling: A tutorial. *Tutorials in Quantitative Methods for Psychology, 5*(1), 11–24.

Badawy, A. H. A. (2012). Students' perceptions of the effectiveness of discussion boards: What can we get from our students for a freebie point? *International Journal of Advanced Computer Science and Applications, 3*(9), 136–144.

Benson, T. A., Cohen, A. L., & Buskist, W. (2005). Rapport: Its relation to student attitudes and behaviors toward teachers and classes. *Teaching of Psychology, 32*(4), 237–239.

Berzonsky, M. D., & Kuk, L. S. (2005). Identity style, psychosocial maturity, and academic performance. *Personality and Individual Differences, 39*(1), 235–247.

DuFour, R. (2004). What is a "professional learning community"? *Educational Leadership, 61*(8), 6–11.

Dweck, C. S. (1999). *Self-theories: Their role in motivation, personality and development*. Philadelphia, PA: The Psychology Press.

Elam, C., Stratton, T., & Gibson, D. D. (2007). Welcoming a new generation to college: The millennial students. *Journal of College Admission, 195*, 20–25.

Fredricks, J. A., Blumenfeld, P. C., & Paris, A. H. (2004). School engagement: Potential of the concept, state of the evidence. *Review of Educational Research, 74*(1), 59–109.

Freeman, S., Eddy, S. L., McDonough, M., Smith, M. K., Okoroafor, N., Jordt, H., et al. (2014). Active learning increases student performance in science, engineering, and mathematics. *Proceedings of the National Academy of Sciences, 111*(23), 8410–8415.

Friedlander, L. J., Reid, G. J., Shupak, N., & Cribbie, R. (2007). Social support, self-esteem, and stress as predictors of adjustment to university among first-year undergraduates. *Journal of College Student Development, 48*(3), 259–274.

Gerdes, H., & Mallinckrodt, B. (1994). Emotional, social, and academic adjustment of college students: A longitudinal study of retention. *Journal of Counseling & Development, 72*(3), 281–288.

Gorham, J., & Christophel, D. M. (1990). The relationship of teachers' use of humor in the classroom to immediacy and student learning. *Communication Education, 39*(1), 46–62.

Griffiths, D. S., Winstanley, D., & Gabriel, Y. (2005). Learning shock: The trauma of return to formal learning. *Management Learning, 36*(3), 275–297.

Guthrie, J. T., & Klauda, S. L. (2014). Effects of classroom practices on reading comprehension, engagement, and motivations for adolescents. *Reading Research Quarterly, 49*(4), 387–416.

Jamieson, J. P., & Mendes, W. B. (2013). Cardiovascular and cognitive responses to stress. *Journal of Experimental Psychology General, 141*(3), 417–422.

Jones, C. (2009). Interdisciplinary approach: Advantages, disadvantages, and the future benefits of interdisciplinary studies. *Essai, 7*, 75–81.

Keeley, J., Zayac, R., & Correia, C. (2008). Curvilinear relationships between statistics anxiety and performance among undergraduate students: Evidence for optimal anxiety. *Statistics Education Research Journal, 7*(1), 4–15.

Keup, J., & Barefoot, B. (2005). Learning how to be a successful student: Exploring the impact of first-year seminars on student outcomes. *Journal of the First-Year Experience & Students in Transition, 17*(1), 11–47.

Klem, A. M., & Connell, J. P. (2004). Linking teacher support to student engagement and achievement. *Journal of School Health, 74*(7), 262–274.

Mueller, C. M., & Dweck, C. S. (1998). Intelligence praise can undermine motivation and performance. *Journal of Personality and Social Psychology, 75*(2), 33–52.

Nagin, D. S., & Tremblay, R. E. (2005). Developmental trajectory groups: Fact or a useful statistical fiction? *Criminology, 43*(4), 873–904.

Pascarella, E. T., & Terenzini, P. T. (2005). *How college affects students: A third decade of research.* San Francisco, CA: Jossey-Bass.

Rhoades, L., & Eisenberger, R. (2002). Perceived organizational support: A review of the literature. *Journal of Applied Psychology, 87*(4), 698–714.

Richardson, M., Abraham, C., & Bond, R. (2012). Psychological correlates of university students' academic performance: A systematic review and meta-analysis. *Psychological Bulletin, 138*(2), 353–387.

Roelofs, K., Bakvis, P., Hermans, E. J., van Pelt, J., & van Honk, J. (2007). The effects of social stress and cortisol responses on the preconscious selective attention to social threat. *Biological Psychology, 75*(1), 1–7.

Schaufeli, W. B., Martinez, I. M., Pinto, A. M., Salanova, M., & Bakker, A. B. (2002). Burnout and engagement in university students: A cross-national study. *Journal of Cross-Cultural Psychology, 33*(5), 464–481.

Shulman, L. S. (2005). Signature pedagogies in the professions. *Daedalus, 134*(3), 52–59.

Solinger, O. N., van Olffen, W., Roe, R. A., & Hofmans, J. (2013). On becoming (un) committed: A taxonomy and test of newcomer onboarding scenarios. *Organization Science, 24*(6), 1640–1661.

Stanton, J. M., Balzer, W. K., Smith, P. C., Parra, L. F., & Ironson, G. (2001). A general measure of work stress: The stress in general scale. *Educational and Psychological Measurement, 61*(5), 866–888.

Sullivan, P. (2002). It's easier to be yourself when you are invisible: Female college students discuss their online classroom experiences. *Innovative Higher Education, 27*(2), 129–144.

Szafran, R. F. (2017). The effect of academic load on success for new college students: Is lighter better? *Research in Higher Education, 42*(1), 27–50.

Ullah, H., & Wilson, M. (2007). Students' academic success and its association to student involvement with learning and relationships with faculty and peers. *College Student Journal, 41*, 1192–1202.

Wang, M. T., & Holcombe, R. (2010). Adolescents' perceptions of school environment, engagement, and academic achievement in middle school. *American Educational Research Journal, 47*(3), 633–662.

Wentzel, K. R., Baker, S. A., & Russell, S. L. (2012). Young adolescents' perceptions of teachers' and peers' goals as predictors of social and academic goal pursuit. *Applied Psychology: An International Review, 61*(4), 605–633.

Wilcox, P., Winn, S., & Fyvie-Gauld, M. (2005). It was nothing to do with the university, it was just the people: The role of social support in the first-year experience of higher education. *Studies in Higher Education, 30*(6), 707–722.

Wingate, T. G., & Tomes, J. L. (2017). Who's getting the grades and who's keeping them? A person-centered approach to academic performance and performance variability. *Learning and Individual Differences, 56*, 175–182.

Yeager, D. S., & Dweck, C. S. (2012). Mindsets that promote resilience: When students believe that personal characteristics can be developed. *Educational Psychologist, 47*(4), 302–314.

Zeng, G., Hou, H., & Peng, K. (2016). Effect of growth mindset on school engagement and psychological well-being of Chinese primary and middle school students: The mediating role of resilience. *Frontiers in Psychology, 7*, 1–8.

Zhao, C. M., & Kuh, G. D. (2004). Adding value: Learning communities and student engagement. *Research in Higher Education, 45*(2), 115–138.

10

Learning in Higher Education: The Role of Sustainability Integration Strategies, Legitimacy, and Teaching Tools

Raquel Antolin-Lopez and Nieves Garcia-de-Frutos

Introduction

The increase in the number and severity of environmental and social problems, along with frequently controversial practices of organizations and managers, requires rethinking business education (Samuelson, 2013; Stoner & Wankel, 2009). University contexts should positively influence business students' willingness to learn (WTL) about sustainability and induce them to act responsibly as leaders of the next generation of companies.

Given this scenario, sustainability is becoming more prevalent in management education as a key component of the business curricula. There have been studies (e.g., Rands, 2009; Rusinko & Sama, 2009; Sammalisto & Lindhqvist, 2008) on implementation strategies (e.g., as a stand-alone course vs. within existing courses) and teaching tools. For instance, Rusinko (2010) developed a matrix of options for integrating sustainability into business education.

R. Antolin-Lopez (✉) • N. Garcia-de-Frutos
University of Almeria, Almeria, Spain
e-mail: ral252@ual.es; gdn779@ual.es

Despite these efforts, integration across business disciplines has been slow and remains a challenge (Starik, Rands, Marcus, & Clark, 2010). In addition, little is known about how different integration strategies might impact on students' perceptions and WTL. Most studies remain at a conceptual level, or address specific cases that make generalization difficult. They seem to be curriculum-centred rather than student-centred.

Moreover, other studies (Thomas, 2005) suggest that sustainability integration within business curricula is not enough to induce students to embrace sustainability as a key managerial criterion. It remains a polarizing topic, with some students diminishing its importance and legitimacy. Given the many different attitudes and a myriad of external influences, sustainability training, to have a real effect on students, should be perceived as a legitimate—indeed, a desirable—component of the business curriculum (Springett & Kearins, 2001). Lack of endorsement from instructors—or from business leaders—may have a negative effect on students' attitudes (Doh & Tashman, 2014).

However, research into students' attitudes towards sustainability, ethics, and Corporate Social Responsibility (CSR) is still in its infancy (Lämsä, Vehkaperä, Puttonen, & Pesonen, 2008). Empirical research has been especially scant (Alonso-Almeida, Fernández de Navarrete, & Rodriguez-Pomeda, 2015) and the studies focus on general attitudes towards sustainability, overlooking specific attitudes in the university context such as WTL about sustainability. This research gap challenges instructors and business school leaders on how to integrate, implement, and endorse sustainability education to reach different students' mindsets.

Sustainability Integration in the Business Curricula

Sustainability is linked to the Brundtland report's definition of sustainable development as:

> *Development that meets the needs of the present generation without compromising the ability of future generations to meet their own needs.* (Brundtland, 1987, p. 43).

It is defined in the academic world in terms of three dimensions—the triple bottom line: economic prosperity, social equity, and environmental responsibility (Bansal, 2005). For example, environmental sustainability encompasses energy conservation, biodiversity, and environmental risks (Martinez-del-Rio, Antolin-Lopez, & Cespedes-Lorente, 2015); social sustainability includes philanthropy, bottom of the pyramid, and local development; and economic sustainability covers profit generation, efficiency, and corruption (Antolin-Lopez, Delgado-Ceballos, & Montiel, 2016). Hence, the integration of sustainability in business education implies the inclusion of environmental and social responsibility principles in addition to economic principles, with the aim of training more responsible future leaders who can help to address, rather than contribute to, the environmental challenges societies face (Stoner & Wankel, 2009).

Due to the severity of such challenges, business schools and higher education institutions worldwide have devoted substantial efforts and resources to developing and integrating sustainability into their curricula (Rusinko, 2010; Samuelson, 2013). Consequently, there has been a remarkable increase in the number of study electives such as sustainability business, corporate sustainability, and business and society (Thomas, 2005), and greater inclusion within existing core courses such as strategic management, financial management, and accounting.

Despite these efforts to legitimize sustainability as a key component of the business curricula, scholars warn about lack of progress and that an effective integration of sustainability in business education remains a major challenge (Doh & Tashman, 2014).

Implementation Strategies for Sustainability Integration

Recent studies have addressed how to better integrate sustainability in both business and management education (Rands, 2009; Rusinko, 2010; Rusinko & Sama, 2009; Sammalisto & Lindhqvist, 2008): whether it should be a stand-alone course through a specific discipline such as CSR, or broadly introduced in the whole business curriculum as part of existing courses as new modules or lessons. Despite disadvantages as well as advantages in the different options, there seems to be consensus that sustainability needs to be broadly integrated in the business curriculum within existing core business courses and across all business-related disciplines beyond management courses (Rusinko & Sama, 2009; Thomas, 2005).

For the purposes of the research, the first assumption was as follows:

H1: *The perceived degree of inclusion of sustainability across the different business subjects in an academic degree will be positively associated with students' WTL about sustainability.*

Sustainability Legitimacy

Thomas (2005) states that even if sustainability is included in management education, there is no guarantee students will regard it as a key managerial principle. Students will only be likely to embrace it if they perceive it to be a legitimate component of the business curriculum. Most would more typically regard economic principles such as profitability, market share, and customer satisfaction as essential corporate objectives.

Nevertheless, students' perceived desirability of sustainability goals—such as fair trade or reducing CO_2 emissions—can differ significantly; they may be considered as valid and a priority, or of minor and secondary importance for others (Swaim, Maloni, Napshin, & Henley, 2014). Moreover, a conflicting logic between sustainability and traditional business goals (e.g., economic goals) can have a negative impact on students' attitudes which tends to diminish the importance and legitimacy of the former, and even when students' attitudes are potentially favourable, any lack of institutional support might inhibit their personal sense of responsibility to the environment (Arbuthnott, 2009).

Social Referents

Research acknowledges that although internal values and beliefs shape students' attitudes towards sustainability, external influences (specific social referents) provide endorsement for sustainability education and impact particularly on college students. This research is grounded in Ajzen's (1985) theory that people will engage in certain behaviour partly because of their internal attitudes, and partly due to subjective norms such as the attitudes of relevant peers and superiors. Instructors are influential in persuading students to regard sustainability as a central aspect of doing business (Benn & Dunphy, 2009), and professors lend it credibility by integrating sustainability with the business school curriculum.

In her study of how a university in the north east of the United States integrated sustainability within business education, Rusinko (2010) found that in addition to high-level university support (rector, department head, etc.), faculty-level support for sustainability was necessary. There were faculty enthusiasts who acted as pioneers in introducing sustainability into their classrooms, raising its desirability as a business topic to teach, and coordinating with professors of different subjects to have a broader impact on students. Likewise, Benn and Dunphy (2009) found faculty commitment to sustainability to be a key to success for an effective integration of sustainably across the curriculum in Australian Business Schools. Therefore, as instructors can build legitimacy for sustainability education, the second research proposition was that:

H2: *A greater perceived attention by the professor to sustainability aspects will be positively associated with students' WTL about sustainability.*

Business leaders also are valid referents in reinforcing students' positive attitudes. For instance, Swaim et al. (2014) found empirical evidence that the opinions of business leaders and politicians exert a positive influence on students' intentions to engage in sustainability behaviours. These social referents provide endorsement to the applicability of sustainability into business practice and that sustainability related skills may be required in the business world. This leads to the third research proposal:

H3: *The perceived importance of sustainability in the business world will be positively associated with students' WTL about sustainability.*

The Position of Sustainability in the Syllabus

It has also been argued that perceptions of the legitimacy of sustainability education will be affected by *where* it is embedded in the business curriculum (Thomas, 2004). If it is a core element, students are more likely to consider it central to business education and be more willing to learn about it—particularly if they need to demonstrate such knowledge to pass the course. Thus the fourth research proposition, in two parts, is that:

H4a: *The inclusion of sustainability aspects within the mandatory bibliography of a subject will be positively associated with students' WTL about sustainability;*

H4b: *The inclusion of sustainability aspects within the supplementary bibliography of a subject will be positively associated with students' WTL about sustainability, but to a lesser degree than the mandatory bibliography.*

Teaching Tools

The teaching tools used to convey sustainability concepts and aspects might also impact on business student's WTL about sustainability. For example, discussions about real world companies' problems might show the importance of knowledge and skills to meet future business requirements for environmental responsibility.

The case method has been argued to be an excellent teaching resource to bring the complexities of sustainability issues to the classroom (ueiró & Raufflet, 2015; Montiel, Antolin-Lopez, & Gallo, 2017). Moreover, applied methods (e.g., the case method) might increase students' positive attitude towards behaving sustainably because they also serve to strengthen the influence of business leaders as a social referent—subjective norm (Swaim et al., 2014). Therefore:

H5: *The use of the case method to teach sustainability will be positively associated with students' WTL about sustainability.*

Lectures that include practical examples of sustainability practices might also have a positive effect on students' WTL by bringing reality to the classroom. Short examples can be linked to:

- Breaking news on sustainability topics,
- Recent international company stories,
- Stories about local companies geographically close to the students.

Combining global and local perspectives helps to reinforce the importance of the topic (Collins & Kearins, 2010), brings students closer to specific sustainability problems and activates a sense of urgency. However, as they are not officially stated in the syllabus, they might be perceived as less central business topic in the subject.

H6: *The use of short examples to teach sustainability will be positively associated with students' WTL about sustainability but in a lower degree than the case study.*

Methodology

Data Collection

Data collection was by online survey. The fieldwork was with undergraduate students from different courses and degrees offered by the Faculty of Economics and Business Studies at the University of Almeria. Data collection was during February and March 2017. From a random selection, the student sample represented more than half the Course 2016/17 enrolment in the Faculty. Students were contacted by e-mail that provided them with a link to the online questionnaire and requested their participation in the survey. The e-mail explained that the questionnaire was part of a research project about teaching methods in general and that their responses would remain anonymous. This avoided self-selection bias by students who might be interested in sustainability issues. The response rate was 19.7%, which—given the size of the sample—can be assumed as acceptable (Nulty, 2008).

Sample Description

The final sample consists of 320 students. As can be seen in Table 10.1, except for a slight overrepresentation of the business administration degree students (38.9% vs. 51.2%), the rest of the sample is similar to the student distribution per degree in the Faculty for the academic year when the data collection took place (University of Almeria, 2017). The sample was also balanced, comprising of 24.4% first-year students, 16.9% second-year students, 19.4% third-year students, 23.8% fourth-year students, and 15.6% of students finishing their degree. As can be seen in Table 10.2, more female (56%) than male (44%) students answered the questionnaire, which closely resembles the actual gender distribution of the Faculty of Economics and Business Studies at the University of Almeria (52.4% females vs. 47.6% males) (National Statistics Institute, 2017). The average age of the sample was 23.57 years.

Measures

The questionnaire consisted of several questions to measure the dependent, independent, and control variables of interest. The dependent variable, students' *WTL about sustainability* in business, was measured as a construct variable using three items on a five-point Likert scale. The three items were:

Table 10.1 Representativeness of the sample according to students' degree

Variables	Total sample (n = 320) (%)	Students enrolled in the Faculty of Economics and Business Studies, Course 2017 (n = 2434) (%)
Degree		
Business Administration	51.2	38.9
Finance and Accounting	14.1	20
Marketing	14.1	13.6
Tourism	10.6	11.3
Economics	10	10.8

Table 10.2 Descriptive statistics of antecedent variables

Variables	M	SD
Age	23.57	5.9
Objective knowledge	2.78	0.93
Neoclassical economic worldview	2.92	1.07
Inclusion of sustainability across the degree	2.87	0.82
Professor attributed importance	2.67	0.82
Importance of sustainability in the business world	3.73	0.79
	Level	Relative frequency (%)
Mandatory bibliography	Yes	24.7
	No	75.3
Supplementary bibliography	Yes	23.8
	No	76.3
Case studies	Yes	53.1
	No	46.9
Professor examples	Yes	60.9
	No	39.1
Gender	Male	44
	Female	56
Academic year	First	24.4
	Second	16.9
	Third	19.4
	Fourth	23.8
	Finished	15.6

- *It is interesting for me to learn about sustainability;*
- *I would like for professors to include more topics related to sustainability in their courses;*
- *I think that learning about sustainability is very important nowadays.*

Principal component analysis of the WTL variables resulted in loadings on one single factor which was able to explain the 77.2% variance. All items featured high-standardized weights. The Cronbach's alpha for the factor was 0.849, well above of the recommended threshold of 0.7 (Hair, Black, Babin, Anderson, & Tatham, 2006).

Students were asked to rate *perceived inclusion of sustainability across the different business subjects in an academic degree* in four separate areas of knowledge related with business studies (i.e., management, finance and accounting, economics, and marketing). A summary variable was built by calculating the mean score of the four areas. This variable was used as a proxy for sustainability integration implementation strategy.

To test the different sources of legitimacy, two potential influences were included related to (1) the professors and (2) the business world. Such constructs were also measured for the separate areas of knowledge in business studies. Two summary variables were created by calculating the mean score of the different areas of knowledge. The final variables were:

1. *Attributed importance of professors to sustainability issues*, which ranged from "it is not important at all" to "it is very important";
2. *Perceived relevance of sustainability knowledge in order to obtain a position in a company* ranged from "little relevance" to "a lot of relevance".

Both variables were measured on a five-point Likert scale.

To measure the different positions of sustainability content within the syllabus, students were asked to select whether or not sustainability topics were presented within their subjects:

1. in the *mandatory bibliography* of the course;
2. in the *supplementary bibliography* of the subject.

Hence two different dummy variables, where the number 1 represents that sustainability content is present and the number 0 means that sustainability content is absent.

The different teaching tools for sustainability were measured by asking students to state whether content about sustainability was presented within their courses through:

1. *case studies*,
2. *examples provided by the professor*.

Thus, two dummy variables (1 = content about sustainability is presented in this teaching tool; 0 = content about sustainability is absent from this teaching tool), each one representing one of the different methods to include sustainability content into management courses.

Control Variables

As controls, three different demographic—that is, gender, age, and year of study—and two psychographic—that is, objective knowledge and worldview—variables were selected.

- *Gender*. It has been posited that women are generally more concerned about sustainability problems than men (Ortega-Egea, García-de-Frutos, & Antolin-Lopez, 2014; Vicente-Molina, Fernández-Sainz, & Izagirre-Olaizola, 2018). Reasons may be found in the socialization of women, which emphasizes altruistic or social values, such as caring, that have been closely matched to sustainability attitudes (Ng & Burke, 2010). Following this, it is expected that women will show a greater WTL about sustainability issues compared to their male counterparts. In our questionnaire, gender was measured with a dichotomous variable that distinguishes between masculine (coded 1) and feminine (coded 2), respondents.
- *Age*. Age is one of the most controversial variables regarding sustainable behaviour (Ortega-Egea et al., 2014). Older individuals tend to have more resources—that is, intellectual development—than their younger counterparts. Hence, it is posited that older individuals will exhibit a greater intention to learn about sustainability (Alonso-Almeida et al., 2015).
- *Year of study*. Sustainability is a complex issue that is linked to multiple problems and potential solutions. Hence, it is expected that, as students move forward during their degree, they will develop the skills and knowledge necessary to understand sustainability and will be more willing to learn (Alonso-Almeida et al., 2015). Students were asked in the questionnaire to indicate in which year of study they were enrolled.
- *Objective knowledge*. Knowledge about sustainability is a fundamental prerequisite for individuals to be able to develop concerns, attitudes, and intentions to act appropriately (Arbuthnott, 2009). In this case, it was expected that students exhibiting more objective knowledge would be more willing to learn about sustainability. In the questionnaire, objective knowledge was operationalized by asking the students to rate whether four different objectives pertained or not to the sustainability

domain. Next, a variable was created by summing the total amount of right answers given by each participant. Thus the final objective knowledge variable ranges between 0 (all answers given about sustainability were wrong) and 4 (all answers given were right, indicating a high level of objective knowledge).

- *Worldview.* Past research on environmental behaviour shows the relevance of a personal worldview—or a broad set of beliefs about the relationship between humans and the environment—on influencing narrower sets of attitudes, intentions, and behaviour (Stern, 2000). These studies focused on the impact of a neoclassical economic worldview, since it is the dominant paradigm and hence, used as a framework by most business courses nowadays (Stubbs & Cocklin, 2008). It is possible that for individuals engaged in this worldview, sustainability learning is seen as less important, since the focus must be on other issues—that is, making the company profitable. As a proxy for students' personal worldviews regarding sustainability in the business field, the questionnaire asked them to rank in a five-point scale their level of agreement with the sentence:

the main objective of a company must be to make as much profit as possible.

It was assumed that greater levels of agreement with the sentence would indicate a more neoclassic economic worldview.

Results

Descriptive Analysis

No missing data were found during the analysis, that is, all participants completed all the questions. Table 10.2 shows some descriptive results of each proposed antecedent of WTL. For scale variables, the mean and standard deviation are provided. In addition, Table 10.2 includes the percentages of different methodologies that students identified to deliver the sustainability content.

The average level of objective knowledge about sustainability issues ranked 2.8, which is moderate-to-high, showing room for improvement. The average level of adherence to a neoclassical economic worldview was 2.9, showing neither agreement nor disagreement. The descriptive results manifest that, on average, students perceived that sustainability content was included on a moderate basis during their degree (2.9).

Comparing the two different sources of legitimacy, professors ranked behind the business world (2.7 vs. 3.7).

Regarding the position of sustainability content in the syllabus, results were similar for mandatory (24.7%) and supplementary (23.8%) bibliography. The results for teaching tools show how more than the half of the students believe their professors include sustainability within their class examples (60.9%). In addition, half of the students (53.1%) were able to identify case studies comprising sustainability content within their courses.

Common Method Variance and Multicollinearity Tests

First, given the reliance on one single source of information to collect all variables, we followed the recommendations of Podsakoff et al. (2003) with regard to the questionnaire's design, to minimize the potential emergence of common method variance. The questions corresponding to our dependent and independent variables were placed in different order from that of the subsequent analysis. There were more questions than the ones included in this report; and the dependent variable consisted of three different items. All these issues made it very difficult for participants to guess the intention of the study, and even less to intentionally alter it.

In addition, we performed Harman's single factor test, to discard common method bias empirically (Podsakoff et al., 2003). The solution without rotation manifested the existence of more than one factor. In addition, the first factor extracted only accounted for 22% of the total variance, which is below the recommended level of 50%. These results show that common method would not be sufficient to explain relationships between variables and then it should not be major issue in our data.

Table 10.3 Correlation tests

	(1)	(2)	(3)	(4)	(5)	(6)	(7)	(8)	(9)	(10)	(11)	(12)	(13)
WTL (1)	1												
Gender (2)	−0.122*	1											
Age (3)	0.175**	0.043	1										
Year of study (4)	0.197**	0.026	0.493**	1									
Objective knowledge (5)	0.090	0.068	0.177**	0.148**	1								
Neoclassic economic worldview (6)	−0.143*	0.043	−0.073	−0.125*	−0.065	1							
Inclusion of sustainability across the degree (7)	0.090	0.081	0.087	0.016	−0.028	0.124*	1						
Professor attributed importance (8)	0.025	−0.022	−0.093	−0.027	0.011	0.130*	0.678**	1					
Importance of sustainability in the business world (9)	0.380**	−0.182**	−0.004	0.008	0.003	−0.051	0.389**	0.301**	1				
Syllabus: mandatory bibliography (10)	−0.067	0.008	0.024	−0.012	−0.035	−0.023	−0.183**	−0.214**	−0.060	1			
Syllabus: supplementary bibliography (11)	0.090	−0.011	−0.083	−0.141*	−0.086	0.122*	−0.080	−0.075	−0.027	0.294**	1		
Teaching tool: case study (12)	0.022	−0.122*	0.003	−0.164**	−0.032	0.007	−0.139*	−0.149**	0.062	0.088	0.039	1	
Teaching tools: professor's examples (13)	−0.150**	−0.022	−0.036	−0.089	0.026	−0.077	−0.138*	−0.232**	−0.118*	0.087	−0.095	0.069	1

Note: *p significant at 0.05; **p significant at 0.01

Next, we ran the variance inflation factor (VIF) test and bivariate correlations to assess potential multicollinearity problems in the data. The VIF values ranged from 1.03 to 2.04, which is under the threshold of 10 (Hair et al., 2006). In addition, as can be seen in Table 10.3, the highest correlation value was 0.68 and the rest were under 0.49, all falling far below the recommended value of 0.8 (Hair et al., 2006). These results led to discard of multicollinearity as a serious issue in the sample. Therefore, both tests show the adequacy of the data for the subsequent analysis.

Determinants of Students' WTL

Stepwise multiple regression analysis identified determinants of WTL about sustainability. The results are presented in Table 10.4.

In Model 1, only control variables were included. This model explained 7.9% of the variance. Regarding the demographics, year of study and gender were found to statistically influence students' WTL about sustainability. This means that men and all students in their last years of their degree are more willing to learn about sustainability. On the other hand, age was found not to be significant. Looking at the psychographic variables, it is possible to find that a neoclassical economic worldview was significant but negatively related to the dependent variable, whereas objective knowledge was not significant.

Model 2 included the controls and the independent variables representing implementation strategy, legitimacy of sustainability content, and teaching tools. Compared with the first, this model explained the greater percentage of WTL variance (25%). Among control variables, two psychographics—that is, year of study and age—were found to be positively and significantly related to the dependent variable, whereas gender was not. The psychographics remained stable in comparison to Model 1, that is, a neoclassical economic worldview was found to be negatively and significant related to students' WTL, whereas objective knowledge remained non-significant.

Contrary to expectations, the results showed that the perceived degree of attention paid to sustainability issues across the degree was not related to WTL. This result does not provide support for H1. Regarding the

Table 10.4 Multiple regression models with WTL about sustainability as dependent variable

Step	Independent variable	R^2	Beta	T	Sig.
Model 1	Gender		−0.128	−2.360	0.019**
	Age		0.099	1.572	n.s.
	Year of study		0.130	2.066	0.040**
	Objective knowledge		0.055	0.992	n.s.
	Neoclassical economic worldview		−0.110	−2.016	0.045**
		0.079			
Model 2	Gender		−0.060	−1.182	n.s.
	Age		0.097	1.668	0.096*
	Year of study		0.136	2.298	0.022**
	Objective knowledge		0.063	1.245	n.s.
	Neoclassical economic worldview		−0.111	−2.162	0.031**
	Sustainability across the degree		0.013	0.188	n.s.
	Professor attributed importance		−0.104	−1.493	n.s.
	Importance for business world		0.374	6.760	0.000**
	Position in the syllabus: Mandatory bibliography		0.104	1.962	0.051*
	Position in the syllabus: Supplementary bibliography		−0.159	−2.990	0.003**
	Teaching tool: case studies		−0.012	−0.238	n.s.
	Teaching tool: professor's examples		0.101	1.940	0.053*
		0.25			

Note: Gender = 1 Male; 2 = Female. Syllabus and tools variables, 1 = sustainability content is present; 0 = sustainability content is absent
*$p < 0.1$; **$p < 0.05$

sources of legitimacy, the results do not support H2, but largely support H3; whereas the perceived degree of attention paid to sustainability by professors was non-significant, the strongest influence on WTL about sustainability comes from the perceived relevance of sustainability knowledge for future work.

With regard to the ways in which sustainability content is included in the syllabus, the results showed different results depending on the position given to the content. On the one hand, mandatory bibliography content was positive and significant, meaning that students who perceive sustainability content present on their courses through mandatory bibliography tend to have a greater interest on learning about such issues. This lends support to H4a. On the other hand, supplementary bibliography was significant and negatively related to the dependent variable, that is, when sustainability content is perceived to be part of the supplementary bibliography; students become less interested about sustainability learning. Hence, H4b does not receive empirical support.

Finally, the teaching tools variables also manifested different impacts on WTL. Whereas examples set by the professor were significantly and positively associated with WTL—providing support to H5; case studies did not have a significant impact on WTL—thus, no support for H6.

Discussion

The results obtained are a useful starting point for understanding different features, strategies, sources of legitimacy, and tools that underlie students' WTL about sustainability issues. Demographic characteristics of students, such as gender or age were shown to have little to no effect on WTL. The extant literature shows that women students tend to be more concerned about sustainability (Alonso-Almeida et al., 2015), but this was not the case in our study. The marginal to non-significant results of age may be explained by the relatively little variance of ages between the students that comprise our sample. Results of year of study manifest how, as students advance in their courses, they become more willing to learn about sustainability issues in business disciplines.

Regarding the psychographic variables, it was surprising to discover that objective knowledge did not show any significant effect on WTL about sustainability. Even more so, considering that knowledge has been claimed as a prerequisite for sustainability concern and action (Ortega-Egea et al., 2014; Vicente-Molina et al., 2018). The results also support the notion that personal worldviews are an important antecedent of WTL. Whereas past evidence was mainly focused on eco-centric worldviews, this study delved into the role of the neoclassical economic paradigm, as an opposite worldview. Therefore, it was found that when students hold more neoclassic economic worldviews—that is, believing companies' main aim must be to be profitable—they become less interested in learning about sustainability issues.

This is in line with past research, where personal worldviews have been considered an important antecedent of other psychographic factors, such as attitude, motivation, or intention (Stern, 2000). To improve the effectiveness of sustainability teaching, it would be necessary to consider additional sustainability frameworks as eco-centric or ecological modernization (Stubbs & Cocklin, 2008).

Regarding the results of the descriptive analysis, it is noticeable that there is still room for introducing more sustainability content to the degrees of the Faculty of Economics and Business Studies at the University of Almeria. Specifically, students perceive that sustainability is only receiving a moderate level of attention from the institution, professors, and even the business world.

Surprisingly, students mark the business world as the place where sustainability is more important. This might be a reason to explain why the implementation strategy, understood as placing more attention to sustainability issues across the degree, was not a good predictor of students' WTL. However, it is more likely that the results of implementation strategy may warn institutions that including sustainability content without a good understanding of other factors that affect its implementation—such as the legitimacy sources and tools—is not effective.

The results for the two legitimacy sources obtained very different results. On the one hand, and in line with the literature (Swaim et al., 2014) the findings show that sustainability relevance in the business world plays a key role on increasing students' WTL. On the other hand, the attributed importance by professors showed no effect. This counterintuitive finding may be better understood when the results of the position of sustainability in the syllabus and teaching tools are considered. In line with Thomas (2005), it is possible to notice that when sustainability content was included in a peripheral way—that is, optional bibliography—the WTL of the students decreased, whereas when sustainability content was included as part of the core of the course—that is, mandatory bibliography—the students were more prone to learn.

The examples set by professors are also powerful tools to induce WTL. This result is very interesting because it may indicate essential features of sustainability training. For instance, examples given in class tend to be selected ad hoc, depending on context. Given their informal nature, examples tend to be more topical and close to students—for instance, of recent events or local companies. These may generate more affective responses, helping students derive greater interest, and find personal relevance in sustainability issues (Montiel et al., 2017).

Case studies did not significantly affect students' WTL. This result calls for further research, given that this could indicate that professors are not using them properly. For instance, Montiel et al. (2017) propose that existing case studies to teach sustainability might be grouped around different typologies (genres) that help to develop different skills and elicit different emotions and feelings, so they need to be adequately selected.

In sum, it is possible to state that, even though sustainability is included in the business curricula, impact on students is not ensured. The findings seem to confirm that the most important factor in fostering students' WTL about sustainable practices is that they are legitimized as a component of business education. Legitimacy might come from leaders in the business world; from presentation of the topic as a core element of management education; and from provision of appropriate teaching tools.

Conclusions

Once the importance of providing business students with sustainability knowledge is widely recognized, the question arises, of which are the best ways to engage them. This study offers some answers, including the importance of curriculum implementation strategies; of legitimization from business and academic sources; and by appropriate teaching tools. To find those answers, 320 students were sampled, enrolled in different degrees of the Faculty of Economics and Business Studies of the University of Almeria (Spain).

Statistical analysis shows how their WTL about sustainability is highly influenced by their individual perceptions of the business field. When students perceive this knowledge will be useful they will be more interested in acquiring it. On the other hand, if they assume the main aim of companies is to make economic profit, they lose interest. Even though the research findings suggest that though instructors on their own do not influence their students' WTL, they can do so if sustainability is embedded within their courses and they use appropriate teaching tools such as case studies. The research results support the idea that when professors place sustainability at the core of the subject—that is, including it on mandatory bibliography—or set specific examples for students, their WTL increases. Paying more attention to sustainability *per se* may have little effect; professors must strategically integrate sustainability into the core of their courses, showing examples of how such practices can be successfully implemented to have a positive impact on companies, society, and the environment. In this way, professors will legitimize the role of sustainability in business success and reinforce the usefulness of such knowledge and related skills to train students in responsible management behaviour as well as to meet job market requirements.

Limitations and Further Research

There are several ways in which this study might be improved and extended. First, it is context-specific, with all the limitations that this entails. Hence, replication is needed, especially in places where sustainability content in business studies has a longer tradition and/or in different cultural settings.

Second, there is room for further improvement in the (moderate) predictive power of the regression model. In this regard, additional variables can be included, such as subject major, work experience, motivation, or perceived effectiveness (Vicente-Molina et al., 2018). Another important issue is that only students' perspectives were studied, hence it should be interesting to make a comparative study of professors' views. Such comparative work would provide evidence of differences between intended versus perceived strategies, methods, and teaching tools.

Notwithstanding this, perhaps the most importantly indicated research path is the one that broadens the ways in which sustainability content can generate more interest and be accepted by students. More empirical evidence is needed on content features such as temporal and geographical proximity, sustainability frameworks, and elicited emotions.

Acknowledgements We acknowledge financial support from the Spanish Ministry of Economy, Industry and Competitiveness, Agencia Nacional de Investigación-AEI, and the European Regional Development Fund-ERDF/FEDER-UE (R&D Project ECO2015-66504).

References

Ajzen, I. (1985). From intentions to actions: A theory of planned behavior. In J. Kuhl & J. Beckmann (Eds.), *Action control: From cognition to behavior* (pp. 11–39). New York: Springer.

Alonso-Almeida, M. D. M., Fernández de Navarrete, F. C., & Rodriguez-Pomeda, J. (2015). Corporate social responsibility perception in business students as future managers: A multifactorial analysis. *Business Ethics: A European Review, 24*(1), 1–17.

Antolin-Lopez, R., Delgado-Ceballos, J., & Montiel, I. (2016). Deconstructing corporate sustainability: A comparison of stakeholder metrics. *Journal of Cleaner Production, 136*, 5–17.

Arbuthnott, K. D. (2009). Education for sustainable development beyond attitude change. *International Journal of Sustainability in Higher Education, 10*(2), 152–163.

Bansal, P. (2005). Evolving sustainably: A longitudinal study of corporate sustainable development. *Strategic Management Journal, 26*(3), 197–218.

Benn, S., & Dunphy, D. (2009). Action research as an approach to integrating sustainability into MBA programs. *Journal of Management Education, 33*(3), 276–295.

Brundtland, G. H. (1987). *Report of the World Commission on Environment and Development: "Our common future"*. United Nations.

Collins, E., & Kearins, K. (2010). Delivering on sustainability's global and local orientation. *Academy of Management Learning and Education, 9*(3), 499–506.

Doh, J. P., & Tashman, P. (2014). Half a world away: The integration and assimilation of corporate social responsibility, sustainability, and sustainable development in business school curricula. *Corporate Social Responsibility and Environmental Management, 21*(3), 131–142.

ueiró, P. S., & Raufflet, E. (2015). Sustainability in higher education: A systematic review with focus on management education. *Journal of Cleaner Production, 106*, 22–33.

Hair, J. F., Black, W. C., Babin, B. J., Anderson, R. E., & Tatham, R. L. (2006). *Multivariate data analysis* (Vol. 6). Upper Saddle River, NJ: Prentice Hall.

Lämsä, A. M., Vehkaperä, M., Puttonen, T., & Pesonen, H. L. (2008). Effect of business education on women and men students' attitudes on corporate responsibility in society. *Journal of Business Ethics, 82*(1), 45–58.

Martinez-del-Rio, J., Antolin-Lopez, R., & Cespedes-Lorente, J. J. (2015). Being green against the wind? The moderating effect of munificence on acquiring environmental competitive advantages. *Organization & Environment, 28*(2), 181–203.

Montiel, I., Antolin-Lopez, R., & Gallo, P. (2017). Emotions and sustainability: A literary genre based framework for environmental sustainability management education. *Academy of Management Learning & Education.* published online.

National Statistics Institute of Spain (INE). (2017). Statistics about university students for the course 2016/17. Retrieved from http://www.mecd.gob.es/servicios-al-ciudadano-mecd/estadisticas/educacion/universitaria/estadisticas/alumnado/2016-2017/Grado-y-Ciclo.html

Ng, E. S., & Burke, R. J. (2010). Predictor of business students' attitudes toward sustainable business practices. *Journal of Business Ethics, 95*(4), 603–615.

Nulty, D. D. (2008). The adequacy of response rates to online and paper surveys: What can be done? *Assessment & Evaluation in Higher Education, 33*(3), 301–314.

Ortega-Egea, J. M., García-de-Frutos, N., & Antolin-Lopez, R. (2014). Why do some people do "more" to mitigate climate change than others? Exploring heterogeneity in psycho-social associations. *PLoS One, 9*(9), 1–17.

Podsakoff, P. M., MacKenzie, S. B., Lee, J. Y., & Podsakoff, N. P. (2003). Common method biases in behavioral research: A critical review of the literature and recommended remedies. *Journal of Applied Psychology, 88*(5), 879–903.

Rands, G. P. (2009). A principle-attribute matrix for environmentally sustainable management education and its application. *Journal of Management Education, 33*(3), 296–322.

Rusinko, C. A. (2010). Integrating sustainability in management and business education: A matrix approach. *Academy of Management Learning & Education, 9*(3), 507–519.

Rusinko, C. A., & Sama, L. (2009). Greening and sustainability across the management curriculum: An extended journey. *Journal of Management Education, 33*(3), 271–275.

Sammalisto, K., & Lindhqvist, T. (2008). Integration of sustainability in higher education: A study with international perspectives. *Innovative Higher Education, 32*(4), 221–233.

Samuelson, J. F. (2013, May/June). Putting pinstripes in perspective. *BizEd*, 66–67. *International Journal of Sustainability in Higher Education, 3*(3): 254–270.

Springett, D., & Kearins, K. (2001). Gaining legitimacy? Sustainable development in business school curricula. *Sustainable Development, 9*(4), 213–221.

Starik, M., Rands, G., Marcus, A. A., & Clark, T. S. (2010). From the guest editors: In search of sustainability in management education. *Academy of Management Learning & Education, 9*(3), 377–383.

Stern, P. C. (2000). New environmental theories: Toward a coherent theory of environmentally significant behaviour. *Journal of Social Issues, 56*(3), 407–424.

Stoner, J. A., & Wankel, C. (2009). The only game big enough for us to play. In C. Wankel & J. A. F. Stoner (Eds.), *Management education for global sustainability*. New York: IAP.

Stubbs, W., & Cocklin, C. (2008). Teaching sustainability to business students: Shifting mindsets. *International Journal of Sustainability in Higher Education, 9*(3), 206–221.

Swaim, J. A., Maloni, M. J., Napshin, S. A., & Henley, A. B. (2014). Influences on student intention and behaviour toward environmental sustainability. *Journal of Business Ethics, 124*(3), 465–484.

Thomas, I. (2004). Sustainability in tertiary curricula: What is stopping it happening? *International Journal of Sustainability in Higher Education, 5*(1), 33–47.

Thomas, T. E. (2005). Are business students buying it? A theoretical framework for measuring attitudes toward the legitimacy of environmental sustainability. *Business Strategy & the Environment, 14*(3), 186–197.

University of Almería. (2017). *Memoria del curso académico 2016/17*. Retrieved from https://www.ual.es/application/files/5115/0667/5402/UNIFICADO_centros.pdf

Vicente-Molina, M. A., Fernández-Sainz, A., & Izagirre-Olaizola, J. (2018). Does gender make a difference in pro-environmental behaviour? The case of the Basque Country University students. *Journal of Cleaner Production, 176*, 89–98.

11

Responsible Managers and Responsible Management Education

Carol Pomare

Introduction

A movement towards more environmental sustainability should mitigate the adverse impact on stranded assets (Baron & Fischer, 2015) but much information on firms' environmental performance is believed to be omitted in financial statements and annual reports (Li, Richardson, & Thornton, 1997). The challenge for responsible managers is not only to evaluate the scale of firms' operational performance but also to assess realistically their environmental performance in terms of the products locked into their reserves (e.g., oil and gas, coal, etc.). This requires responsible management education (RME).

C. Pomare (✉)
Mount Allison University, Sackville, NB, Canada
e-mail: cpomare@mta.ca

Responsible Managers and RME

Corporate Social Responsibility and Business Ethics

This section explores the definitions of corporate social responsibility (CSR) and related concepts. Recent academic debates have identified an increasing overlap between, and lack of clarity in, concepts related to CSR (Fassin, Van Rossem, & Buelens, 2011). Further, the application of CSR-related concepts may differ between multinational enterprises (MNEs) and small and medium enterprises (SMEs), as well as from original academic definitions.

CSR refers to modern managerial practices to reduce environmental or societal problems. The terms CSR and business ethics are used interchangeably in the literature (Cacioppe, Forster, & Fox, 2008; Epstein, 1987; Ferrell, 2004; Joyner & Payne, 2002; Vogel, 1991). To provide clarity, Christensen, Peirce, Hartman, Hoffman, and Carrier (2007) identify two aspects of corporate ethics:

1. Corporations' ethical role in society (CSR),
2. The role of corporations in minimizing the destruction to, and maximizing the preservation of, resources for future generations (sustainable management).

However, the roles seem to have merged in recent years (Staurer, Langer, Konrad, & Martinuzzi, 2005; Waddock, 2004), due to actions of stakeholders in regulating corporate behaviour (Donaldson & Preston, 1995; Garriga & Melé, 2004). Triple bottom-line management (Savitz & Weber, 2006), corporate governance, and accountability have been fragmented into sub-concepts such as safety, product liability, and human rights (Carroll & Buchholtz, 2006; Crane & Matten, 2004), and Carroll's pyramid of CSR includes economic, legal, ethical, and philanthropy-related dimensions.

Responsible managers have an important role to play in the orientation of MNEs and SMEs towards CSR. The challenge is to evaluate operational performance and to assess environmental performance. Substantial adjustments of regulating practices are required for firms to realistically alter balance sheets, and such changes require RME.

Responsible Managers and RME

Since business students collectively constitute the future leadership of corporations and small businesses, it has been argued, for example, by Albaum and Peterson (2006), that business students should be prioritized as a target group for RME. Some studies (Ferraro, Pfeffer, & Sutton, 2005; Frank & Schulze, 2000; Smyth & Davis, 2004) have shown that traditional business education tends to result in students who are less ethical and more corruptible. Wang, Malhotra, and Murnighan (2011) have shown that elements of the traditional business education, such as exposure to some specific courses, lead to higher levels of comfort with "greed". Luthar and Karri (2005) observed a significant disconnect in students' perceptions between ethics and professional performance, and that students did not believe it "pays to be good". Arguably students saw the line between right and wrong as increasingly blurry and expected managers to behave unethically.

Giacalone and Thompson (2006) claimed the main problem was the worldview underpinning management education, as some business professors may have emphasized the benefits of economic and materialistic thinking in their classes (Alsop, 2003). However, a substantive amount of information (Bekmezci, 2015) indicates this worldview is flawed, as it fails to serve humanity in ways that are sustainable. As a result, even when CSR was taught in traditional curricula, it was based on a pragmatic approach, focused on shareholders' wealth, rather than a moral approach focused on stakeholders' needs (Giacalone & Thompson, 2006). This has led to a call for business schools to become more socially responsible, to be more than institutions educating graduates in a narrow shareholder value ideology (Matten & Moon, 2004), most of all after the series of corporate scandals happening during the 2008 global financial crisis (Crossan, Mazutis, Seijts, & Gandz, 2013; Giacalone, 2007; Podolny, 2009).

The concept of RME is related to business education, including teaching, research, and dialogue, to develop students to become responsible generators of sustainable values for business and society at large. Haski-Leventhal, Pournader, & McKinnon (2017) refer to six Principles for Responsible Management Education (PRME) as a basis for RME: purpose, values, method, research, partnership, and dialogue. PRME values, from stakeholders management, social inclusion, and practicalities, allow an active—instead of passive—learners' role for business students (Christensen, Peirce, & Hartman, 2007).

Some business schools have shifted from a focus on rankings and alumni salaries, to a commitment to help in creating a more ethical and moral business environment (Haski-Leventhal et al., 2017). One example has been the increasing number of business schools committed to the United Nations support for PRME—over 500 in 2013—and many examples of schools that integrate RME throughout their curriculum can be found on the PRME website (www.unprme.org).

In 2007, Christensen et al. (2007) explored CSR in MBA classrooms and how education in CSR has evolved since 2002. They found that many business school administrators had long debated its role in the classroom and challenged its role in the profit-maximizing world of business schools. These writers' research is supported, for example, by Alsop (2003), Evans and Robertson (2003), Hartman and Hartman (2005), (Rossouw, 2002), Sims and Brinkmann (2003), Sims (2000), Swanson and Frederick (2005), and Weber (1990).

Christensen et al. (2007) conducted a survey of the top 50 business schools, as identified in the Financial Times 2006 rating of global MBA programmes. They show how, since 2012, MBA programmes have expanded their focus on:

1. The ethical role of corporations in society (CSR),
2. The role of corporations in minimizing the destruction to, and maximizing the preservation of, resources for future generations (sustainable management).

The authors found that nearly one-third of the responding schools required coverage of all topics in the MBA curriculum. They identified how students' involvement was a driver for continued change and concluded their investigation by describing key programmes in sustainability, as well as key programmes in ethics and CSR in the early 2000s.

To better understand how business schools have been moving towards RME up to 2017, Haski-Leventhal et al. (2017) investigated four indicators of business students' moral approach, with a focus on the most relevant indicators to RME, namely:

1. Business students' values
2. Their attitudes towards CSR
3. Their priorities for CSR
4. Their suggestions for CSR suggestions

Based on an international sample of nearly 1300 business students in RME-signatory schools, the authors were able to highlight the impact of gender and age on these four indicators of students' moral approach. They observed that business students, particularly females and older students, wanted to learn more about responsible management and leveraged theories of gender socialization (Gilligan, 1982) as well as life stages (Kohlberg, 1981) to assess how moral approach may be partially related to gender or age. Also they explored the implications for business schools and their various groups of stakeholders for including all students' worldviews in an active learning approach to a CSR curriculum.

If business schools are to move more towards RME and to be more inclusive of students, innovative teaching methods may be needed. This may be both a challenge and an opportunity. Formerly, professors have focused on the cognitive understanding of CSR but recent studies have called for a shift of paradigm (e.g., Shrivastava, 2010; Starik, Rands, Marcus, & Clark, 2010). This may require more holistic pedagogical approaches and experiential methods to integrate emotional, spiritual, and physical learning (Christensen et al., 2007). Some evidence exists already for new technologies (e.g., Jagger, Siala, & Sloan, 2016; Lozano, Folguera, &Arenas, 2003) to teach CSR-related courses, using smartphones, Web 2.0 platforms, and/or mobile apps.

New technologies offer an opportunity for students to relate theories to their daily experiences. For example, the GoodGuide mobile app was decsribed as a way to translate complex data—on health, environment, and social impact of food and consumer products—into average sustainability ratings using a barcode scan (O'Rourke & Ringer, 2015). Thus, the app may have the potential to educate about corporate sustainability, non-financial ratings, and responsible consumption (O'Rourke & Ringer, 2015). Another example is the Buycott app that was described as allowing users to join "support" or "boycott" campaigns related to social and environmental causes (O'Rourke & Ringer, 2015).

Therefore, the challenge for future responsible managers is to be educated not only in terms of traditional business curricula but also within an RME framework and to integrate these newly learned skills.

Conclusions and Implications

Global economic systems are moving towards more environmental sustainability, by taking a firm's environmental performance into consideration when valuing firms financially—for example, greenhouse gas emissions, carbon taxes, and cap-and-trade programmes. However, the challenge for responsible managers is not only to evaluate the firm's operational performance but also to assess realistically its environmental performance. This requires better understanding of how to implement RME in business schools. This chapter has discussed RME within a context of environmental economic performance.

The outcome of this review of litterature is the argument that business schools should maintain and increase RME. They should take a proactive role in both teaching and research (Haski-Leventhal et al., 2017); CSR and ethics teaching should be embedded in all core units and subjects, as well as being taught as a separate course (Haski-Leventhal et al., 2017). CSR students should be offered internships and visits to socially responsible companies (Haski-Leventhal et al., 2017); Students should be involved in RME discussions and RME should be integrated throughout the entire curriculum, and be made available online (Haski-Leventhal et al., 2017).

These practices and ideas should be shared with the entire PRME community as well as with external readers, through "Sharing Information on Progress" reports which could be uploaded to the relevant websites of all signatory schools and to the PRME website (www.unprme.org). RME should be of interest to other stakeholders, including faculty, employers, and policy makers.

Finally, there are business schools that shift their mission statements, curricula, faculties, and students towards RME (e.g., The Copenhagen Business School, and Bentley University), and students who feel strongly about RME might prefer to study at one of these institutions—as might academics seeking university teaching positions. For current faculty, there is great scope for leading bottom-up change towards RME.

References

Albaum, G., & Peterson, R. A. (2006). Ethical attitudes of future business leaders: Do they vary by gender and religiosity? *Business and Society, 45*(3), 300–321.

Alsop, R. (2003, September). Right and wrong: Can business schools teach students to be virtuous?' *Wall Street Journal*, R9.

Baron, R., & Fischer, D. (2015). Divestment and stranded assets in the low-carbon transition. Background paper for the *32nd Round Table on Sustainable Development*, 28 October 2015, OECD Headquarters, Paris.

Bekmezci, M. (2015, May). Companies' profitable way of fulfilling duties towards humanity and environment by sustainable innovation. *Procedia—Social and Behavioral Sciences, 181*(11), 228–240.

Cacioppe, R., Forster, N., & Fox, M. (2008). A survey of managers' perceptions of corporate ethics and social responsibility and actions may affect companies' success. *Journal of Business Ethics, 82*, 681–700.

Carroll, A., & Buchholtz, A. (2006). *Business and society: Ethics and stakeholder management*. Mason: Thompson Learning.

Christensen, L., Peirce, E., Hartman, L., Hoffman, W. M., & Carrier, J. (2007). Ethics, CSR, and sustainability education in the Financial Times top 50 global business schools: Baseline data and future research directions. *Journal of Business Ethics, 73*(4), 347–368.

Crane, A., & Matten, D. (2004). *Business ethics: A European perspective*. Oxford: Oxford University Press.

Crossan, M., Mazutis, D., Seijts, G., & Gandz, J. (2013). Developing leadership character in business programs. *Academy of Management Learning & Education, 12*(2), 285–305.

Donaldson, T., & Preston, L. (1995). The stakeholder theory of the corporation: Concepts, evidence, and implications. *Academy of Management Review, 20*(1), 65–91.

Epstein, J. (1987). The corporate social policy process: Beyond business ethics, corporate social responsibility, and corporate social responsiveness. *California Management Review, 29*(3), 99–114.

Evans, F. J., & Robertson, J. W. (2003). Business school deans and business ethics. *AACSB Annual Meeting*, New Orleans, LA.

Fassin, Y., Van Rossem, A., & Buelens, M. (2011). Small-business owner-managers' perceptions of business ethics and CSR-related concepts. *Journal of Business Ethics, 98*(3), 425–453.

Ferraro, F., Pfeffer, J., & Sutton, R. I. (2005). Economics language and assumptions: How theories can become self-fulfilling. *Academy of Management Review, 30*(1), 8–24.

Ferrell, O. (2004). Business ethics and customer stakeholders. *Academy of Management Executive, 18*(2), 126–129.

Frank, B., & Schulze, G. G. (2000). Does economics make citizens corrupt? *Journal of Economic Behavior & Organization, 43*(1), 101–113.

Freedman, M., & Jaggi, B. (2010). *Sustainability, environmental performance and disclosures*. Emerald Group Publishing.

Garriga, E., & Melé, D. (2004). Corporate social responsibility theories: Mapping the theory. *Journal of Business Ethics, 53*(1/2), 51–71.

Giacalone, R. A. (2007). Taking a red pill to disempower unethical students: Creating ethical sentinels in business schools. *Academy of Management Learning & Education, 6*(4), 534–542.

Giacalone, R. A., & Thompson, K. R. (2006). Business ethics and social responsibility education: Shifting the worldview. *Academy of Management Learning & Education, 5*(3), 266–277.

Gilligan, C. (1982). *In a different voice: Psychological theory and women's development* (p. 326). Cambridge, MA: Harvard University Press.

Hartman, L., & Hartman, E. (2005). How to teach ethics: Assumptions and arguments. *Journal of Business Ethics Education, 1*, 165–121.

Haski-Leventhal, D., Pournader, M., & McKinnon, J. (2017). The role of gender and age in business students' values, CSR attitudes, and responsible management education: Learnings from the PRME International Survey. *Journal of Business Ethics, 146*, 219.

Jagger, S., Siala, H., & Sloan, D. (2016). It's all in the game: A 3D learning model for business ethics. *Journal of Business Ethics, 137*(2), 383–403.

Joyner, B., & Payne, D. (2002). Evolution and implementation: A study of values, business ethics and corporate social responsibility. *Journal of Business Ethics, 41*, 297–311.

Kohlberg, L. (1981). *The philosophy of moral development: Moral stages and the idea of justice. Essays on moral development* (Vol. 1). San Francisco, SF: Harper & Row.

Li, Y., Richardson, G. D., & Thornton, D. B. (1997, Fall). Corporate disclosure of environmental liability information: Theory and evidence. *Contemporary Accounting Research, 14*(3), 435–474.

Lozano, J. M., Folguera, C., & Arenas, D. (2003). Setting the context: The role information technology in a business ethics course based on face-to-face dialogue. *Journal of Business Ethics, 48*(1), 99–111.

Luthar, H., & Karri, R. (2005). Exposure to ethics education and the perception of linkage between organizational ethical behavior and business outcomes. *Journal of Business Ethics, 61*(4), 353–368.

Matten, D., & Moon, J. (2004). Corporate social responsibility education in Europe. *Journal of Business Ethics, 54*(4), 323–337.

O'Rourke, D., & Ringer, A. (2015). The impact of sustainability information on consumer decision making. *Journal of Industrial Ecology, 20*(4), 882–892.

Podolny, J. M. (2009). The buck stops (and starts) at business school. *Harvard Business Review, 87*(6), 62–67.

Rossouw, D. (2002). Three approaches to teaching business ethics. *Teaching Business Ethics, 6*, 411–433.

Savitz, A. W., & Weber, K. (2006). *The triple bottom line: How today's best-run companies are achieving economic, social and environmental success—And how you can too*. Jossey-Bass.

Shrivastava, P. (2010). Pedagogy of passion for sustainability. *Academy of Management Learning & Education, 9*(3), 443–455.

Sims, R. (2000). Teaching business ethics: A case study of an ethics across the curriculum policy. *Teaching Business Ethics, 7*, 69–86.

Sims, R., & Brinkmann, J. (2003). Business ethics curriculum design: Suggestions and illustrations. *Teaching Business Ethics, 7*, 69–86.

Smyth, M. L., & Davis, J. (2004). Perceptions of dishonesty among two-year college students: Academic versus business situations. *Journal of Business Ethics, 51*(1), 63–73.

Starik, M., Rands, G., Marcus, A. A., & Clark, T. S. (2010). From the guest editors: In search of sustainability in management education. *Academy of Management Learning & Education, 9*(3), 377–383.

Staurer, R., Langer, M., Konrad, A., & Martinuzzi, A. (2005). Corporations, stakeholders and sustainable development: A theoretical exploration of business-society relations'. *Journal of Business Ethics, 61*, 263–281.

Swanson, D., & Frederick, W. C. (2005). Denial and leadership in business ethics education. In O. C. Ferrell & R. A. Peterson (Eds.), *Business ethics: The new challenge for business schools and corporate leaders*. Armonk, NY: M.E. Sharpe.

Vogel, D. (1991). Business ethics: New perspectives on old problems. *California Management Review, 33*(4), 101–117.

Waddock, S. (2004). Parallel universes: Companies, academics, and the progress of corporate citizenship. *Business and Society, 24*(1), 32–39.

Wang, L., Malhotra, D., & Murnighan, J. K. (2011). Economics education and greed. *Academy of Management Learning & Education, 10*(4), 643–660.

Weber, J. (1990). Measuring the impact of teaching ethics to future managers. *Journal of Business Ethics, 9*, 183–190.

12

Sustainable Business Ethics Education

Meena Chavan and Leanne M. Carter

Introduction

The chapter argues the existence of an ethical "hole" in recent international business practices that requires urgent repair. For example, Matthews and Heimer (2016) reported that 2016 was a year dominated by corporate scandals, including pharma giant Mylan imposing big price increases on users of its life-saving EpiPen, the batteries exploding in the new Samsung Galaxy Note 7, and Wells Fargo's employees creating fake accounts in the names of real customers.

The need for an ethical workforce has always been high (Carucci, 2016), but this apparent vacuum in business standards prevents transfer of ethical values to subsequent generations of corporate managers. As a result, the academic community faces increasing demands for

M. Chavan (✉) • L. M. Carter
Macquarie University, Sydney, Australia
e-mail: meena.chavan@mq.edu.au; leanne.carter@mq.edu.au

better and more sustainable ethics education in business programmes (Nijhof, Wilderom, & Oost, 2012). Society needs professionals who can be trusted and relied on to behave ethically for the benefit of all stakeholders.

Business ethics education by tradition is taught from a cognitive perspective—by transmission of knowledge, reasoning, and intuition. To meet the current demand for more corporate social responsibility, it is necessary not only to review current mechanistic educational paradigms (Lozano, Lukman, Lozano, Huisingh, & Lambrechts, 2013) but also to provide credible and practical alternatives (Sterling, 2004). New methods need to be identified to apply these ideas to real-life practices (Maclagan, 2012), and one that has been under-explored is teaching ethics from affective and behavioural perspectives.

Learning through experience was first popularized in 1938 by John Dewey (2007). His idea of creation of meaning through direct experience was later developed by Lewin (1951) and then Knowles (1980). Experiential learning activities (ELAs) and critical action learning (CAL) are contemporary models designed to empower students to achieve real and material changes in how they interact with others and the environment, and what theories and frameworks they use to interpret the world around them (Kemmis & McTaggart, 2005).

The ELA model has been researched extensively, based on Kolb's (1984) theory of learning styles. Applied to the study of ethics, it indicates possibilities for helping students to become more ethical citizens by increasing their ability to transfer university-acquired knowledge to their workplaces (Beard & Wilson, 2006). CAL is an approach to individual development where students work in small groups, tackle important organizational issues or problems, and learn from their attempts to solve them (Trehan in Pedler, 2011). CAL concerns the ways in which individuals classify data and how these might be channelled into more productive relationships between learning and practice (Anderson & Thorpe, 2004). There is growing consensus (Vince, 2008) that ELA and CAL engage students not only cognitively (as they acquire new knowledge, in this case of ethics) but also emotionally—for example, they might be encouraged to feel empathy towards victims of unethical practices (Werhane, Hartman, Archer, Bevan, & Clark, 2011).

Ethics Education

The issue of ethics in business has come under a brighter spotlight of late due to corporate corruption scandals that have plagued international business. In dire need of higher ethical standards, the business community has turned to higher education programmes for help. Therefore, there has emerged a sense of urgency and readiness to include business ethics subjects in curricula in higher business education.

It is important to understand that business ethics education is relatively young, as major American universities began teaching it only around 33 years ago (Velasquez, Freeman, Gentile, Friedman, & Hanson, 2003). Bampton and Cowton (2002) found that in the early years of the twenty-first century few classroom teachers taught ethics issues explicitly; the longest reported teaching period being five hours in an accounting subject. Reasons were lack of training for teachers, lack of time or materials, lack of motivation, a view that ethics is not really part of an accountant's rigorous practical training, and the prevailing culture of business schools.

The development in the field has shown some progress, including a very important integration of business and ethics. Some reports (Velasquez, 2003) have noted that in study areas such as the environment, race relations, and consumer relations, the frequency of unethical behaviour has decreased, demonstrably due to the effectiveness of business ethics education (Chawla, Khan, Jackson, & Gray, 2015; Dzuranin, Shortridge, & Smith, 2013; Floyd, Xu, Atkins, & Caldwell, 2013). Yet the overall results of teaching business ethics at universities are at best piecemeal and at worst irrelevant, with academic commentators noting that business ethics have not permeated the business world (Freeman & Newkirk, 2011; Freeman, Stewart, & Moriarty, 2009).

There are differing opinions on how best to teach ethics at a higher education level. One argument is that little has been accomplished because of marginalization of business ethics outside the mainstream discourse on business at universities (Martin & Freeman, 2004). To create a new type of inclusive relationship between business ethics and the curriculum, educators can apply three approaches. Business ethics subject matter can be incorporated:

- Through micro-insertions of mini lessons lasting only a few minutes each;
- As complete business ethics modules (large insertions of ethics instructions) integrated in business-related courses, including marketing, accounting, and finance (Slocum, Rohlfer, & Gonzalez-Canton, 2014);
- As free standing ethics courses (Davis & Riley, 2008).

The effectiveness of the more integrated approaches have been demonstrated to be greater, although there has been limited research in this area (Davis & Riley, 2008). Bampton and Maclagan (2005) state that what is required is research which shows that goals, content (rules and stages or moral philosophy), methodology (stand-alone courses or integrated courses), pedagogy (experiential or non-experiential) can all be linked.

Teaching Business Ethics

Ethics are extensively taught using cognitive approaches including didactic and cognitive learning activities (Hartman, Wolfe, & Werhane, 2008). It is argued this is the best method because it equips students with theoretical frameworks to spring off, shows them their underlying assumptions, and invites them to critically analyse those. This makes students more capable of making grounded judgements in ethically challenging situations and more aware of, and courageously not to follow blindly, the rules and regulations (Sia, 2008).

Nielsen (2001) argues that a cognitive understanding of both policy and individual level ethics is important; however, there can be cognitive understanding without affective, emotive concern—which can lead to understanding without motivation. An action-learning approach to organizational ethics can join cognitive understanding of policy and individual level issues with affective concern, to stimulate and enable ethical character.

Cognitive activities encourage students to identify stakeholders by looking at all possible decisions and being aware of each decision's impact on each stakeholder (Hartman et al., 2008). It is claimed that this creates integrity in their decisions, as they are looking at the whole picture and considering all implications. Hartman et al. (2008) suggest that ethics are best taught by showing both positive and negative cases of ethics in business, which are then analysed and discussed by the students using ethical theory. Advocates of cognitive approaches argue that such presentations of dilemmas allow the students to find the morality that fits within "what we are and where we are" (Wishloff, 2003, p. 91). This method assumes that though students should receive this information passively, yet changes to their ethical systems will still occur.

The effectiveness of this approach to teaching business ethics requires further research. Purely cognitive approaches may lack emotional connection to the issues and result in generalized knowledge with little emotional understanding of actions (Rest, Turiel, & Kohlberg, 1969). An experiential learning model may be a more effective teaching method (Loescher, Hughes, Cavico, Mirabella, & Pellet, 2005; McPhail, 2001). McPhail (2001) passionately appeals for examination of the very purpose of teaching ethics in higher education, advocating that it should entail disruption of existing beliefs and assumptions, and encouragement of cognitive dissonance to prepare students to learn. Teaching should include the development of a broad social and political ethical context for organizational management and the development of students' moral sensibility.

The experiential learning model, then, is argued to be beneficial to students because it involves them emotionally, disrupting their old beliefs and assumptions while providing a safe environment for change, through discussions, small group activities, real-life case studies, role plays, simulation exercises, films, literature, and personal reflective journals (Chavan, 2011, 2015; Loescher et al., 2005; McPhail, 2001).

The Research

The research question—in what ways do ELAs and CALs appear to help undergraduate students make connections between business ethics theory and practice?—arose from lack of research into the effects on students of business ethics teaching. In seeking answers, it was not the ELAs and the CALs *per se* that were the focus, but the role they play in making learning business ethics relevant and useful to students.

Answering the question entailed development of an interpretive framework, based on a qualitative analysis—using focus groups and interviews—of the sampled students' experiences of ethics teaching by action and ELAs. It investigated the extent to which students were able to learn cognitively from the various exercises and whether, affectively, they enjoyed the experience, because liking a learning activity is directly related to the degree of learning acquired (Church, Baskwill, & Swain, 2007).

Research Design

The research design took a mixed method approach and included focus groups, followed by individual semi-structured interviews to achieve breadth and depth of understanding (Hesse-Biber & Leavy, 2011). The focus groups allowed the researchers to tap into the social nature of students' shared experiences and gave them a chance to understand the social fabric of the student group that participated in the ELA and CAL activities.

Following the experiential activities, 50 students participated in five focus groups with approximately 10 students in each focus group (five international and five domestic students). The number of students per group was as recommended by Patton (2002) as an optimal number for sustaining and controlling a discussion.

Individual semi-structured interviews are argued (Yin, 2009) to generate deeper meanings and to evoke more nuanced insights into student experiences of ELAs and CALs. Interviews in the study lasted approximately 20 minutes and were face-to-face, in which open-ended questions served as the *a priori* structure, guiding students in discussing what they learnt about business ethics when they participated in ELAs and CALs during their course (Yin, 2009). Students who were individually interviewed also participated in the focus groups. Examples of ELAs and CALs are attached in theAppendix.

The interview questions in the semi-structured individual interviews included the following:

Q1. Which of the ELAs did you enjoy/like the most and why?
Q2. Which of the ELAs helped you learn the most and why?
Q3. In which situations were you able to apply ethics material learnt through ELAs and CALs to real-life situations?

Data collected through both the focus groups and the individual interview were rich, and combining the two allowed for the comparison between emergent individual and group interview patterns and reinforcement of the main developing themes. Narratives of individual students were checked against their performance in the focus group and interview settings, thus providing triangulation of the data.

The Research Samples

Students from a large undergraduate unit were invited to participate in both focus groups and interviews. Students attended a large metropolitan Australian university and were undertaking commerce undergraduate degrees in their final year of study. Local and international students were equally represented. Students who are Australian citizens or residents were regarded as local and students who arrived from other countries were considered international students. In this study, the international respondents were predominantly from Asia and specifically from China, Hong Kong, India, Indonesia, Pakistan, Singapore, Sri Lanka, Taiwan, and Vietnam. This study was approved by the ethics committee.

Analysis

The process of research was inductive and supported the interpretive nature of this qualitative study, because analytic induction has a goal "to discover meaning and to achieve understanding" (Benner, 1994, p. 10). NViVo was used to manage the coding process and upgrade codes to group and model levels (Bazeley, 2007; Richards, 2005). The software helped to organize data in an ascending, inductive process to higher levels of abstraction (Bazeley, 2007).

A three-step approach to data analysis involved preliminary observations of the transcripts, identifying themes through clustering (resulting in formation of constructs), and categorizing through grouping (resulting in formation of categories). Data analysis became a conceptual activity of clustering "the particulars into the general", in which "the analyst shuttles back and forth between first-level data and more general categories, which evolve and develop through successive iterations" (Miles, Huberman, & Saldaña, 2014, p. 286), whether the units of meaning are called themes, dimensions, codes, or categories (Creswell, 2014; Denzin & Lincoln, 2011).

Findings

Selected data are presented to answer the research question, in what ways do ELAs and CALs appear to help undergraduate students make connections between business ethics theory and practice? The focus group and interview data revealed that ELAs and CALs allow students to gain confidence in applying business ethics to a range of issues in a safe learning environment. There were some interesting outcomes concerning social benefits and co-creation that emerged from the relevant ELAs and CALs for understanding business ethics.

Indicative Quotations from Focus Groups and Interviews

Data analysis, supported by reports of the focus groups and interviews identified *social benefits* and *co-creation* as two important student needs that educators designing ELAs should be aware of, to maximize the learning potential of ELAs and CALs. Applied to a business ethics context, *co-creation* refers to joint activities between teachers and students, and between students, that involve effort from both parties. This and the identified *social benefits* were found to influence students' perceptions of value derived from the experience of the learning activities.

Social Benefits

Six constructs are said to contribute to formation of the category of *social benefits* as an emotional aspect of student and teacher relationships in a process of self-efficacy and belonging (Bandura, 1997; Curtin, Stewart, & Ostrove, 2013; Pool & Qualter, 2012; Maslow & Lowery, 1998).

Friendship

Making friends through participation in ELAs and CALs was one of the most consistently identified themes. It was discussed at length in all the focus groups and during the individual interviews, with findings from the two methods reinforcing each other. Most of international and some of domestic students spoke about their initial loneliness and the contrast between high school, where they "knew everyone" to sitting in a lecture theatre and knowing very few, if any, other people. Examples are as follows:

> *I was motivated to come to class every week as I got to know new (students) every week, particularly the ones from Korea as my parents are from Korea but I was born and bought up in Australia. I got to know a lot about Korea from these students and how and why their perspectives on ethics differed from mine* (Local Student).

> *In India we get to know the lecturers and they know every one's names which is a good thing and a bad as sometimes there is favouritism.... I like the experiential activities as we do get to know the lecturer more than when we did in the face to face lectures and make more friends* (International Student).

Language

The theme of improving one's English or awareness of the need to improve it was a consistent theme discussed by international students. After participating in the experiential activities, they reported in both the interviews and focus groups that their interactions had been affected by their English language proficiency (or lack of). This theme related strongly to ideas of self-worth and social acceptance. This is reflected in the following quotation:

> *I liked (the experiential activities) because every student had to speak and there was no right and wrong answer. It was a discussion which improved my language skills and I got to learn a lot and take part in the role plays and share my views and thoughts about how it was done in China and that it was not unethical to give a job to your relative. I learned a lot on how things were done differently in varied countries* (International Student).

Engagement with Academics

This was a prominent theme in the accounts of both international and domestic students. Given the inherently relational nature of social benefit, as the dynamics between students and teachers, ELAs and CALs shift the responsibility for learning from the teacher towards a student (Moon, 2002). This is evidenced in the following:

> *It was good as the lecturer too took part in the activities too and we got to know her better and she helped us and directed us with the ethics game we played and it was a really fun interactive way of learning because it brought together the knowledge we learnt* (International Student).

Working with People (in Career)

The data from both the focus groups and interviews confirmed existing literature on the contribution of experiential activities to the development of students' abilities to see the application of the business ethical issues in their work situations. The students shared their perceptions of becoming more sensitive to ethical issues in the workplace and the exercise of caution was considered important. This is witnessed in the following:

> *I started to analyse every operation and activity in my work place and tried to apply what I had learned in class and I could see what I had learned and how it has been beneficial to critically look at the way things are done ... more aware of how ethics plays role in business and managerial decisions* (Local Student).

> *The activities in class demonstrated real cases and incidents and..... the consequences of unethical behaviour which were frightening ...forced us to think more in depth about how ethics affects business* (Local Student).

Networking

ELAs, as the data demonstrated, provided opportunities for students to network and to acquire networking skills, which could help them in their working life in the future:

> *Earlier I hardly got to know anyone in class, but because of these group activities and submissions we had to work together and email each other all the time so made more friends ....perhaps not a huge impact but allowed me to read other people's/peers views* (Local student).

> *As we worked in groups for the experiential activities I got an opportunity to learn a lot about my Thai group member and we caught up for drinks later and he invited me over for the Thai festival in the weekend which was awesome* (Local student).

Satisfaction with University Experience

Participation in experiential activities appeared to involve excitement about new insights to about business ethics, and overall greater satisfaction with the course. The latter has been correlated in research with overall satisfaction with university experience (*2014 UES National Report,* 2016), to which students in the focus groups and interview settings attested:

> *Most units that I took at this university had a unique element to it which encouraged a lot of interactive activities and this unit was the best as it had a double edge. Made me think a little broader and prioritise certain ethical issues and it helped us make friends from the first class and assisted us understand the consequences of unethical behaviour through play* (Local Student).

Co-Creation

The category of co-creation is formed by six themes in a dynamic process of knowledge co-construction: *motivation, engagement, teamwork, experiencing another culture, experiencing different learning styles,* and *self-discipline* (Bowden & D'Allesandro, 2011).

Student Motivation

The theme of motivation was identified as characteristic of domestic students. It involves an understanding by students of the social nature of knowledge creation and the interdependence of students' relationships:

> *I think it is indispensable in our current world to learn on ethics. It was mandatory to participate in these activities, so it was not like we could procrastinate as we did with our other studies, you learned if you participated and you got the marks if you were active, so students were motivated all the time Experiential exercises were a good way to practice what was learnt* (Local Student).

Student Engagement

ELAs by their very nature involve and engage students as they participate and co-create knowledge with teachers and fellow students. It was an interesting way to communicate ethical and cultural issues between students. They had to take on more responsibility for the learning and apply business ethics to the situations by which they were confronted. The engagement was compared to more traditional styles of teaching and learning such as lecturing:

> *Every week we had a new activity or a guest lecture or a game or a movie and it was never boring so I looked forward to this class although it was a lot of work because it increased my awareness and knowledge regarding different cultural values.... It's great to see how important ethics is and that it is seriously being addressed.*

Teamwork

Teamwork emerged strongly as a force in co-creation of knowledge as the teams progressed through the ELAs. Whilst group work is often disliked by many undergraduate students, the experiential activities appeared to change this attitude. It was the sense of team that appeared to added value to the knowledge created:

> *Every member in the group was allocated a task hence every student in the team had to co-operate to win the game. It was a competition so every team wanted to win so they all took active part in the activities* (International Student).

> *This course is quite challenging and it was an appropriate level with increased knowledge and a more superior and mature approach to work, both University and professional work.*

Experience of Other Cultures

Focus groups' reports were very strong on the theme of experiencing other cultures within the ELAs. Culture sharing provided a social aspect to knowledge co-creation as students worked with each other during the ELAs and CALs to understand and apply the given ethical situations. It served as a pragmatic tool to expand their horizons and increase their understanding of different cultures to tackle business ethical dilemmas in the future:

> *I did not expect to be taught about (business) ethics in a cross-cultural unit, and was surprised to learn how ethics varied across culture and what was unethical in one culture could be just fine in another* (Local Student).

> *The experiential exercises helped me to listen to the views of local students and helped me understand how they feel about (business) ethics... it was good to know their views* (International Student).

> *I learned that ... giving and taking gifts (in this country) were not allowed which was surprising for me...increased knowledge on facts of other countries because of the cross cultural facet included in the unit taught* (International Student).

> *I learned that if I have to run my family business successfully internationally it is important for me to understand what is considered ethical globally* (International Student).

Experience with Different Learning Styles

In both focus groups and interviews, international and domestic students emphasized the importance of learning in different ways. They saw ELAs and CALs as an opportunity to expand their own repertoire of styles as well as to become more aware of the styles of others. ELAs and CALs allow students to learn by doing rather than simply cognitively processing theory:

> *I felt that all was interesting …it was definitely a good practical way of teaching (business) ethics… all those things are learned throughout life experience, the class, though, provided an awareness. I thought ethics is common sense, based on personal judgment. No point learning it, but have changed my perspective* (Local Student).

> *The assignment had allowed me to integrate a real-life business problem and apply it academically to the course content. It was a good hands-on activity which had engaged all group members* (International Student).

Self-Discipline

The theme of self-discipline emerged strongly in focus groups and interviews in both student cohorts. Students were sometimes confronted by the freedom inherent in experiential learning. Experiencing it through learning activities, they suddenly realised the weight of responsibility associated with freedom of learning, and the importance of self-control and self-discipline when preparing for and participating in experiential activities.

> *In the beginning some students did not like the activities as it was a lot of work every week and a new task too and it needed a lot of homework too, but then everyone did get used to it and they all participated… I became more confident than before and yes, I think I learned a lot and it will affect how I act in a position of authority* (International Student).

> *The activity was very interactive and engaging which made learning much easier as opposed to the conservative techniques of reading or receiving boring lectures from tutors* (Local Student).

Concluding Remarks

Results show that business ethics can be taught effectively using ELAs and CALs. These activities appear to enable students to gain confidence in applying ethics to a range of issues in a safe learning environment.

Moreover, student needs that ELAs and CALs satisfied included social benefits, improved ethical standards and language skills, increased engagement with academics, improved employability, networking opportunities, and satisfaction with university life.

The perceived effects of ELAs when applied to study of business ethics in real-life situations involved co-creation, that is, increased student motivation and engagement with learning, improved teamwork, greater understanding of different cultures and learning styles, and increased self-discipline.

The results of this study demonstrate the potential value of ELAs in the context of teaching business ethics in undergraduate education. As witnessed in the focus groups and interviews, ELAs appear to assist undergraduate students to make connections between theory and practice through affective learning. In addition, they reported being able to extend the application of this knowledge into other areas such as employability skills and overall satisfaction with their university education.

The adoption of these experiential activities tested the efficacy of Kolb's (1984) model, by providing real time real-life experiences to students in a classroom setting, and demonstrated that not only can ethical education develop an opportunity for reflection on business ethics but also can extend learning to other graduate capabilities.

From this experience, ELAs and CALs can be developed and applied in large classes to teach ethics, enabling students to make connections between business ethical issues in theory and in practice that can be applied beyond the classroom setting.

Limitations and Further Research

Further research is required to compare this affective style of learning with cognitive learning in other cultures and ethical contexts, such as medicine, nursing and engineering, to further prove this finding. Another possible area for further study is the effect of ethics education on behaviour, that is, how students act after being taught about ethics (Liebler, 2010). A longitudinal study may also be helpful in understanding ethical behaviour of students after they have graduated and are working in business settings, as there is concern as to the level of transference of ethics education into real world applications. The earlier students are exposed to ethics in the classroom, the more likely they will be to engage in ethical behaviour and to adopt ethical attitudes in their daily lives (Borkowski & Ugras, 1998; Desjardine, 2012; Rossouw, 2002).

Appendix. Sample Ethics-Based Experiential Learning Activity (ELA) and Critical Action Learning (CAL) Used in the Course

Activity I: Simulation in Genetically Modified Food

This simulation is designed to develop skills at cross-cultural negotiations with an emphasis on multi-stakeholder dialogue and exchange. It raises ethical questions of selling and using genetically modified food. This exercise provides an interactive case simulation in which students are assigned to a group that will assume the role of one of several stakeholder groups in the actual dispute between the United States and the European Union (EU) over trade in genetically modified organisms (GMOs).

In this case, the US government, on behalf of US farmers and the biotech industry, argued that the EU is in violation of global trading rules. Europe responded that it has the right to protect the health and safety of its population and domestic crops, given the uncertainties over the effects of GMOs on humans, animals, and plants. This simulation assumes that the United States and the EU proceed through the World Trade Organization (WTO) dispute-settlement procedures, and it places participants in the roles of the various disputants: the US government, the European Union, a consortium of GMO companies, a group of interested developing countries, a group of NGOs, and a WTO Dispute Settlement Panel.

Activity II: The Bribery Scandal at Siemens AG—Case Study

In December 2008, the Munich, Germany-based Siemens AG agreed to pay fines to the tune of €1 billion towards settlement of corruption charges that had hit the company since 2006. This is an eleven-page case study where students must analyse the ethical and corporate responsibility issues and participate in a case presentation and discussion and submit a written analysis with recommendations. The case study is on the unit webpage on Black Board (online learning platform).

Activity III: Sample International Bribery Scenario

Students are placed in a role of an International Executive, informed by the Company's African market Sales Representative that the newly formed African Organization for Protective Economics (AOPE) has adopted a Resolution authorizing its executive management to selectively exclude overseas manufacturers and exporters from its markets where the management in its sole judgement deems appropriate.

While the Executive is processing the information about the Resolution that had appeared in the Wall Street Journal, Business Week, and Fortune, the events in the African market start developing rapidly with the receipt of an email from the Sales Representative stating that a Senior Official advised that in order to operate in the African market new regulations require the Company to secure an import licence from AOPE.

The Sales Rep subsequently requests the Executive's urgent presence in Africa to conduct negotiations to secure a license. Upon arrival, the Executive and the Sales Representative commence discussions with the Senior Head of the AOPE Department dealing with the Executive's product group. The negotiations of specific terms dealing with product specifications and quality, price levels, technical support to be provided and logistic details as well as submission of relevant financial data proceed smoothly and are apparently completed satisfactorily.

On the final day of negotiations, however, the Senior Department Head extends the Executive the invitation to a private luncheon meeting with the Minister-Director of AOPE. Upon arrival, the Executive is warmly greeted by the Minister-Director and introduced to the only other person present, his "Consultant" on importer qualifications. At the conclusion of the luncheon and over brandy and coffee, the Minister-Director expresses his pleasure at the culmination of the negotiations but advises the Executive that the import licensing agreement must be countersigned by the "Consultant" who remained silent and did not participate in the luncheon discussion.

The Minister-Director further explains that the Consultant's fee of $500,000 must be borne by the Executive, and paid immediately. The tone of the request, however, indicates that the Consultant might be agreeable to a lower amount. The Executive starts explaining that this fee, as a new development, has not been factored into the cost component of the negotiations, while internally weighing in such factors as existence of The Foreign Corrupt Practices Act (FCPA) of 1977, mounting pressure to revoke it, and the possibility of being excluded from the growing market in case of the refusal to pay.

Students are then asked, if in the shoes of the Executive, whether they would agree or refuse to pay. They are also asked to explain their decision and outline the plan of dealing with its consequences.

Activity IV: The Global Strategy Game

An International Business Ethics Simulation. This was an online game that students played during the semester as a part of their assessments competing with students from other universities.

References

Anderson, L., & Thorpe, R. (2004). New perspectives on action learning: Developing criticality. *Journal of European International Training, 28*(8–9), 657–668.

Bampton, R., & Cowton, C. J. (2002). The teaching of ethics in management accounting: Progress and prospects. *Business Ethics: A European Review, 11*(1), 52–61.

Bampton, R., & Maclagan, P. (2005). Why teach ethics to accounting students? A response to the sceptics. *Business Ethics: A European Review, 14*(3), 290–300.
Bandura, A. (1997). *Self-efficacy: The exercise of control.* New York: W.H. Freeman.
Bazeley, P. (2007). *Qualitative data analysis with NVivo.* London, UK: Sage Publications.
Beard, C., & Wilson, J. P. (2006). *Experiential learning: A best practice handbook for educators and trainers.* London: Kogan Page.
Benner, P. (1994). *Interpretative phenomenology: Embodiment, caring, and ethics in health and illness.* Newbury Park, CA: Sage.
Borkowski, S. C., & Ugras, U. J. (1998). Business students and ethics: A meta-analysis. *Journal of Business Ethics, 17*(11), 1117–1127.
Bowden, J., & D'Allesandro, S. (2011). Co-creating value in higher education: The role of interactive classroom response technologies. *Asian Social Science, 7*(11), 35–49.
Carucci, R. (2016, December 16). Why ethical people make unethical choices. *Harvard Business Review.*
Chavan, M. (2011). Higher education students' attitudes towards experiential learning in international business. *Journal of Teaching in International Business, 22*(2), 126–143.
Chavan, M. (2015). Alternative modes of teaching international business: Online experiential learning. In V. Taras & M. A. Gonzalez-Perez (Eds.), (2007). *The Palgrave handbook of experiential learning in international business* (pp. 202–222). New York: Palgrave Macmillan.
Chawla, S. K., Khan, Z. U., Jackson, R. E., & Gray, A. W. (2015). Evaluating ethics education for accounting students. *Management Accounting Quarterly, 16*(2), 16.
Church, S., Baskwill, J., & Swain, M. (2007). *Yes, but ... if they like it, they'll learn it!* Portland, ME: Stenhouse Publishers.
Creswell, J. W. (2014). *Research design: Qualitative, quantitative, and mixed methods approaches* (4th ed.). Thousand Oaks, CA: Sage Publications.
Curtin, N., Stewart, A. J., & Ostrove, J. M. (2013). Fostering academic self-concept: Advisor support and sense of belonging among International and domestic graduate students. *American Educational Research Journal, 50*(1), 108–137.
Davis, M., & Riley, K. (2008). Ethics across graduate engineering curriculum. *Teaching Ethics, 8,* 25–42.
Denzin, N. K., & Lincoln, Y. S. (Eds.). (2011). *The SAGE handbook of qualitative research* (4th ed.). Thousand Oaks, CA: Sage Publications.

Desjardine, M. (2012). Making the right decision: Incorporating ethics into business education. *Teaching Innovation Projects, 2*(1), 1–6.

Dewey, J. (1938). *Experience and education.* New York: The Macmillan Company.

Dzuranin, A. C., Shortridge, R. T., & Smith, P. A. (2013). Building ethical leaders: A way to integrate and assess ethics education. *Journal of Business Ethics, 115*(1), 101–114.

Floyd, L. A., Xu, F., Atkins, R., & Caldwell, C. (2013). Ethical outcomes and business ethics: Toward improving business ethics education. *Journal of Business Ethics, 117*(4), 753–776.

Freeman, R. E., & Newkirk, D. (2011). Business school research: Some preliminary suggestions. In W. Amann, M. Pirson, C. Dierkmeier, E. Von Kimakowitz, & H. Spitzeck (Eds.), *Business schools under fire: Humanistic management education as the way forward* (pp. 273–290). London: Palgrave.

Freeman, R. E., Stewart, L., & Moriarty, B. (2009). Teaching business ethics in the age of Madoff. *Change: The Magazine of Higher Learning, 41*(6), 37–42.

Hartman, L. P., Wolfe, R., & Werhane, P. H. (2008). Teaching ethics through a pedagogical case discussion: The McDonald's case and poverty alleviation. *Teaching Business Ethics, 9*(1), 103–133.

Hesse-Biber, S. N., & Leavy, P. (2011). *The practice of qualitative research* (2nd ed.). Thousand Oaks: Sage Publications.

Kemmis, S., & McTaggart, R. (2005). Participatory action research: Communicative action and the public sphere. In N. K. Denzin & Y. S. Lincoln (Eds.), *The Sage handbook of qualitative research* (pp. 559–603). Thousand Oaks, CA: Sage Publications.

Knowles, M. S. (1980). *The modern practice of adult education: From pedagogy to andragogy.* Englewood Cliffs, NJ: Cambridge Adult Education.

Kolb, D. A. (1984). *Experiential learning: Experience as a source of learning and development.* Englewood Cliffs, NJ: Prentice-Hall.

Lewin, K. (Ed.). (1951). *Field theory in social science: Selected theoretical papers.* New York: Harper & Row.

Liebler, R. (2010). Action and ethics education. *Journal of Academic Ethics, 8*(2), 153–160.

Loescher, K. J., Hughes, R. W., Cavico, F., Mirabella, J., & Pellet, P. F. (2005). The impact of an "Ethics across the curriculum" initiative on the cognitive moral development of business school undergraduates. *Teaching Ethics, 5*(2), 31–72.

Lozano, R., Lukman, R., Lozano, F., Huisingh, D., & Lambrechts, W. (2013). Declarations for sustainability in higher education: Becoming better leaders, through addressing the university system. *Journal of Cleaner Production, 48,* 10–19.

Maclagan, P. (2012). Conflicting obligations, moral dilemmas and the development of judgement through business ethics education. *Business Ethics: A European Review, 21*(2), 183–197.

Martin, K. E., & Freeman, R. E. (2004). The separation of technology and ethics in business ethics. *Journal of Business Ethics, 53*(4), 353–364.

Maslow, A., & Lowery, R. (Eds.). (1998). *Toward a psychology of being* (3rd ed.). New York: Wiley & Sons.

Matthews, C., & Heimer, M. (2016, December 28). The 5 biggest corporate scandals of 2016. *Fortune Magazine.*

McPhail, K. (2001). The other objective of ethics education: Re-humanising the accounting profession—A study of ethics education in law, engineering, medicine and accountancy. *Journal of Business Ethics, 34*(3–4), 279–298.

Miles, M. B., Huberman, M., & Saldaña, J. (2014). *Qualitative data analysis: A methods sourcebook* (3rd ed.). Thousand Oaks, CA: Sage Publications.

Moon, J. A. (2002). *A handbook of programme and module development.* London, UK: Routledge Falmer.

Nielsen, R. P. (2001). Can ethical character be stimulated and enabled? An action learning approach to teaching and learning organizational ethics. In J. Dienhart, D. Moberg, et al. (Eds.), *The next phase of business ethics: Integrating psychology and ethics* (Vol. 3). Greenwich, CT: Elsevier Science/JAI Press.

Nijhof, R. A. H. J., Wilderom, C. P. M., & Oost, M. (2012). Professional and institutional morality: Building ethics programmes on the dual loyalty of academic professionals. *Ethics and Education, 7*(1), 91–109.

Patton, M. Q. (2002). *Qualitative research and evaluation methods* (3rd ed.). Thousand Oaks, CA: Sage Publications.

Pool, L. D., & Qualter, P. (2012). Improving emotional intelligence and emotional self-efficacy through a teaching intervention for university students. *Learning and Individual Differences, 22*(3), 306–312.

Rest, J., Turiel, E., & Kohlberg, L. (1969). Level of moral development as a determinant of preference and comprehension of moral judgments made by others. *Journal of Personality, 37*(2), 225–252.

Richards, L. (2005). *Handling qualitative data: A practical guide.* London, UK: Sage Publications.

Rossouw, G. (2002). Three approaches to teaching business ethics. *Teaching Business Ethics, 6*(4), 411–433.

Sia, S. (2008). Ethics and religion. *New Blackfriars, 89*(1024), 702–709.

Slocum, A., Rohlfer, S., & Gonzalez-Canton, C. (2014). Teaching business ethics through strategically integrated micro-insertions. *Journal of Business Ethics, 125*(1), 45–58.

Sterling, S. (2004). *Sustainable education: Re-visioning learning and change.* Bristol, UK: J. M. Arrowsmith Ltd.

Trehan, K. (2011). Critical action learning. In M. Pedler (Ed.), *Action learning in practice* (4th ed.). Farnham: Gower Publishing Company.

UES National Report. (2016, April 17). Retrieved from https://docs.education.gov.au/system/files/doc/other/ues14_report_final_access2a.pdf

Velasquez, M. (2003). Debunking corporate moral responsibility. *Business Ethics Quarterly, 13*(4), 531–562.

Velasquez, M., Freeman, R. E., Gentile, M., Friedman, D., & Hanson, K. O. (2003). *Has business ethics teaching and research had any discernible impact on business practice in the US and around the world?* Sponsored by the Markkula Center for Applied Ethics and the Institute on Globalization, Santa Clara University.

Vince, R. (2008). 'Learning-in-Action' and 'Learning Inaction': Advancing the theory and practice of critical action learning. *Action Learning: Research and Practice, 5*(2), 93–104.

Werhane, P., Hartman, L., Archer, C., Bevan, D., & Clark, K. (2011). Trust after the global financial meltdown. *Business and Society Review, 116*(4), 403–433.

Wishloff, J. (2003). Responsible free enterprise: What it is and why we don't have it. *Teaching Business Ethics, 7*(3), 229–263.

Yin, R. K. (2009). *Case study research: Design and methods* (4th ed.). Thousand Oaks, CA: Sage.

13

Creating an Organization in the Classroom: Students Living Management Theories in Action

Elyssebeth Leigh and Anne Herbert

Introduction

Socially responsible work modes and sustainable business formats are changing more rapidly and less predictably than ever before, while higher education systems remain relatively stable (Herbert & Leigh, 2018). Lack of flexibility in higher education systems limits students' opportunities to learn from contextual issues, to become more socially responsible and more adept at making choices on ethical reasoning. The dissonance between academic curricula and the real world seems especially observable in management education. A new paradigm is needed to challenge received wisdom concerning the relative importance of "content" and "process" knowledge, and the chapter proposes a rearrangement of priorities. The authors argue that responsible management of twenty-first century complex adaptive systems (Lansing, *Annual Review of Anthropology, 32*, 183–204, 2003) is

E. Leigh (✉)
Aalto University, Espoo, Finland

A. Herbert
RMIT University, Melbourne, Australia

most effectively studied through immersion in an experiential learning environment that replicates this type of knowledge domain (Snowden & Boone, *Harvard Business Review, 85*(11), 69–76, 2007).

Dissonance in Management Education

Management is a practice, around which much theory has been constructed. Managers act and may—or may not—have time to analyze and assess. Educators impart *knowledge about* management in formal academic settings, but their *practice of* management theories they espouse is less evident. For example, experienced and dedicated lecturers may teach about building integrated, supportive, collaborative teams as effective and efficient as good management, while their students sit silent and isolated from each other, and impersonal, standardized, results of post-lecture tests are assumed to be valid indictors of what they learned. In effect, students receive messages diametrically opposed to the words of the lecturer. On the one hand, they are told that good managers should build effective and efficient teams, while, on the other hand, they are subjected to classroom treatment that supports and maintains separation, anxiety, and competition.

The educator's spoken message is clear: "Accept and obey my injunctions and advice, because the theory supports it", but there is misalignment between their words and their behavior (Argyris 1983). Arguably, this dissonance between verbal and non-verbal messages will lead to many students' failure to understand how to apply the theory—and even to find fault with themselves as learners rather than with their lecturers' failure to model the theory in practice.

Moreover, there seems to be increasing dissonance between teaching processes and the content of management education, which may be contributing to current problems of lack of managerial social responsibility. For example, Kerr (1995) cited many examples of reward systems that favor undesirable management practices, while failing to reward good management. Dattner and Dahl (2011) explored such disconnects in the context of business operations and found that many are created because of faulty incentives and flawed reward systems that are set up to accomplish one thing but actually motivate people to do another, or even the opposite.

Kerr (1995) notes that in academic contexts it is assumed that a primary goal is to transfer knowledge from educator to student, and grades are a means toward that goal: but in practice, the grades become more important in themselves than the knowledge they are supposed to signify.

These observations raise many questions. How might lecturers adjust their non-verbal behavior to align it with the content of their verbal communication? How might they adapt their spoken messages, for example, about teamwork, to model the intent of those messages? How might other educational stakeholders adjust their expectations to align with such a change? Such questions suggest the need for the teaching assumption to change from "Do as I say, not as I do" to "do as I say, *and* as I do".

There are some problems with enacting the latter in higher education. Students may not react positively to unfamiliar teaching formats, however much they can be shown to model the spoken message and increase learners' ability to link theory and practice in meaningful ways. Educators, who face conflicting demands between research output and teaching loads, are unlikely to welcome new and more complex ways to expedite their students' learning. Educational institutions confront tough and complex environments where stability is receding and uncertainty increasing, creating conditions where anything that challenges currently stable processes may be deemed immediately suspect.

However, it is not possible to teach and learn about practices and dealing with their complexity if educators and learners remain confined to the "simple domain" of a lecture hall (Snowden & Boone, 2007). One way to reset expectations—called 'classroom as organization' (CAO)—is to create the means and methods for theory and practice to operate as components in a holistic approach to learning *how to* manage, as well as *about* managing.

CAO—Theory into Practice

CAO is a teaching method whose roots lie in the work of Cohen (1976), who expressed its educational objectives as:

> *to create genuine organizational issues for students, to put them in the position of an organizational member who must deal with such problems as: how does*

work get allocated; how does one work with others who bring different expertise to tasks (p. 13).

The process has been researched extensively since then and this chapter draws on that research but primarily on the authors' extensive first-hand experience of using CAO to reduce the dissonance between management theory and delivery mode. It invites students to undertake work that engages their tacit knowledge (Polanyi, 2009) and allows them scope and opportunity to display it in action. Bright, Turesky, Putzel, and Stang (2012) propose that professors who intend to use students' self-organization in the classroom as a key learning mechanism should take a CAO approach. McDonald, Spence, and Sheehan (2011) write that CAO:

> *involves making organizational properties salient to [participants] within the classroom context, giving them the responsibility for planning, organizing, leading, and controlling the class mechanism of learning* (p. 67).

Herbert and Leigh (2018) define this approach as:

> *a teaching/learning methodology designed to guide students through the process of making their own living connections between abstract theories of management and the art, science and skill of managing* (p. 12).

Educators in higher education accept there are many expectations about how management education will be organized. If courses are to be delivered face to face in classrooms, the process usually is anticipated to be "teacher-centered", with educators deciding on syllabus content and delivery, and conducting all assessment of students' learning within the overall institutional framework. Normally students accept these arrangements and any learning material their educators identify as important. Students adjust to each educator's preferences, often without taking responsibility for critical analysis of their learning habits.

On the other hand, CAO begins with assuming the class as an organization. Educators set up initial activities deliberately to transfer to students the responsibility for organizing themselves to enact the syllabus.

Educators explain that this process will help each student to learn and account for their own learning while contributing to and supporting others' learning. This shift in responsibility, from educators to students, requires commitment and courage from educators and students because it may unsettle assumptions about how education "works". Consequently, this may give rise to uneasiness among students, academic peers, and administrators. Sheehan, McDonald, and Spencer (2009) note that:

> *Those who question the model's value argue that the CAO approach disorients students who have little experience and ability working in teams and are more accustomed to a passive learning environment (traditional lecture format). As a result, these students become uncomfortable, frustrated, and their learning experience may be impaired. Those who favor the CAO approach do not dispute any disorientation that students may experience, believing that such disorientation in the context of the CAO is representative of what they will experience in the real world and is therefore a valuable learning tool* (p. 78).

Such disorientation is associated with reconfiguring the classroom. Participants are told at the outset they should assume they will be part of an organization whose business is maximizing each and everyone's learning, and that they are responsible for its success. An "organizational chart" outlines the framework for students preferably to self-assign, or to be assigned, to working groups in identified Departments, and Groups within each Department, and delineates specific roles and responsibilities. Subject content is distributed logically among Departments and sub-Groups whose members are assigned administrative responsibilities, teaching/working projects, and assessment and feedback tasks. The educator's role is that of senior manager. Educators must be knowledgeable in their respective fields and willing and able to use that knowledge as a guide by which students may explore concepts and ideas, rather than imposing it as a map of certainties. The educator must be able to enact a stance whereby—as far as is humanly possible—their espoused beliefs about management theory are enacted in their daily interactions with students. The entire process resonates with Klabbers' (2009) concept of simulation as a 'magic circle' within which reality is to be replicated for learning purposes.

One CAO format is based on Kolb's (1984) action learning cycle. Kolb identified four approaches to learning which he named concrete experience, reflective observation, abstract conceptualization, and active experimentation. In the CAO format these become, respectively, Departments for Responsibility, Observation, Understanding, and Doing. Study and teaching projects associated with each approach to learning are distributed to the relevant departments. The Responsibility Department is charged with securing members' commitment to the organization's values, mission, goals, and objectives. The Observing Department must provide and ensure feedback to help class members perceive, and describe their own and each other's behavior and the consequences of such actions—without judging them. The role of the Understanding Department is to provide the means for members to articulate the theories, concepts, and models underlying their actions. The Doing Department monitors the work toward student-defined personal, team, and Departmental objectives. Everyone is learning, planning, and teaching relevant management theories associated with their designated tasks, meanwhile supporting each other as they practice, take risks, and reflect on their actions. Some students on their own responsibility will research literature that helps them to become more reflexive.

Inevitably there is initial discomfort and uncertainty. One student captured this vividly in his observations about the early moments of the experience:

At first, I was ... confused about this course. We didn't have a [clear] structure but instead had to figure it out ourselves utilizing the manual for learning Mikkeli managers. The progress was slow, and I felt like a turtle on dry land. Many of us had different ideas about how the course should be set up and different objectives [to be] achieved and sometimes we were moving [in different] directions as departments (unpublished student assignment).

In contrast a student in a parallel course was more focused:

Learning even more about the role of my team really helped me and my team members to start working on the right things more efficiently. In these early stages, our team is quite dependent on other teams such as the planning team and the observing department before we can fully start doing, for example, the monitoring policy. Therefore, we focused on the planning a lot, which had many benefits in my opinion. The textbook showcases similar benefits of planning as I noticed today such as "intensified effort, persistence, direction, and creation of task strategies". I have learned that discussing different concepts in groups can really make you understand things better when you get to hear insights from others. Your contribution will also have an effect on others' learning. Planning has also showed to be a great asset and hopefully it will make a good foundation for the rest of our team's work (unpublished student assignment).

The version of CAO to which these students contributed is conducted daily over three weeks—three hours over 15 days with two intervening weekends. Students are also expected to allocate up to 115 hours of independent and/or team-based study overall, outside class hours. They study one subject at a time in an undergraduate degree taught in English in Finland. During that three-week period, starting on day 3, students begin working out how to operate the process as described above, to achieve as many as possible of an extensive list of "behaviourally stated learning objectives'" (BSLOs). The senior manager's tricky task is to oversee a gradual shift in students' perspectives on responsibilities. This intensive CAO was designed specifically for the academic program of which it is part. Other delivery modes of CAO operate on a weekly schedule of classes for a full semester, and others use CAO principles as a discrete component within a semester-long subject.

Three Initiating Conditions for CAO

Since Cohen (1976) first introduced CAO at the University of New Hampshire, a range of adaptions have been reported—for example, Sheehan et al. (2009) and Barry (1990). Herbert and Leigh (2018) write about CAO in the context of preparing employees for knowledge-based workplaces in Finland in the twenty-first century, with the goal of identifying CAO both as a disruptive and an enabling teaching strategy. This ongoing research has identified three co-existing conditions in environments where CAO might emerge as an acceptable teaching/learning option:

1. Educators have become dissatisfied with merely "telling" the students about management theory and are prepared to dedicate time to going beyond being a "teacher".
2. Students reveal themselves as open to engage with the act of managing, are prepared to deal with unfamiliar learning processes, and similarly are able (with help) to step beyond standard "student" passivity.
3. Administrators are willing to tolerate alternative processes, if standards are maintained (in whatever format they are locally established).

Co-existing with these three conditions are forces external to the immediate teaching/learning environment, including dramatically changing work contexts and modes, and employer requirements for staff to work in ethical and sustainable businesses, where employment conditions are unpredictable. Such changes in employment, and social conditions and contexts, are occurring faster than educational habits can change in higher education settings that have maintained relatively stable processes for more than a hundred years. This stability has recently been described, somewhat unkindly, by Baggini (2018), as years of academic training in desiccation, because it seems often to value standardization of content over individualization of learning opportunities (Robinson, 2013). CAO challenges such values because its "disruptive" nature replaces standardization with originality and encourages engagement with a wide range of social, economic, political, and existential forces at work in the world.

Educators Dissatisfied with "Telling"

Becoming dissatisfied with continuing enactment of familiar teaching roles may emerge slowly—or arrive suddenly. For Putzel (1997), who developed a CAO handbook called *XB—manual for a learning organization*, the change emerged from a dissatisfying early experience of teaching management theory. For Sheehan et al. (2009), a sports marketing professor's venture in running a basketball tournament in 1990 morphed into an ongoing sports management version of CAO. For one of the authors of this chapter it was the result of an effort to align the hard-won experience of conducting workplace learning with the demands of an academic teaching role.

In each instance, the disparity—between how things are said and what is being said—made itself evident and led to a search for ways to close the gap. Each "conversion" is, in its own way, an example of Kuhn's (1970) paradigm shifts that are achieved only by discarding some previously held beliefs or procedures and replacing them with others.

Such changes are more easily achieved by individuals or small groups or teams. It is harder for an entire university or institution to do so. Thus, the uptake of CAO as a teaching/learning process is occurring at lower, operational, levels of teaching and still tends to find itself in conflict with the surrounding environment. However, it also is proving to be a lively factor in changing perspectives on what constitutes "appropriate" teaching at tertiary levels, not least because it challenges norms. Educators who use CAO are better prepared for future educational contexts than are those fixed in established parameters and paradigms, because managing CAO requires development and ongoing maintenance of a capacity for dealing with complexity and uncertainty.

Students' Opportunities to Engage

According to Henny (2016) some educators worry that technology will take over many tasks and abilities on which they have been relying for decades. However, education will never disappear; it will just take different forms, and CAO is one. Students are aware of the changing nature of education, learning, and workplace expectations; their future is at stake. They know that work will less often confine them to conventional offices and that information is available on demand for conversion to knowledge, as required. They are beginning to recognize that their capabilities will be assessed as much on what they do as on what they know and are becoming more willing to take the risk of moving from passively receiving to actively engaging with knowledge and its enactment.

CAO provides both a framework for asking questions, and opportunities to engage with the kinds of answers that emerge when students ask:

- How is this theory relevant to my specific career goals?
- Why bother with other "domains of knowledge" when I'm going into (e.g.) marketing?
- What does knowing about how I work in a team have to do with becoming a solo operator?

CAO works best with students who are prepared to take risks, are curious about their future and are willing to step into action. That it is different, is unnerving, and has unknown outcomes and mixed feedback is often an inviting challenge for students interested in engaging in their learning journey. However, not all students will be receptive. Some demand more guidance from educators; they prefer traditional lectures, and they like to work individually.

Administrative Environment: Tolerating Alternative Processes

For those charged with managing the complexity of modern educational systems, maintaining an ongoing tolerance of ambiguity is not easy. Dependence on order and stability can often feel like the only possible course when everything is happening at once, various stakeholders are pressing contradictory demands and costs are ever increasing. In such conditions stable, repeatable teaching processes that have been tested by time, are familiar to everyone and bring no surprises are welcome oases of stability. Any impetus to unsettle such stability is unlikely to be welcomed.

It takes courage to tolerate change and maintain willing support for individuals or small groups intent on implementing teaching practices that cannot guarantee stability. A key factor in achieving and sustaining that support is trust that, although demonstrably helping to build students' resilience and flexibility, CAOs will not unduly disturb more conventional teaching practices. When complaints emerge (e.g. "this is not traditional"), it takes an effort, and precious time, to sustain that support.

However, ongoing support for use of a CAO strategy can lead to emergence of a more complex and fulfilling educational system.

> *... In such an environment, ... characterized by connectedness and feedback loops, students may develop greater awareness about themselves and about complex organizations* (Bright et al., 2012, p. 159).

Creating and Guiding a CAO

The following is a summary of a three-week CAO program, including provision of job descriptions, performance expectations, and background information on key thematic tools.

Beginning to Shift Responsibility

Day 1

Setting up a "world café" (Brown, Isaacs, & Community, 2005), designed for peer participants to meet and converse, to reduce reservations commonly experienced when entering new contexts—especially learning ones (Tuckman, 1990). This is followed by an introductory session on managing and being managed, on learning about how to learn, and team role preferences and contributions. An operational text, the "Manual for Mikkeli Learning Managers" (Herbert & Leigh, 2016) is distributed, to allow participants time to begin reading about what lies ahead. This is a process-oriented text, and relevant sources of "content information" are available via online resources: the library, items posted to the local learning management system (LMS), and an assigned text.

Day 2

Students are guided through an exploration of the concepts of complexity and adaptive systems as an introduction to this new learning environment. A series of short activities gradually moves students' attention from familiar domains into a state of temporary confusion and uncertainty and eventually to a critically analytical debriefing of these experiences. Finally, students are invited to review their assumptions about "how to" be a student and to consider how passive learning strategies might be ineffective for management roles.

Student perceptions about learning as a process and about *who* is responsible for learning vary widely. Course materials are as explicit as possible about the importance of "taking risks and making first-time mistakes" but post-course feedback indicates that this is not always fully appreciated. Some students want only to be told what to read and how to respond. Such dependency on external motivators may not be unusual in academic settings, but it is unlikely to serve students well in the independent and interdependent world of work they are studying to enter.

Day 3: Structure and Ambiguity

This is the first day of the CAO experience, and there is some confusion, as the full implications of the advertised shift in responsibility take hold. Traditional organizational structures are based on some form of departmentalization, of subdividing workers into separate units to take responsibility for completing different tasks. On Day 3 the CAO is formally divided into the four Departments of Doing, Observing, Responsibility, and Understanding. Diversity of responses continues for some time after Day 3, as daily reports ("memos") are filed every night—recording events, reactions, and analysis—to be read and commented on by peers.

Days 4–7

Events during this period are determined by the ways the four Departments and their sub-Groups take up their tasks. All activities, including the daily schedule itself, are the responsibility of class members. For example, in a recent CAO, a sub-Group of the Doing Department managed the university-mandated LMS (with the senior manager's agreement and help) and set up Google Drive and WhatsApp accounts to manage daily communication traffic.

Days 8–14

The second half of a CAO course can move along smoothly as the operation picks up the pace to meet deadlines. Focus is on performance, though the occasional conflict may occur as the strains of sustaining the complex environment take their toll, and the senior manager sometimes needs to provide a steadying hand. More often a class member, or the combined efforts of the Department heads, relieves the tensions.

Overall Sequence

In many CAOs the whole sequence is divided into two parts, to mark a "half way" point to allow for reflection on what has occurred in the first half and to allow for readjustments for future action in the second half. By the halfway point a sub-Group will have interviewed all class members to establish their satisfaction level with their role and performance. The results are published to all member of the CAO. The same sub-Group arranges transfer requests, acting as negotiators between individuals and the Departments they wish to leave and join respectively. Around this time students' memos reflect a clearer understanding of how to operate, using a wider range of resources to identify theories that help to explain events and experiences and reflect on personal behavior. As the senior manager can read all memos and feedback comments, it is possible to identify those who remain confused and provide them with individual support.

Day 15: The Final Day

The last day is an "exhibition day" when all participants present their final assessment task—a three-dimensional representation that invites participants to integrate and summarize their learning. Students display their own artifacts, explanations, and interpretations and examine each other's work. Images (mirrors, stairs, music, X-Box controllers, etc.) reoccur regularly, but in 20 years of running CAOs the authors have never had a problem with plagiarism. This assessment task—as with others completed during the three weeks—promotes creativity and originality.

Concluding Comments

This chapter sets out to provide answers to the following questions:

- Is it possible to create a corporate social performance model as a coherent, integrative framework for teaching managerial ethics and social responsibility?
- What are some examples of how to teach principles of managerial social responsibility at institutional, organizational, and individual levels?
- Granted that sustainable development is a complex series of continuously negotiated business and social projects requiring ongoing learning, action, and change, how might management students be taught to examine those networks that span business organizations and stakeholders in society?
- What might be the content of a management education course on how environmental management can provide firms with a competitive advantage and serve to develop new links between operations and corporate strategies?

Experience with the CAO approach to collaborative learning in undergraduate management programs indicates that:

- CAO creates a living, coherent framework to help students integrate their behavior with awareness and understanding of management precepts, including corporate social responsibility and ethically responsible behavior. Such learning will not be without difficulties—and students are encouraged to understand that they will encounter similar problems in the workplaces they will enter.
- While enactment of a CAO takes place at the classroom and individual student level, the results impinge on organizational and institutional values and practices. Introducing and sustaining CAOs are not an easy or simple endeavor; direct experience of the authors and anecdotal evidence from other CAO users reveals they can be very unsettling for all involved. However, the authors' ongoing research indicates that the benefits—in terms of student learning outcomes—are well worthwhile.

- CAOs foster analysis of work-related tasks and relationships and encourage exploration of how these may create trust or distrust, while supporting business activity.
- CAOs promote stakeholder analysis and exploration of organizational networks.

Regarding content/process, a CAO classroom attempts alignment of words and actions. The content of management theory informs the process—and vice versa. Learners and educators together are creating events and activities to model the content of management theory. They are learning to accept that there will be failures and glitches and shortcomings. It becomes clearer over time that progress is not made by giving up and reverting to "didactic" teaching but through use of "first-time" mistakes as objects for analysis and application of relevant theory in a cycle of continuous improvement.

As a final note on "doing as we say, and as we do", the use of a CAO strategy continues to assign significant power to the educators. This will continue as long as educational institutions insist that educators are solely responsible for grading. However, Foucault (1980) noted that people are likely to win more for freedom by declining to define in advance all the forms that freedom could possibly take—which implies a refusal to latch on to static definitions of power.

This is at the core of CAO activity. It makes the power relationships in a classroom visible, creating possibilities for students to assume ever more power. This in turn encourages learning how to use such power to better understand management practices and associated theories and their potential contribution to their own development as mature, ethical, and responsible adults working in complex, evolving, and challenging workplaces.

References

Argyris, C. (1983). *Reasoning, learning, and action*. San Francisco, CA: Jossey-Bass.
Baggini, J. (2018). I still love Kierkegaard. *Aeon.com*. Retrieved January 7, 2018.

Barry, D. (1990). Twincorp: Extensions of the classroom-as-organization model. *Journal of Management Education, 14*(1), 1–15.

Bright, D. S., Turesky, E. F., Putzel, R., & Stang, T. (2012, Winter). Professor as facilitator: Shaping an emerging, living system of shared leadership in the classroom. *Journal of Leadership Education, 11*(1), 157–176.

Brown, J., Isaacs, D., & Community, W. C. (2005). *The World Café book: Shaping our futures through conversations that matter.* Oakland, CA: Berrett-Koehler.

Cohen, A. (1976). Beyond simulation: Treating the classroom as an organization. *Journal of Management Education, 2*(1), 13–19.

Dattner, B., & Dahl, D. (2011). *The blame game: How the hidden rules of credit and blame determine our success or failure.* New York, NY: Free Press.

Foucault, M. (1980). *Power/knowledge: Selected interviews and other writings, 1972–1977.* Pantheon Books.

Henny, C. (2016, June 1). 9 things that will shape the future of education: What learning will look like in 20 years? *eLearning Industry*.

Herbert, A., & Leigh, E. (2016). *Mikkeli learning managers: Manual for courses on introduction to management.* FutureSearch.

Herbert, A., & Leigh, E. (2018). Classroom as organization: An educational strategy for emergent learning. In A. Eskola (Ed.), *Navigating through changing times: Knowledge work in complex environments.* New York: Routledge.

Kerr, S. (1995). On the folly of rewarding A, while hoping for B. *The Academy of Management Executive, 9*(1), 7–14.

Klabbers, J. (2009). *The magic circle: Principles of gaming & simulation* (3rd ed.). Rotterdam: Sense Publishers.

Kolb, D. (1984). *Experiential learning: Experience as the source of learning and development.* Englewood Cliffs, NJ: Prentice Hall.

Kuhn, T. (1970). *The structure of scientific revolution* (2nd ed.). University of Chicago Press.

Lansing, J. S. (2003). Complex adaptive systems. *Annual Review of Anthropology, 32,* 183–204.

McDonald, M., Spence, K., & Sheehan, B. (2011). Classroom-as-organization: An integral approach. *Journal of Integral Theory and Practice, 6*(2), 67–81.

Polanyi, M. (2009). *The tacit dimension.* University of Chicago Press.

Putzel, R. (1997). *XB: Manual for a learning organization: Containing basic principles, tools and theories of management and organizational behaviour.* St. Michael's College.

Robinson, K. (2013). How to escape education's death valley. *TED Talks Education*. Retrieved March 03, 2018, from https://www.ted.com/talks/ken_robinson_how_to_escape_education_s_death_valley

Sheehan, B. J., McDonald, M. A., & Spencer, K. A. (2009). Developing students' emotional competency using the classroom-as-organization approach. *Journal of Management Education, 33*(1), 77–98.

Snowden, D. J., & Boone, M. E. (2007, November). A leader's framework for decision making. *Harvard Business Review, 85*(11), 69–76.

Tuckman, B. W. (1990). Development sequence in small groups. *Psychological Bulletin, 63*, 384–999.

14

Reflections on the Development and Delivery of an Experiential Learning Capstone Project Course

Dan Murray and Michael Wood

Introduction

SEED is the acronym of the School of Environment, Enterprise, and Development at the University of Waterloo, Canada. Its mission is to develop knowledge, tools, and expertise that integrate business and development activities with environmental and social objectives to realize a sustainable world. The focus of the chapter is SEED's Environment and Business (E&B) program. Specifically, the chapter critically examines the experiential learning-focused final-year capstone course, where students work in groups to address real sustainability problems within a business setting.

D. Murray (✉) • M. Wood
School of Environment, Enterprise and Development,
University of Waterloo, Waterloo, ON, Canada
e-mail: d4murray@uwaterloo.ca; mowood@uwaterloo.ca

Experiential Learning

The motivation behind SEED's E&B program is to deliver a business degree that trains a new type of graduate, one that is uniquely prepared to address emerging business sustainability challenges. The innovative design of the program integrates two traditionally separate disciplines and trains graduates to see and value a multitude of perspectives, think critically and analytically, provide a more holistic understanding of complex phenomena, and to leverage this knowledge in corporate decision-making. The program is a response to calls to integrate sustainability, both in management education and across business schools (see Rusinko, 2010).

Those involved in the development of the program perceived experiential learning to be a critical component, as experiential learning has been identified as a way to broaden students' perspectives and to foster the development of a wide range of skills, including general leadership competence, working in cross-cultural teams, networking, and effective communication (Gitsham, 2012). From a Theory-First perspective, which is most common for students with little to no work experience before entering their post-secondary education, experiential learning provides an opportunity for participants to ground the theory that they learn in class by bringing abstract concepts to life (Kolb & Kolb, 2009). From a Practice-First perspective, which is most common for those pursuing post-secondary education after having work experience (e.g. MBA or EMBA), experiential learning provides a way to illuminate past practical experience through theory and then allowing for applying this new understanding back to practice (Gitsham, 2012). In both cases, experiential learning acts as a bridge to reduce the gap between conceptual and practical experience, thereby highlighting the importance of both theory and practice.

Experiential learning has been identified also as an effective way of integrating sustainability into the business school curriculum (see Baden & Parkes, 2013; Gitsham, 2012). According to Kolb (1984) it is a teaching method simply described as a process that includes:

1. experience or action,
2. reflection, and
3. testing conclusions.

The interaction between individuals and their environment is critical (Kolb & Kolb, 2009); students are empowered to explore and apply concepts in real-world settings. These elements of experiential learning were explicitly considered in the design of the capstone course.

The Capstone Course

A core (required) two-semester capstone course is provided for final-year undergraduates, in which they work in groups of four to six members, preparing for and executing a major project. Ideally, the groups work with clients from the business community, to gain valuable real-world experience. Students are tasked with applying previously acquired knowledge and skills to address real-world problems that integrate environment and business concepts. They are challenged to develop and demonstrate problem-solving, critical thinking, integration, and communication skills. Course deliverables are flexible enough to allow the student groups to match outcomes to the needs of the client and include a comprehensive written report and an oral poster presentation at the end of the second term, and may also include presentations to clients, annotated slide decks, briefing notes, and websites.

While all student groups are responsible for conducting their own research, they work closely with instructors, who take on roles quite different from those in traditional approaches to course instruction. Instructors act as mentors, as sounding boards for ideas, and as resources, and are there to answer any questions or help solve any problems. They work *with* the student groups to develop knowledge. Class time is a mix of lectures, designed to build skills and reiterate relevant material from previous courses, and open-class time. Lecture topics include conflict management, recapitulations of research methods, and strategies for literature reviews and presentations. In open-class time, students work on their projects with instructors on hand to offer advice or answer questions.

Opportunities and Challenges

Experimental learning not only presents wonderful learning and teaching opportunities but also presents some key challenges.

Opportunities

Key opportunities related to the capstone course come under two headings: relationship building with external stakeholders and integrating theory and practice.

Relationship Building with External Stakeholders

As part of the E&B program, instructors actively seek out clients from the business community and work with them to develop projects with scope and challenge to fulfill the academic requirements of the course but also to provide value and benefit to the client. This strategy enables the university to engage with the broader community, building its brand and making connections that help students to find employment and instructors to develop relationships for future research. Working with real projects and clients also engages students more fully and provides them with experience directly relatable to their future careers. They can include it on their resumes and refer to it job interviews

The process begins with a kick-off meeting with the client, preparation of a non-disclosure agreement, and a project scoping exercise. Students delve into the literature to find what has been done before, what gaps exist, and what can be learned from previous experience. Ongoing interactions with the client provide opportunities to gain insights into business operations, the applicability of potential solutions, and feedback on progress. The entire exercise is designed to teach students how research is needed to address business problems, as well as giving them experience of working with clients and on large projects. The experience prepares them for life after university, helps them identify the areas they are passionate about (to inform future employment or graduate studies choices), and allows them to develop the skills necessary to become leaders in their field.

The capstone course also promotes innovation within the business community by building a bridge to current research within the university. Involved clients gain insights into the latest developments in their field and new perspectives, strategies, and tools to address the problems they have encountered. Clients often return another year, either to address new challenges within their business or to advance or operationalize ideas developed through earlier course projects. A key part of the course is client evaluation of the student projects.

Integrating Theory and Practice

The capstone course aims to integrate theory and practice by encouraging students to draw on previous work and course work experience to creatively solve complex problems. Students are encouraged to apply concepts, models, and tools from previous academic courses to their problem solving. Additionally, the E&B program is fortunate to be a participant in the University of Waterloo co-op program where students take five years (instead of four) to complete their undergraduate degree by alternating four paid work placements with course work at regular intervals throughout the program. Students gain valuable experience that both build employment opportunities and provide the means to put their academic lessons into practice. Approximately 85% of enrolled students participate in the co-op program, providing a strong foundation of work experience that students can bring to the capstone course.

Challenges

These opportunities do not come without costs. Key challenges come under three headings: student perspectives, instructor challenges, and challenges to the E&B program and the University.

Student Perspectives

Experiential learning is quite challenging for students. They are asked to work with external clients and to apply their knowledge to real-world environments, and some students are better equipped than others to be successful in this context. Organizing meetings, taking minutes, professional communication, and related activities challenge students with no prior work experience. Additionally, while all students are required to complete the capstone course, every year there are a few who do not see the value in research or have no interest in applying themselves to the project. Students who plan to pursue further studies (and therefore have an interest in research) typically do well. Those who fail to perceive the value of research can be difficult to motivate. This presents a challenge, as commitment is a critical component of a successful project.

Within groups, a different level of commitment to the project from students can create tension, impede progress, and may result in conflict—though conflict can also be a normal part of decision-making. Students work in the same group, on the same project, for two semesters. Conflicts emerge over which direction to take, the scope of the project, data collection choices, as well as more everyday conflicts concerning roles and responsibilities. Experiential learning introduces pressure that students may never have experienced before. To address these challenges, academic instructors need to be mentors, not just educators, and be willing to address students' anxieties and worries.

Instructor Challenges

Experiential learning is resource intensive. Outreach to the business community is an ongoing process that involves bringing in potential clients and working with them to develop projects that are academically rigorous, valuable to the client and that suit both the academic calendar and corporate timeframes. From an instructor perspective, an experiential learning course requires a time commitment far in excess of a traditional university course. Within the capstone course, instructors work with groups as advisors and mentors, frequently meeting with group members and working through decisions and problems together.

Teaching a course with over 100 students, working on more than 20 unique projects year after year, requires a broad knowledge base. Depending on client problems and student group skills, projects range from a focus on industrial ecology to climate adaptation plans and to market analysis. Furthermore, projects may include both qualitative and quantitative approaches to data collection; instructors need knowledge of such areas or to find colleagues to assist them. In any case instructors should have a strong research background.

Challenges to the E&B Program and the University

Students represent the program and the university when they interact with external clients, and it is imperative that students adopt professional behavior, communication skills, and work habits. The reputation of both can be damaged by negative incidents or poor deliverables. These risks increase demands on instructors to ensure that all projects are executed well. Often extra time and meetings with student groups, comments on drafts, and detailed feedback are required for those groups that struggle to develop strong outcomes.

Evolution

The capstone course has been continually examined and improved over the past decade to address the above-mentioned challenges and in response to increase enrollment linked to the growing popularity of the E&B program (student numbers were 18 in 2007 and 107 in 2017, with a total of 895 who completed the program). Challenges change from year to year, depending on the nature, experience, and enthusiasm of the student body, and the course is adapted accordingly, to reduce any negative impact on students' learning experience.

Addressing Student Perspective Challenges

As educators, we recognize that students are not all the same. Each student brings with them to the course their own unique set of experiences and skill sets and this is taken into consideration in group formation. In a pre-course survey, all students are asked to identify their strengths and the role within the group that they are best suited to fill (e.g. project manager, client liaison, researcher, and editor in chief). Each group is required to have a designated client liaison, and that person must demonstrate previous experience to support their appointment.

The pre-course survey is also used proactively to identify where students' key interests lie. In some years, student cohorts have overwhelmingly expressed a desire to work on projects with a corporate sustainability angle. In other years, the majority of students may express a desire to work on projects with an industrial ecology focus. This changing nature of student interests may be tied to experiences within previous courses or reflect the electives or interests each brings to the capstone course.

Regardless, the changing nature of student interests presents both a challenge and an opportunity. The pre-course survey attempts to identify the key interest areas each year. Instructors work to tailor the projects to reflect the interests of the students before the course commences. The approach is designed to ensure that students work on projects that interest them, to encourage work of high quality and to encourage students to maintain enthusiasm for the two-semester course. It also reduces the risk of poor performance when students work with external clients.

Addressing Instructor Challenges

The capstone course requires at least double the resources (time and personnel) for a 'traditional' university course with the same number of students. It evolves every year as new clients come on board and new projects are developed. Within the E&B program, this challenge has been addressed through the appointment of two instructors for the capstone course. Each advises 11 student groups, in addition to sharing course preparation and teaching responsibilities. Such an approach has been particularly useful when the co-instructors complement each other's skill set. For example, having one instructor with strong experience of qualitative research can be complemented with a co-instructor with a strong background in quantitative research.

Instructors bring their own experience and a broad range of skills to projects (both in the developmental stages and in advising how projects might be implemented). However, additional expertise is sometimes required, and broad support from all faculty members within the School means that the course can draw on their knowledge and experience to meet with students, discuss their work, or connect them with external people within their own professional networks. The take-away from this consideration of instructor/administrator challenges is that to design and implement experiential learning requires commitment, advanced planning, and investment from the host institution.

Dealing with Conflict

While significant (i.e. project ending) conflict has never emerged in the ten-year history of the capstone course, there have been times when student groups experience divisions that impact project success. Four key strategies have emerged to address such conflict: team contracts and peer group evaluations, early diagnosis, threat of removal, and minimizing risks.

Team Contracts and Peer Evaluations

The design of the capstone course includes a team contract as the first assignment and four-group peer evaluations (two per semester). For the team contracts, groups are provided with a general template that poses questions about each member's expectations for the course, roles and responsibilities, decision-making, conflict management, and accountability. Each group is asked to discuss and agree to the rules of the contract, which is used throughout the course to guide decision-making and address conflicts.

The peer evaluations effectively work as performance reviews. Groups review the team contract and assess themselves and other group members against their predetermined expectations. Peer evaluations affect group marks (individual members can be penalized for underperformance) and ensure that all members pull their weight on the project.

Early Diagnosis

Course instructors work closely with groups to make sure that all conflict is addressed early. They hold regular meetings with groups, review the outcomes of the peer evaluations, and sit in on internal group meetings (when invited) to ensure that decision-making and conflict management techniques are applied.

Threat of Removal

The course outline explicitly states that instructors can remove individuals from groups, should there be a serious conflict. As of now, it has never been required, but the threat of removal from a group (and having to complete the course requirements as an individual) serves as a disincentive for bad behavior.

Minimizing Risks

Changes have been made to the course to minimize the risk of damaging the reputation of the school or university. Over the last few years, instructors have adopted a model whereby multiple groups (up to three) work with the same external client. This ensures that clients receive a range of perspectives on their project and minimizes the impact should any group fail to perform to expected standards.

Multiple groups working with the same client mean they must work together and communicate with one voice to the client. An added advantage of this approach is that it alleviates some of the extra work associated with the capstone course. Fewer clients (previously each group worked with a single client) mean less of a learning curve for instructors.

Future Directions

One new change will be the development of a parallel course that mirrors the capstone course but will be focused on entrepreneurial students who bring their own products or business ideas to the course. Students will still follow a similar research-based approach to advance their ideas, but they will work on their own projects that they bring to the table. Such a change will add new challenges for course design and delivery but will address existing challenges related to maintaining student enthusiasm and providing avenues for students who are particularly interested in practical application of their ideas.

Conclusion

This chapter has provided a summary of an experiential learning capstone course and how it has evolved over ten years in the hope that the knowledge gained of student motivations, opportunities, and challenges can be applied to new programs to increase learning outcomes.

The motivation for integrating experiential learning courses into business and management school curricula is clear. Experiential learning holds great value and promise for student development (Kolb & Kolb, 2009). In challenging students to move beyond the comforts and familiarities of the classroom to engage in practical application of concepts (in this case sustainability), they learn to appreciate and understand the complexities and nuance of the real world. Experiential learning helps to integrate multiple concepts, skills, and knowledge developed through previous education and work experience. In articulating the motivations and values associated with experiential learning, it is hoped this chapter will serve as a resource for program makers seeking to expand beyond the walls of the classroom.

The chapter has identified several opportunities and challenges associated with developing and delivering an experiential learning course over the past ten years. Opportunities include building relationships with external stakeholders, providing students with valuable real-world experience, and encouraging innovation through the application of academic research to address business and sustainability problems in practice. Challenges include the need for students to demonstrate professional behavior, communication skills, and work habits; for staff to manage conflict; and to find the additional teaching and administrative resources required for experiential learning, and instructors with broad experience in research design and methods.

Explanation was given of how the program has changed in response to student, instructor, and client needs. Changes to the course include engaging the interest of students prior to commencement, so that projects can be tailored to their needs; integrating multiple mechanisms within course design to manage potential conflict, appointing co-instructors, having broad support throughout the School to provide students with access to a range of expertise; and engaging multiple groups to work with the same client to reduce risk of project failure. Future evolutions for the program include developing a parallel stream for more entrepreneurially focused students, where they can work on their own (approved) projects focused on product or business idea development.

Recommendations have been made for integrating experiential learning into business and management school curricula, and strategic considerations for institutions seeking to develop a similar program, including a clear understanding of the additional resources required for implementing an experiential learning program. Hiring and staffing considerations should be planned well in advance of course commencement, and strong connections made between the teaching institution and the wider business community so that clients' project needs will fit with course objectives.

References

Baden, D., & Parkes, C. (2013). Experiential learning: Inspiring the business leaders of tomorrow. *Journal of Management Development, 32*(3), 295–308.

Gitsham, M. (2012). Experiential learning for leadership and sustainability at IBM and HSBC. *Journal of Management Development, 31*(3), 298–307.

Kolb, A. Y., & Kolb, D. A. (2009). Experiential learning theory: A dynamic, holistic approach to management learning, education and development. In S. J. Armstrong & C. V. Fukami (Eds.), *The Sage handbook of management learning, education and development* (pp. 42–68). SAGE.

Kolb, D. A. (1984). *Experiential learning: Experience as the source of learning and development*. FT Press.

Rusinko, C. A. (2010). Integrating sustainability in management and business education: A matrix approach. *Academy of Management Learning & Education, 9*(3), 507–519.

15

Shaping Managerial Values: Incorporating Experiential Learning in Management Education

Pallvi Arora

Introduction

Management institutions across the globe are now laying emphasis upon the creation of responsible future leaders who are self-motivated, intrinsically driven as well as ethically appropriate. Most postgraduate training seems to be for executive roles, for students who are already well acquainted with business knowledge and managerial competencies that can facilitate their careers (Baruch & Leeming, 1996), but in terms of expected deliverables of ethical learning, there seems to be a significant gap between teaching and learning, which may eventually have serious implications in societal, environmental and humane contexts.

The abundance of corporate scandals and unethical business practices in public and private organisations suggest a deterioration in the teaching of managerial values in business schools (Segon & Booth, 2009) that has resulted in irresponsible behaviour by managers and

P. Arora (✉)
University of Jammu, Jammu, India

business graduates (Ghoshal, 2005) for whom the term business is synonymous with profitability.

It is the responsibility of faculty teaching staff in management education to shape students' attitudes towards responsible behaviour (Koljatic & Silva, 2015), but research suggests that teachers seem disinclined to deal with ethical and CSR issues—perhaps partly because these areas of expertise are not particularly relevant to their academic careers (Crane, Matten, McWilliams, Moon, & Siegel, 2008). Moreover, merely including elements of societal, environmental and ethical concerns in a management course would achieve no purpose. On the contrary, cursory treatment is likely to send a signal to the students that such concerns are not eminent for business functioning (Crane et al., 2008).

There is need for a broader agenda for management education than nonchalant teaching of merely economic benefits. The whole range issues across organisations need to be covered, including ethical, moral, societal or environmental factors in management. The objectives of management education are complex. They should be not only to train students to be business leaders but also to be value-oriented individuals who are sensitive to global concerns. Curricula need to be designed with enough scope for addressing societal, environmental and ethical concerns, for value creation amongst the participants (Falkenstein, 2014).

Management institutions have a responsibility to identify and evaluate methodological and pedagogical techniques to create thoughtful leaders with a broadened vision capable of acknowledging societal and environmental concerns. Management education should be to motivate future leaders and organisational members with an innate will to support societal and environmental concerns and to contribute to society, and experiential learning methods, as a central component of management education programmes, are claimed to deliver extraordinary results along these lines. This chapter describes how implementation of Kolb's (1984) learning style theory can assist in creating a holistic approach to management education, whereby educators, curricula and students combine to establish connections between individual value systems and contemporary realities. The task is to train the educators, management students and others at the grassroots level to nurture self-dedicated managers who will help to build societies that exist in harmony with natural and created ecosystems.

Essentially, the future of the world is significantly dependent upon how its future leaders are nurtured in institutes for management education, and to influence the entire outlook of students, a blend of training in leadership skills and competencies with a strong value system will make a difference. Business education can truly act as the change agent, whose interventions can alter unacceptable behavioural patterns.

Review of Literature

The number of academicians and researchers showing interest in ethics education and responsible management training for future global leaders and decision-makers is increasing (Jennings, 2004). Particularly, the post-1990s, with numerous corporate scandals, financial crisis and corporate misconducts, gave a start to serious questions about the foundation of such behavioural patterns of leaders, many of whom were graduates of prestigious educational institutions. Since unethical behaviour by organisational leaders leads to serious repercussions for stakeholders, including society at large (Giacalone & Jurkiewicz, 2003), the orientation of business schools towards responsible management education has come under increasing scrutiny, as seen in the following review of literature.

Cornelius, Wallace, and Tassabehji (2007) discussed the need for established CSR models in business schools, having analysed and evaluated their content and commitment in offering ethics education. Pfeffer and Fong (2004), quoting US business schools, have thrown light upon the responsibility of business schools to convey social and environmental values to future management professionals. Gardiner and Lacy (2005) address the fact that educational programmes on business in society should incorporate CSR education into their curricula and establish their role in shaping society at large.

Bruce and Edgington (2008) determined the need to include ethics and CSR issues as a mandatory part of the management education curriculum, with case studies and exemplary models to augment students' knowledge. Baruch and Leeming (1996) and Neelankavil (1994) argue the needs of management students for including courses such as ethics that can further aid their decision-making processes as individuals. Gardiner and Lacy (2005) and Cornelius et al. (2007) support this by writing that ethics and CSR education must form a compulsory feature of the business curriculum, for students to comprehend the significance of responsible management as well as shaping their moral reasoning. Crane (2004) posits the relevance of training management professionals with suitable tools to challenge ethical situations more skilfully to shape the perception of individuals to see the connection between ethical decision-making and its ultimate implications for business and society.

However, the challenge is for appropriate implementation as well as reappraisal of the business ethics domain in light of corporate scandals, globalisation and so on (Crane & Matten, 2004). Phillips (2004) draws attention to this when he urges the need to integrate ethics education as an important element of the business curriculum and points out that there is no fixed mandate or prescriptive technique for doing so, but Rossouw (2002) has provided a threefold preview of teaching business ethics which includes cognitive, behavioual and managerial competence. Adler (2002) argues the failure of business schools to relieve the bottleneck in the teaching–learning process of ethics education and suggests an expansive methodology encompassing greater brainstorming over ethical concerns and the creation of suitable learning conditions to fit ethical contexts.

Matten and Moon (2004) researched social responsibility concerns in both teaching and research in Europe. They found that almost 47% of their respondent educational institutes offered discrete courses in the domain of CSR or related fields, while 38% included CSR issues only as a component of other courses. The authors also investigated administrative measures to ensure that CSR education has a prominent position in management curricula. They found that several institutional players have an eminent role in this decision, including business stakeholders as well as faculty.

Cowton and Cummins (2003) found that there has been a transformation in the business education system wherein many institutions have recognised the importance of ethics education by offering it either as a core subject or as a combination with the core offerings. However, they found that despite 58% of institutions in the UK offered ethics, only 18 out of 105 UK institutions offered it as a mandatory subject. The authors pointed that students have demonstrated their willingness for inclusion of ethics into their curriculum and that availability of qualified staff, along with case-based material, can act as facilitators.

Felton and Sims (2005) argue the importance for business schools to recognise the desired outcomes and timely delivery of ethics education. The authors insist that management professionals, especially students, must be well acquainted with the heightened need for ethics education including their personal responsibility to act on this teaching.

Akrivou and Bradbury-Huang (2015) argue that business schools need to transform their curricula to encourage dialogue and interpersonal discussions as learning methods by which the moral and cognitive abilities of students may be honed. They confirm that conventional teaching methodologies need to be revisited to meet sustainability issues and concerns.

Michaelson (2016) reports that a narrative pedagogical methodology for imparting ethics education can transform business students' attitudes, and that study of classical novels will reveal the requisite quality and content in the domain and result in a long-lasting impact.

A study by Rasche, Gilbert, and Schedel (2013) reveals that despite the increase in numbers of ethics-related courses across disciplines in business schools, the faculties often face impediments in fully integrating ethics education into their curricula—particularly as a core subject. The authors of the study suggest that business education curricula need structural transformation to fully incorporate these values.

A study by Power and Lundsten (2001), of students' perspectives on, and orientation towards, the inclusion of ethics education in their curriculum, revealed a positive response that supports the inclusion of ethics education in management education. Pless, Maak, and Stahl (2011) found it essential to incorporate service-learning programmes, with a view to develop responsible global leaders. This view was based on their study of "Project Ulysses" (Synergos, 2018). Under the programme, launched in 2001, the company sends small teams of PriceWaterhouseCooper partners into developing countries to apply their business expertise to complex social and economic challenges. The cross-cultural PwC teams work on a pro bono basis in field assignments for eight weeks with NGOs, community-based organisations and intergovernmental agencies in communities struggling with the effects of poverty, conflict and environmental degradation.

Hanson and Moore (2014) found that student's moral development is affected by the ethical approach adopted by the university. They identified five factors—institutional moral reinforcement, service activities, experiential challenges, moral amplifiers and evolving moral identities—that shape students' moral development process. The authors argue that students actively seek direction for their moral development and look to their institutions to provide it.

Mande (2012) indicates that student participation in business ethics courses strongly influences them to function and manage ethically and that teaching methodology and curriculum content reinforce it. Lau (2010) argues the significance of ethics education to augment both ethical awareness and moral reasoning by students. Not only does ethical education bring a holistic approach but also students' willingness to learn.

From the research it is evident that business schools and management institutions have a great responsibility—and to some extent accountability—for contribution to the moral development of professional managers, but the question that remains whether their courses are structured to develop appropriate value systems in students or to graduate morally unstable individuals, incapable of addressing legitimate leadership concerns as well as ethical dilemmas (Ghoshal, 2005).

This has created a strong need to rethink how managerial values taught in business schools can be embedded into a core programme to change student behaviour towards a genuine wish to act responsibly for their stakeholders. Over the past decade, many researchers have expressed concern that management education should shape students' managerial values through training in responsibility (Miller, 2009; Moon & Shen, 2010; Nicholson & DeMoss, 2009; Swanson & Fisher, 2008) and that business schools should incorporate such teachings with core curricula or as part of existing modules. However, more recent research explores alternative ways to enhance and build upon newer methodologies for developing future global leaders.

Experiential Learning

This section describes how implementation of Kolb's (1984) learning style theory can assist in creating a holistic approach to management education, whereby educators, curricula and students combine to establish connections between individual value systems and contemporary realities.

Kolb's (1984) Experiential Learning Theory

Drawing on the interpretations of John Dewey (Dewey, 1996), Kurt Lewin (Lewin & Gold, 1999) and Jean Piaget (Piaget & Inhelder, 2008), Kolb (1984) developed an experiential learning theory (ELT) to describe the crucial role of experience if learning is to result in behaviour change. The theory assumes that learning occurs from an amalgamation of experience and concepts, and the transition from observation to action; and focuses on learners' internal cognitive processes. It proposes a four-stage cycle of four learning styles:

- Concrete Experience
- Reflective Observation
- Abstract Conceptualisation
- Active Experimentation

Concrete experience and abstract conceptualisation describe how experiences are perceived and interpreted. Reflective observation and active experimentation describe how action is decided, based on interpretation of the relevant experience of the external environment. Learning (behaviour change) occurs when all four stages are in harmony and each indicates a logical approach to the next in the cycle.

Kolb identified four learning styles, depending on which stage in the cycle is preferred by the learner. He claimed that a cognitive preference for concrete experience and reflective observation signifies a "divergent" learning style characterised by diversity of perspectives, questioning and reasoning. Open-mindedness and knowledge-seeking enhance the owners' imagination and creativity and need for feedback. On the other hand, a preference for abstract conceptualisation and reflective observation denotes an "assimilating" style that encourages brainstorming over issues and focuses on learning through lectures and reading. This style takes a logical focus on theoretical understanding rather than practical work.

The third of Kolb's learning style is that of the "converger" whose cognitive strengths are abstract conceptualisation and active experimentation. Individuals who own this style tend to want to work independently to explore the practicality of issues. They opt for a technical rather than an interpersonal approach and seek to apply theories and ideas to practical purposes. The fourth style belongs to "accommodators", who learn most effectively from a combination of concrete experience and active experimentation. These individuals work more on intuition than logic, prefer practical learning and doing in contrast to thinking and lecturing.

Thus, holistically, Kolb's ELT framework suggests that teaching methods, to facilitate learning for all students, should incorporate experience, reflection, theory and action (Kolb & Kolb, 2005). On the assumption that learning outcomes are primarily influenced by students' preferred learning styles, ELT provides a useful foundation for creating management programmes with appropriate methodologies to involve all students in societal, environmental and ethical concerns.

Shaping Managerial Values through Experiential Learning Methods

Learning methods, including those for management education, focus on three domains: knowledge, attitudes and skills (Bloom, Engelhart, Furst, Hill, & Krathwohl, 1956), that is:

- *Cognitive*: encompassing mental skills (knowledge domain)
- *Affective*: encompassing emotional development (attitude domain)
- *Psychomotor*: encompassing physical functioning (skills domain)

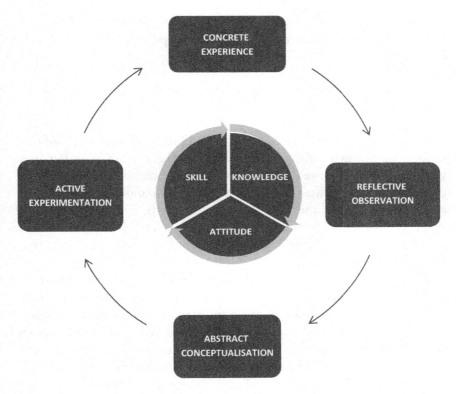

Fig. 15.1 Creation of a climate of understanding

Experiential learning in management education (Steiner & Watson, 2006) may help students to develop a responsible orientation to society. Applying Kolb's ELT framework, Fig. 15.1 illustrates how instructors might nurture a climate of understanding that is likely to minimise students' future inadequate, unresponsive and irresponsive behaviour towards society, environment and the stakeholders.

Value Creation Framework

Educational theory (Quiñones & Ehrenstein, 1997) suggests that behaviour change occurs in a phasic manner by which new knowledge results in new attitudes and values, which lead to the attainment of relevant skills. In Kolb's framework, concrete experience provides new knowledge:

> *(Learning)... is a process whereby knowledge is created through the transformation of experience.* (Kolb, 1984, p. 38)

Knowledge is augmented by reviewing and reassessing elements of that experience through reflective observation. "There is no meaning in a given situation until we relate our own experiences to it" (Jarvis, 1987, p. 164). Thus, individuals' experiences lead them to more intricate knowledge. On reflection, they derive concepts that generate attitudes that shape a course of action—and gain new skills as a result

Table 15.1 indicates how management education might apply an experiential learning strategy.

The importance of applying an experiential learning framework to management education is that students are encouraged in a phasic manner, over time, to seek their own solutions to ethical business issues. This model fits well with most management curricula that run between one or two years and is an appropriate means by which students can learn that business is not just about profitability but also responsibility and credibility. Additionally, feedback and reflection during the several stages of the model should provide all students with opportunities for self-introspection.

Important Considerations

Some considerations for applying Kolb's ELT to management education include the following:

1. Selection criteria for instructors/mentors of experiential learning are of paramount concern. They need the requisite motivational and leadership capabilities. They must be capable of mentoring, directing and providing suitable feedback to the students.

Table 15.1 Application of Kolb's experiential learning theory (ELT)

Strategy	Description	Process
Stage 1 Knowledge Creation	*(Concrete experience-reflective observation)* *Value creation*: students engage in activities that generate awareness and knowledge of ethical, societal and environmental aspects of business. *Implementation time*: beginning of the programme/semester/course	Preparation of compulsory modules that present business knowledge from multiple perspectives, not restricted to theoretical models. Knowledge is generated through student involvement. Students gain information from local, regional, national and international case studies—both negative and positive. Some cases are of business unresponsivenesss that has led to detrimental outcomes. Others are examples of corporate social responsibility. Case studies are shared in class; knowledge is shared and discussions encourarged to promote learning. Case studies are supported by lectures, tutorials and short movies.
Stage 2 Attitude Building	*(Reflective observation-abstract conceptualisation-active experimentation)* This is crucial for shaping students' attitudes and values that will affect their decisions as future managers.	Students report their responses to the cases, instructors promote discussion so students will gain insights from each other, and explain implications of the cases. Students and instructors build models to align business success with ethical reasoning and decision-making, to demonstrate the social and environmental roles of corporate managers, and how decisions in these roles will bring positive outcomes.

(continued)

Table 15.1 (continued)

Strategy	Description	Process
Stage 3 Skill Development	*(Active experimentation-concrete experience)* The objective at this stage is to reinforce the notion that business managers should take responsibility not only for profitability but also for the morality of their decisions.	Assessment of learning outcomes from Stage 2 by putting students in situations (similar to role plays) in which they have to assume certain responsibilities and make crucial decisions, both small and large. The instructors' role is to create a conditioning environment that supports the students in their decision-making.
Value Creation and Assessment	*(Holistic Feedback)*	All the three stages require feedback. Moderators/instructors help students to draw a road map of "why", 'how", "when" and "where" for their effective and responsible decision-making as future business leaders.

2. Experiential learning should be holistic—substantiated by cases, lectures, simulations, brainstorming, idea generation and so on—and should constitute a significant proportion of the curriculum. This can be done in two ways. First, the pedagogical approach must cover the ethical, moral, societal and environmental issues pertaining to responsible management education. Second, a full teaching module on responsible management should run throughout the whole management education programme, to enable the students to comprehend the significance of corporate responsibility from all dimensions of business management.
3. As students may come from diverse backgrounds and set-ups, acknowledgement of a variety of values is necessary. Instructors need to gather relevant background information to find out how each student views the conduct of the business world, to find a teaching style that most effectively instils new values, should this be needed.

Limitations and Future Research Directions

The present research is conceptual and builds upon an experiential learning framework that can be applied to management curricula. Empirical testing is needed to determine the influence that it may bear on framing the mindsets, orientations and value systems of the participants. This may initially be adapted at a smaller level and then applied holistically to determine its impact on basic functioning as well as decision-making of the participants.

Repeated exposure to students of an experiential learning methodology should give them practice in drawing inferences about the kind of behaviour they would need as business managers who can fit into natural as well as created ecosystems, and motivate others to achieve the same harmony.

References

Adler, P. S. (2002). Corporate scandals: It's time for reflection in business schools. *Academy of Management Executive, 16*(3), 148–150.

Akrivou, K., & Bradbury-Huang, H. (2015). Educating integrating catalysts: Transforming business schools toward ethics and sustainability. *Academy of Management Learning & Education, 14*(2), 222–240.

Baruch, Y., & Leeming, A. (1996). Programming the MBA Programme—The quest for curriculum. *Journal of Management Development, 15*(7), 27–36.

Bloom, B. S., Engelhart, M. D., Furst, E. J., Hill, W. H., & Krathwohl, D. R. (1956). *Taxonomy of educational objectives, handbook I: The cognitive domain.* New York: David McKay Co Inc.

Bruce, G., & Edgington, R. (2008). Ethics education in MBA programs: Effectiveness and effects. *International Journal of Management and Marketing Research, 1*(1), 49–69.

Cornelius, N., Wallace, J., & Tassabehji, R. (2007). An analysis of corporate social responsibility, corporate identity and ethics teaching in business schools. *Journal of Business Ethics, 76*(1), 117–135.

Cowton, C. J., & Cummins, J. (2003). Teaching business ethics in UK higher education: Progress and prospects. *Teaching Business Ethics, 7*(1), 37–54.

Crane, A., & Matten, D. (2004). Questioning the domain of business ethics curriculum. *Journal of Business Ethics, 54*(4), 357–369.

Crane, A., Matten, D., McWilliams, A., Moon, J., & Siegel, D. S. (2008). *The Oxford handbook of corporate social responsibility*. Oxford: Oxford University Press.

Crane, F. (2004). The teaching of business ethics: An imperative at business schools. *Journal of Education for Business, 79*(3), 149–151.

Dewey, J. (1996). *Theory of the moral life*. Ardent Media.

Falkenstein, M. (2014, December 18). *Ethics, sustainability and responsibility in business and management education*. Retrieved from European Association of International Education: http://www.eaie.org/blog/ethical-business-and-management-education/

Felton, E. L., & Sims, R. R. (2005). Teaching business ethics: Targeted outputs. *Journal of Business Ethics, 60*(4), 377–391.

Gardiner, L., & Lacy, P. (2005). Lead, respond, partner or ignore: The ole of business schools on corporate responsibility. *Corporate Governance: The International Journal of Business in Society, 5*(2), 174–185.

Ghoshal, S. (2005). Bad management theories are destroying good management practices. *Academy of Management Learning & Education, 4*, 75–91.

Giacalone, R. A., & Jurkiewicz, C. L. (2003). Right from wrong: The influence of spirituality on perceptions of unethical business activities. *Journal of Business Ethics, 46*(1), 85–97.

Hanson, W. R., & Moore, J. R. (2014). Business student moral influencers: Unseen opportunities for development? *Academy of Management Learning & Education, 13*(4), 525–546.

Jarvis, P. (1987). Meaningful and meaningless experience: Towards an analysis of learning from life. *Adult Education Quarterly, 37*(3), 164–172.

Jennings, M. M. (2004). Incorporating ethics and professionalism into accounting education and research: A discussion of the voids and advocacy for training in seminal works in business ethics. *Issues in Accounting Education, 19*(1), 7–26.

Kolb, A. Y., & Kolb, D. A. (2005). Learning styles and learning spaces: Enhancing experiential learning in higher education. *Academy of Management Learning and Education, 4*, 193–212.

Kolb, D. A. (1984). *Experiential learning: Experience as a source of learning and development* (Vol. 1). Englewood Cliffs, NJ: Prentice Hall.

Koljatic, M., & Silva, M. (2015). Do business schools influence students' awareness of social issues? Evidence from two of Chile's leading MBA programs. *Journal of Business Ethics, 131*(3), 595–604.

Lau, C. L. (2010). A step forward: Ethics education matters! *Journal of Business Ethics, 92*(4), 565–584.

Lewin, K., & Gold, M. (1999). *The complete social scientist: A Kurt Lewin reader*. American Psychological Association.

Mande, W. M. (2012). Business ethics course and readiness of MBA students to manage ethically. *African Journal of Business Ethics, 6*(2), 133–142.

Matten, D., & Moon, J. (2004). Corporate social responsibility education in Europe. *Journal of Business Ethics, 54*(4), 323–337.

Michaelson, C. (2016). A novel approach to business ethics education: Exploring how to live and work in the 21st century. *Academy of Management Learning & Education, 15*(3), 588–606.

Miller, R. E. (2009). The ethics narrative and the role of the business school in moral development. *Journal of Business Ethics, 90*(Suppl. 3), 287–293.

Moon, J., & Shen, X. (2010). CSR in China research: Salience, focus and nature. *Journal of Business Ethics, 94*(4), 613–629.

Neelankavil, J. P. (1994). Corporate America's quest for an ideal MBA. *Journal of Management Development, 13*(5), 38–52.

Nicholson, C. Y., & DeMoss, M. (2009). Teaching ethics and social responsibility: An evaluation of undergraduate business education at the discipline level. *Journal of Education for Business, 84*(4), 213–218.

Pfeffer, J., & Fong, C. T. (2004). The business school 'business': Some lessons from the US experience. *Journal of Management Studies, 41*(8), 1501–1520.

Phillips, S. M. (2004). *Ethics education in business schools*. Report of the Ethics Education Task Force to AACSB International's Board of Directors.

Piaget, J., & Inhelder, B. (2008). *The psychology of the child*. Basic Books.

Pless, N. M., Maak, T., & Stahl, G. K. (2011). Developing responsible global leaders through international service learning programs: The Ulysses experience. *Academy of Management Learning & Education, 10*(2), 237–260.

Power, S. J., & Lundsten, L. L. (2001). MBA student opinion about the teaching of business ethics: Preference for inclusion and perceived benefit. *Teaching Business Ethics, 5*(1), 59–70.

Quiñones, M. A., & Ehrenstein, A. (1997). *Training for a rapidly changing workplace: Applications of psychological research*. American Psychological Association.

Rasche, A., Gilbert, D. U., & Schedel, I. (2013). Cross-disciplinary ethics education in MBA programs: Rhetoric or reality? *Academy of Management Learning & Education, 12*(1), 71–85.

Rossouw, G. (2002). Three approaches to teaching business ethics. *Teaching Business Ethics, 6*(4), 411–433.

Segon, M., & Booth, C. (2009). Business ethics and CSR as part of MBA curricula: An analysis of student. *International Review of Business Research Papers, 5*(3), 72–81.

Steiner, S. D., & Watson, M. A. (2006). The service learning component in business education: The values linkage void. *Academy of Management Learning & Education, 5*(4), 422–434.

Swanson, D. L., & Fisher, D. G. (2008). If we don't know where we're going, any road will take us there. In D. L. Swanson & D. G. Fisher (Eds.), *Advancing business ethics education* (pp. 1–23). Charlotte, NC: Information Age Publishing.

Synergos. (2018). PricewaterhouseCoopers' Project Ulysses—Linking global leadership training to community development. Retrieved January 19, 2018, from www.synergos.org

16

Management Education for Women—and Men?

Elizabeth Christopher

Introduction

In 2011 for the first time in the United States, women made up slightly more than half the workforce (van der Gaag, 2014), but when a university lecturer (Bell, 2011) asked her class of MBA students whether they would prefer a male to a female manager, 90% of the women raised their hands and only a few men. When she asked how many would prefer a female manager, several men raised their hands, but only one or two women.

These students were not alone. The same year Hall (2011) commented that in a survey of 2000 British women in full- or part-time employment, 63% responded they would prefer a male over a female boss, and in 2009 London's *Daily Mail* (*Daily Mail* Reporter, 2009) stated that women prefer to work for male bosses because they're 'better managers and less prone to moods'.

Most women will insist they have the right to equality at work but often express doubt of their confidence to ask for a raise, a promotion, or

---

E. Christopher (✉)
Independent Scholar, Avoca Beach, NSW, Australia

equal pay (Sandberg, 2013). Statistics, though gradually improving, are certainly not in women's favour, even though research (The Globalist, 2014) confirms a direct correlation between the gender gap in economic opportunities and economic growth and that the smaller the nation's gender gap, the higher its economic productivity. Although women perform 66% of the world's work, they earn 10% of incomes and own 1% of property globally. Out of 197 countries, only 22 (11.2%) have women currently serving as heads of state. In business, in the United States, for example, *Fortune* magazine (Fortune editors, 2017) boasted that as of 2017, there were 32 female CEOs on their list, meaning that 6.4% of the United States' biggest companies (by revenue) were run by women, and this was the highest proportion of female CEOs in the 63-year history of the Fortune 500.

Explanations for these discrepancies vary but most blame women for causing their own woes. For example, Bell and Villarosa (2011) suggest that some women go into the workplace looking for more than a mentor; they want a father-figure and may become so dependent on their male managers that they lose the will to change their behaviour along more independent lines. Another suggestion is that employers become frustrated by a succession of women managers who choose to become pregnant and leave (Wells, 2016). A 2017 study at Curtin University (Shad, 2017) found that the pay gap between men's and women's salaries is even greater in female-dominated workplaces (17% in workplaces where women represent more than 80% of management, versus as low as 8% when management was largely dominated by men). The authors of the study concluded that male managers in heavily female-dominated organizations are more highly valued and more likely to be fast tracked to senior positions and receive greater pay.

Women, especially white women, are sometimes stereotyped as 'queen bees', super competitive, bright, and ambitious but not friendly and supportive—a corporate code for 'not a team player', 'can't be trusted', 'will stab you in the back'. Black women (Bell & Nkomo, 2003), confronting the twin evils of sexism and racism, are often labelled as 'angry black women'—a stereotype Michelle Obama struggled with during her husband's presidential campaign (Landsbaum, 2016). Asian women are stereotyped as passive—a synonym for 'having low emotional intelligence', being 'poor communicators', and 'not leadership material'.

Perhaps because of these negative stereotypes, bias against women is seldom cited as a reason for their lack of upward professional mobility, though undoubtedly it exists. Wan (2014) reported a field experiment by researchers from Wharton, Columbia, and NYU. Pretending to be students, they e-mailed over 6000 professors at top US universities, asking to meet them. The e-mails were identical except for the senders' invented names, all associated with gender or race, such as John Anderson, Meredith Roberts, LaToya Brown, Juanita Martinez, Deepak Patel, Sonali Desai, Chang Wong, and Mei Chen. The researchers found that faculty members were most likely to respond to e-mails from white males and were most likely to ignore messages from senders who seemed to be women, Asian, or Indian—indicating a high level of racial and gender bias.

Perceptions and Realties

Two studies show that perceptions differ between men and women, of the importance of gender diversity to the success of a company and that female managers are 'queen bees' is more stereotype than reality. The first (Grabitz, 2012) is based on a poll conducted by management consultancy McKinsey among 500 top managers in 53 German companies. The second is a report based on interviews with graduates of 26 leading business schools in the United States, Canada, Europe, and Asia.

The McKinsey results are surprising, given the strong political focus in Germany on the importance of gender diversity to company success, because the study reveals that only about a third of male managers believe it. Sixty per cent of women, on the other hand, believe that it is. Three out of four men also expressed the view that men and women in their company were treated the same, whereas only one in three (32%) of the women thought this. Thirty-six of male managers also believed that the company was doing enough for job equality, while only 16% of women did. These figures demonstrate that much still needs to be done to cancel differences of perception; although most companies actively support equality principles, it will take hard work and time to incorporate them into everyday business life at all levels of the hierarchy.

The second study was by Catalyst, a non-profit organization supporting women in business (Carter & Silva, 2010), and shows that, contrary to popular views, women in top positions do support subordinate women on their way up. According to this study, the Queen Bee syndrome is a myth, and highly qualified women do not try to trump other women. On the contrary, apparently there is a higher probability that women, rather than men, will support same-sex colleagues; between 2008 and 2010, the salaries of women who supported other women were over $25,000 higher than those who did not. One of the motivations for giving support, the researchers believed, was that a woman's own visibility increases within the company if she supports others—and the higher the visibility, the greater the chance of being offered a helping hand up the ladder oneself. Another hypothesis is that women who have been mentored by other women follow the example of their mentors.

Informal Management Education for Women

Mentoring

Mentoring is a form of management education, and the researchers interviewed a representative group of over 700 male and female MBAs who graduated between 1996 and 2007 from top business schools. They found several examples of this kind of 'education', from good advice to helping to open doors for mentees to gain more senior positions. The researchers also found there was a 66% chance that anyone with experience of a 'door opener' would themselves later open doors for someone else, whereas only 42% of those looking out for themselves were likely to do so. In all forms of on-the-spot 'management education' by senior for junior colleagues, women showed themselves to be more committed than men. Seventy-three per cent of women in the study chose to mentor other women, while 70% of men chose to mentor other men.

Spreading the Word

Perhaps partly because of being mentored at work, women managers have become more adept at educating others on the status of women at work by 'spreading the word' of their professional competence. For example, Ozga (1993) collated women managers' accounts of their various career paths and day-to-day experiences of their minority status. Besides presenting positive arguments for women as managers, their stories should help to combat stereotypical images of women somehow managing 'differently' from men (with the implication that men's ways are better) and that management is a 'masculine' activity. The contributors were women managers in the United Kingdom at all levels, and descriptions of some of their problems should help other women identify barriers and how to overcome them.

Besides publication, ways of enhancing the status of women include conferences, workshops, and summits. For example, plans for the Women in Project Management Leadership Summit in Sydney, Australia (Educationcareer, 2018), on 6 March 2018 include a series of lectures by women in prominent management positions on how women can succeed as project management professionals. Speakers will include representatives from the ANZ Bank, the Australian Department of Environment and Energy, the Australian National Maritime Museum, Bupa, the National Australia Bank, Port Authority of NSW, and Westpac. The manifesto of the organization is that, despite being still a male-dominated environment, there is a positive shift in gender balance in project management. More women are taking on challenges across a range of industries, to overcome all obstacles through improved skills and leadership.

'Women in business' Groups

Many of these groups have been set up in various industries, to empower women (Barron, 2017) and many women attend them, not only to be inspired by their counterparts but also to form business relationships and network with each other.

The tech industry, traditionally male-dominated, hosts events that allow women to network, to upskill themselves, and seek solidarity among other women working in similar environments (Alba, 2015). One disadvantage for women who seek a career in the tech industry is lack of good 'foot-in-the-door' contacts. Companies tend to hire from pools of candidates who already have connections, and in a predominantly male industry, men have an easier entrée than women.

Dr Telle Whitney, CEO of the Anita Borg Institute (ABI), believes women should be involved to a much greater extent in creating technology and that business leaders everywhere need to wake up to that idea (King, 2016). Backed by Google, the ABI is a non-profit institute and in 2015 inaugurated its 'ABI.Local' programme on the first day of its annual Grace Hopper Celebration—the world's largest event for women in computing. The idea is to help women technologists around the world connect with each other locally to form networks that will help build their ranks in the tech industry. Internationally, 'ABI.Local' groups organize technical talks, networking receptions, panels, hackathons, and workshops featuring local women technologists, and a beta (experimental) version serves as an online networking hub for women in tech (Anita B.org, 2018).

Formal Management Education for Women

In a global, diverse and interconnected world, there is recognition in corporations, in the public sector, in government, and in civil society of the need for more creative and ethical leadership as a key ingredient for political, social, and economic success. For example, Knapp (2007) backgrounds recent scandals from the corporate world, of political chicanery and within religious institutions, to offer the recommendations of leading scholars, Nobel prize-winners, and politicians who argue the need for a new kind of leadership committed to the greater good of society. Hence, leading organizations are embracing gender diversity and recognizing the value that women can create.

Unfortunately, most women lack strategies to develop their leadership potential. As a result, they experience difficulties with systems of corporate structures designed by men and traditionally male-dominated. Perhaps in consequence there is a growing trend to educate women for management through collaboration between universities and businesses. Examples include:

- Carleton's Advancing Women in Leadership Program (AWLP) (Carleton, 2018) in partnership with a corporate sponsor, Goldcorp Inc.;
- The Industry Task Force, established by the Australian Federal Government (Smith & Hutchinson, 1994) to commission a core MBA curriculum unit on Effective Organizations; Gender Issues in Management;
- MGSM'S Women in MBA programme. In 2014, Macquarie University Graduate School of Management (MGSM), Sydney, Australia (MGSM, 2014), announced the largest investment by any Australian business school in postgraduate business education for women: $4 million in a Women in MBA programme, with a matching $4 million from corporate and government partners;
- The Women's Director Development Programme (Kellogg Northwestern, 2018) on the university's Evanston Campus.

Counter-Arguments

What is missing so far is evidence that any of these or similar programmes are effective. For example, Simpson (1995) expressed doubts about their success for women managers. Among other factors she identifies men's formal and informal networks as a significant barrier, meaning, for example, that an MBA is less successful for women than for men in terms of career advancement and salary levels. Kitroeff and Rodkin (2015) reported that women with MBAs face a gender-based pay divide that starts as soon as they graduate and plagues them throughout their careers. Within a few years of graduation, women with MBAs earn lower salaries, manage fewer people, and are less pleased with their progress than men with the same degree.

The Missing Ingredient

These findings suggest that whether they are offered by industry or academia, the content of all programmes of management education needs to be re-examined. Not only should it try to mitigate the special career problems women face but it should address also the social assumptions held by both men and women of the 'natural' differences between the genders that inevitably disempower women from senior management. There is a missing ingredient in all 'women in management' programmes: the presence of men. What is needed is not education (through MBAs or by any other means) for women to become 'better' managers but education for both men and women, built into the curricula, to negate gender stereotypes and replace them with a deeper understanding and acknowledgement of the roles of men and women in society.

The Way Forward? Transformative Learning

In the early 1920s, the American sociologist John Mezirow (Kitchenham, 2008) wanted to help US women who were resuming their education or considering employment after an extended period out of university or the workforce. He conducted a qualitative study to identify factors that characteristically impeded or facilitated women's progress in the re-entry programmes. He concluded that their educational success was a transformative process, in that after initial disorientation, including feelings of inadequacy, they were reassured by recognizing that other students shared the same feelings. This led to exploration of options for new roles, relationships, and action plans for acquisition of knowledge and skills. Experimentation with new roles and relationships resulted in increased competence and self-confidence, leading to a new look on life.

Based on his other studies, including Kuhn's (1962) notion of paradigm shifts, Mezirow developed the concept of 'transformative learning' by which participants might move from a paradigm in which women are assumed (by themselves as well as men) to be poor managers in need of masculine support, to another which empowers women to recognize their unique strengths and capitalize on them. He perceived transformational learning to be a deep, constructive process that goes beyond simple knowledge acquisition to enable learners consciously to make new meanings for their lives. He believed it could bring about a fundamental change in their worldview: a shift from mindless or unquestioning assumptions to becoming critically aware of them and assessing their relevance. These fresh interpretations often lead to profound changes in thoughts, feelings, perspectives, beliefs, and behaviour, due to a radical shift of consciousness that permanently alters previous worldviews.

A 2011 study reported by Debebe (2011) used qualitative data to describe transformational learning in a women-only training (WOT) programme. The rationale for the programme was that an all-women student contingent, and instructors with gender-sensitive teaching and learning skills, would create an environment conducive to transformational learning. It would provide a safe environment in which to experiment with new behaviours and induce in participants a willingness to break with habitual patterns, in a paradigm shift.

In 2016, Knipfer, Shaughnessy, and Hentschel (2016) wrote how women in academia face unique challenges in advancing to professorship and presented a training curriculum tailored to the unique demands of women in, and aspiring to, leadership positions. The curriculum takes an evidence-based approach, with a transformative focus on self-directed leadership development, and aims to enhance women's motivation to lead, increase their knowledge about academic leadership, and empower them to seek the support they need to work towards appointment to professorship.

The Nature of Management

Curricula such as these suggest that all higher education programmes such as the MBA might be of more service to both women and men students, were instructors to recognize that most women—and almost all men—bring to their studies an unacknowledged set of assumptions about what management 'is' and why men are more naturally suited to it than women. These assumptions comprise a set of beliefs, socialized into both men and women since birth, that men are mentally tougher, more decisive, and therefore more competent managers, that a man's sense of self is defined through his ability to achieve results, but a woman's sense of self is defined through her feelings and the quality of her relationships, and that for organizational leadership, tasks are more important than relationships. Gray (2012) expressed these popular sentiments in the title of his book, *Men are from Mars, Women are from Venus*, and its runaway success testifies to the strength of these stereotypes. Ferree and Hess (2002) claim that for two millennia, 'impartial experts' have compiled a never-ending list of female characteristics, for example, that women's heads are too small, their wombs too big, their hormones too debilitating, and that they think with the wrong side of the brain.

Fine (2011) comments that though in the twenty-first century parents are trying to rear unisex children, they have failed and that though the glass ceiling is cracked, most women are content to stay beneath it because they feel unwilling or unable to fill senior management roles. She denounces the 'myth' of 'hardwired' differences between male and female brains and claims it only validates a *status quo* in which both men and women accept that women are too intuitive for logical thinking and men too focused for housework; that men's brains are not wired for empathy and women's brains are not made to understand technology. Instead, she offers a different explanation of the dissimilarities between men's and women's behaviour: that biological sex, hormones, culture, and evolution work together in ways that make gender a collaborative dynamic, not a fixed set of differences.

Fine is not alone in questioning assumptions about gender distinctions. McKie (2010) reports that a growing number of scientists are challenging the theory of neurosexism, an argument that there are fixed differences between female and male brains, and these explain women's inferiority or unsuitability for certain roles. By spotting sex-dependent activity in certain brain regions—such as those associated with empathizing, learning languages, or spatial processing—neurosexist supporters have voiced a litany of sex differences that include men being more logical and women better at languages or nurturing. Such opinions reflect a belief in 'biological determinism', the idea that biological differences reflect the natural order of things, to be meddled with at society's peril.

In fact, there are no major neurological differences between the sexes (Wheeling, 2015), but the implications of neurosexism are concerning. By telling parents that boys have poor chances of acquiring good verbal skills and girls have little prospect of developing leadership qualities, serious and unjustified obstacles are placed in the paths of children's education that remain throughout adulthood unless they are broken down.

Transformative Learning Methods

This suggestion returns to the idea that transformational or transformative learning methods should be critical ingredients in MBA and other higher education programmes. Transformative learning theory proposes that perception change is in three dimensions: psychological (changes in understanding of the self), convictional (revision of belief systems), and behavioural (changes in lifestyle) (Mark & Todd, 1983).

If these claims were to be applied to management education, the result might be that women would benefit from it by gaining more confidence in their abilities—by viewing them in a new perspective, and men might be readier to recognize those abilities and more willing to support women's careers towards senior management positions.

Transformative learning is a teaching method applied already in many institutions of higher education, particularly in the United States (Chadwick-Blossey & Robertson, 2004), but it is not a common element, much less a key element, in management education programmes. One advantage of including it is that it requires a social context (Grabove, 1997) of long-term work with others, including faculty members genuinely interested in teaching (p. 735) and this is relevant to MBA and other management programmes, characterized by group work, in which instructors often serve as mentors or provocateurs, to guide learners' self-direction.

Imel (1998) is another writer on the importance of establishing a community of learners and because instructors in postgraduate management education are instructing students who may already be practising professional managers, educators' roles should change from expert directors of learning to those of helpers as they shift power, responsibility, and decision-making onto the learners—a critical transition if transformative learning is to occur.

The purpose of management education is to enable deeper understanding and discovery of learners' abilities. Increased knowledge is only one vital outcome to be achieved; another is to create opportunities for learners to critically reflect and re-conceptualize, to find deeper understanding of management and leadership roles—not only of women in management but also to make affective as well as cognitive transformations for a broader range of personal development.

Teaching a Management Curriculum to Foster Transformational Learning

There are many ways of teaching adults, but Taylor (2000) listed some key actions to apply transformational learning in practice. He wrote that instructors should begin by creating a classroom environment conducive to learning by promoting a sense of safety, openness, and trust. 'Icebreaker' games or short exercises at the start of the semester can be useful tools to create group solidarity. For example, the game Matrix (see Appendix) has been found to be very successful in 'warming up' a group of strangers who are going to work together.

Taylor's second injunction is that instructors should take a learner-centred approach that will promote student autonomy, participation, and collaboration. A useful activity might be based on Edward de Bono's (2017) 'Six Thinking Hats' as an introduction to a problem-solving exercise—it offers different viewpoints to the same situation, thus forcing participants to move outside their habitual thinking style. Management education content is structured on very rational, positive lines, and rightly so, but the possibility remains of failure to look at a problem from emotional, intuitive, creative or negative perspectives, resulting in underestimating difficulties, no creative leaps, and no essential contingency plans.

Whether or not it is true that more women than men tend to take subjective views of situations and events and men tend to be more objective, 'Six Thinking Hats' is an experiential exercise that demonstrates the importance of using all approaches to problem-solving and that decisions and plans should mix ambition, skill in execution, social sensitivity, creativity, and good contingency planning. Role plays such as this can explore confrontations that occur when people with different thinking styles discuss the same problem. Each 'Thinking Hat' represents a different problem-solving style.

de Bono illustrates the problem-solving characteristics of each Hat within an imaginary scenario of a board of directors of a property company who are considering whether to construct a new office building as an investment; the economy is doing well, and vacant office space to rent is becoming harder to find.

In the role play, a student (or several, depending on class numbers) plays one (or more) of the directors, wearing a White Hat, and has been briefed to analyse the data, examine the trend in vacant office space, anticipate a severe shortage by the time the office block is completed, and report to the Board that current government projections show steady economic growth for at least the construction period. Another student (or more) in role as a second director is asked to don a Red Hat and to maintain to the Board that even though it will be cost-effective, businesses will be reluctant to rent office space in such an ugly building and employees will not be comfortable or happy working there. A third actor or actors is given a Black Hat and under its influence to argue to the Board that government projections may be wrong; the economy may be about to enter a 'cyclical downturn', in which case the office building may be empty for a long time, and if the building is not attractive, companies will choose to work somewhere more pleasant at the same rent.

The actor(s) with the Green Hat is asked to play a director who considers a change of design—to build prestige offices that people would want to rent in any economic climate; alternatively, the Board should invest the money in the short term to buy up property at a low cost when a recession comes. However, the actor/director wearing the Yellow Hat is to remain confident that if the economy holds up and their projections are correct, the company stands to make a great deal of money; if they are lucky, maybe they could sell the building before the next downturn or rent to tenants on long-term leases that will last through any recession. The Blue Hat is given to an actor playing the Chair of the Board, who facilitates arguments by the different thinking styles and negotiates conflicts to reach a decision.

In summary, Six Thinking Hats is a good technique for looking at the effects of a decision from many different points of view. It allows necessary emotion and scepticism for what otherwise would be purely rational decisions. It opens the opportunity for creativity within decision-making and helps, for example, persistently pessimistic people to be positive and creative. de Bono argues that plans developed using the 'Six Thinking Hats' technique will be sounder and more resilient than would otherwise be the case. It may also help to avoid public relations mistakes, and spot good reasons not to follow a course of action before being committed to it.

Summary and Conclusion

This chapter presents an account of social stereotypes of women, held by women as well as men, that categorize women as somehow unfit by their very nature for senior management status. It describes informal attempts to improve the status of women at work—but not necessarily to alter the stereotypes—and support from industries, private institutions, and collaborative efforts by universities and business sponsors to offer management degree programmes tailored to 'women's needs'. The argument of this chapter, however, is that the usual, accepted, content of these and most MBA and other management curricula needs to be questioned. It needs to be reconstructed to promote a paradigm shift in students' perceptions (both men and women). Previously held assumptions about the nature of women as a gender need to change to a new mental model in which there are no major neurological differences between the sexes and in which every man and woman contributes equally and uniquely, and in collaboration, to the world of work. Management requires logic and intuition, planning and people, thoughts and feelings, future orientation, and dealing with the present.

Transformative learning methods have been proposed as a means of promoting this paradigm shift, and their theoretical background explained. Such methods are applied already in many teaching institutions worldwide, but they are not common in management education programmes: yet their emphasis on teamwork, on self-directed learning, is highly relevant to MBA and other management programmes for mature adults who may already be practising professional managers.

Suggestions have been offered for the content of a transformative learning curriculum, including warm-up activities (an example has been provided) and learner-centred exercises such as role plays in which participants try on various 'thinking hats'.

In conclusion, the central argument of this chapter is that many efforts to support the cause of 'women as managers' do so by treating the symptoms of gender bias with no attempt to identify and eliminate the cause: which is that everybody, from time immemorial, is socialized from birth to view the differences between men and women in terms of power, with the consequent disempowerment of women. If they are to find their rightful place in society, side by side with men in every sphere and at every level, women as well as their male counterparts must make a paradigm shift from outdated stereotypes to a new set of assumptions about 'women's work', and transformative learning methods in management education programmes should help them to do so.

Appendix

Matrix

An active learning exercise designed by Elizabeth Christopher
 Echristopher051@gmail.com
 February 2018

Purposes

The purposes of this activity are that it shall be:

- A 'warm-up' at the start of a teaching or training session whose participants are from widely different backgrounds and mostly unknown to each other;

- An introduction to the subject matter of the session, especially useful for transformative learning, that is, when learners are shown how to use their previous interpretations of given situations, events, people, concepts and so on, to enable new or revised perceptions and possibilities for change in behaviour.

The activity involves students experientially in several ways:

- They move around the room, meeting many or all their fellow participants for the first time and engaging with them.
- They learn something about each other.
- Because the statements can be changed by the session presenters, the activity can be tailor-made to suit specific teaching and learning needs.
- Because the activity is both entertaining and personal, it creates a comfortable and mutually supportive learning environment for the teaching or training session to follow.

Procedure

Size of group: probably around 20 people, but the activity will work well with fewer (though probably no fewer than, say, 8) or as many as the space will permit.

Playing time: About half an hour, including discussion, and depending on numbers.

Classroom layout: Participants must be free to move around. If a sufficiently clear space is not available in the classroom, presenters might make use of an adjacent room or somewhere outside the building, for example, in a garden, then recall the players for a plenary session in the classroom when the game is over (15–20 minutes).

Resources:

- Each player will need a copy of the set of statements. These will not necessarily be the same statements as illustrated below. Presenters may want to change them, depending on the nature of the programme to follow the warm-up, but the format and number of statements should remain.

- Each set should be printed on paper as heavy as possible. Alternatively each set might be pasted onto a cardboard backing, cut to fit.
- Each player will need a pen or pencil.
- One, two, or three small prizes will be needed for the winner or winners.

Briefing and Administering the Game

1. Presenters explain that the object of the game is for players to gain insights to their own and others' culture-related values (depending on how these are understood in the context of the teaching or training session to follow).

   Players will move around to find somebody who can truthfully reply 'yes' to ONE of the statements on the sheet they will be given. When they do so, the respondent (including themselves) will sign their name across the relevant box and move on. No player may sign more than one box. The winner(s) will be players whose papers have the most signatures after a playing time of 20 minutes, and each will receive a small prize.

2. All players are then issued with a copy of the statements (as in the example below but the statements can be changed to fit the occasion) and the game begins. Presenters call a halt after 15–20 minutes. If any player submits a winning entry before that time, presenters keep it on hand and allow the game to continue. They do the same for any other winners before time is up.

Debriefing: When the game is over, presenters initiate a general discussion and respond to players' comments on their experience.

Matrix

Instructions

The object of the game is to gain insights to your own and others' culture-related values. Find somebody (you can include yourself) who can truthfully reply 'yes' to ONE of the above statements. Ask them to initial the relevant box and move on. No player may initial more than one box. The winner(s) will be the player(s) whose paper has the most signatures! You have 20 minutes to complete this exercise and the winner(s) will receive a small prize. Good hunting!

I believe that men are from Mars and women are from Venus	Democracy is the best form of government for all nations	I have friends from different backgrounds including race and sexual orientation	My parents are of different nationalities (from each other or from me)
I have been arrested by the police	I support gay marriages	I have experienced discrimination	I need to spend time on my own each day
I have taken part in a protest demonstration	I am a member of a social minority	If facts appear to refute a theory, I will question the facts before rejecting the theory	I hold strong views (for or against) Brexit
I am a people-person	Each country should have its own form of government	I have climbed a mountain and/or been deep sea diving	Same-sex marriages should be banned
Personal use of recreational drugs should be decriminalized	There is no such thing as 'society'; only individuals	Society is more important than individuals	Never mind the theory, give me the facts
I judge by first impressions	I listen first and speak last	My country is part of ASEAN	I speak first and listen afterwards
I believe my seniors are wiser than I	I live in the present	I look to the future	I believe in myself
I like to travel	Home is best	I am open to new ideas	I am cautious about change

References

Alba, D. (2015, October 14). Google backs groups that help women network in tech. *Wired*.

Anita B.org. (2018). Join a local. Retrieved January 14, 2018, from https://community.anitab.org/groups/

Barron, B. (2017, March 9). 9 powerful professional organizations for women in business. *GoDaddy.*

Bell, E. L. J. E. (2011, November 17). When mean girls go to work. *Huffington Post.*

Bell, E. L. J. E., & Nkomo, S. M. (2003). *Our separate ways: Black and white women and the struggle for professional identity.* Harvard Business Review Press.

Bell, E. L. J. E., & Villarosa, L. (2011). *Career GPS: Strategies for women navigating the new corporate landscape.* HarperCollins.

de Bono, E. (2017). *Six thinking hats.* Penguin UK

Carleton. (2018). Retrieved January 14, 2018, from https://carleton.ca/creww/registration-awlp/

Carter, N. M., & Silva, C. (2010, March). Women in management: Delusions of progress. *Harvard Business Review.*

Chadwick-Blossey, S. (Ed.), & Robertson, D. R. (Associate Ed.). (2004). *To improve the academy: Resources for faculty, instructional, and organizational development* (Vol. 23). Wiley.

Daily Mail Reporter. (2009, August 13). Women prefer to work for male bosses... because they're 'better managers and less prone to moods'. *Daily Mail UK.* Retrieved from http://www.dailymail.co.uk

Debebe, G. (2011). Creating a safe environment for women's leadership transformation. *Journal of Management Education, 35*(5). First published April 6, 2011.

Educationcareer. (2018). Retrieved January 14, 2018, from http://www.educationcareer.net.au/events/the-6th-women-in-project-management-leadership-summit-2018

Ferree, M., & Hess, B. (2002). *Controversy and coalition: The new feminist movement across four decades of change.* Routledge

Fine, C. (2011). *Delusions of gender: How our minds, society, and neurosexism create difference.* W. W. Norton.

Fortune editors. (2017, June 7). These are the women CEOs leading Fortune 500 companies. *Fortune.*

Grabitz, I. (2012, June 12). Managers consider women support sufficient. *Die Welt* (translated from German).

Grabove, V. (1997). The many facets of transformative learning theory and practice. In P. Cranton (Ed.), *New directions for adult and continuing education: No. 74. Transformative learning in action: Insights from practice* (pp. 89–95). San Francisco, CA: Jossey-Bass.

Gray, J. (2012). *Men are from Mars, women are from Venus: A practical guide for improving communication and getting what you want in your relationships.* HarperCollins.

Hall, A. L. (2011). *The IPINIONS journal: Commentaries on the major events of our times* (Vol. 6). iUniverse.

Imel, S. (1998). Transformative learning in adulthood. *ERIC Document Reproduction Service No. ED42326*. Washington, DC: Office of Educational Research and Improvement. Retrieved January 15, 2018, https://eric.ed.gov/?id=ED423426

Kellogg Northwestern. (2018). The journey to the boardroom. *Kellogg Northwestern.* Retrieved from http://www.kellogg.northwestern.edu/executive-education/individual-programs/executive-programs/women.aspx

King, L. (2016, September 29). Anita Borg Institute chief on how tech women will have 'a place at the table'. *Forbes.*

Kitchenham, A. (2008, April). The evolution of John Mezirow's transformative learning theory. *Journal of Transformative Education, 6*(2), 104–123.

Kitroeff, N., & Rodkin, J. (2015, October 21). The real payoff from an MBA is different for men and women. *Bloomberg Business Week.*

Knapp, J. (2007). *For the common good: The ethics of leadership in the 21st century.* Greenwood Publishing Group.

Knipfer, K., Shaughnessy, B., Hentschel, T. (2016). A curricular example for developing female leaders in academia. *Journal of Management Education, 41*(2), 272–302, 2017. First published October 13, 2016.

Kuhn, T. (1962). *The structure of scientific revolutions.* Chicago: University of Chicago Press.

Landsbaum, C. (2016, December 19). Michelle Obama said she was hurt by the 'angry black woman' label. *The Cut.* Retrieved from www.thecut.com

Mark, L. S., & Todd, J. T. (1983). The perception of growth in three dimensions. *Perception & Psychophysics, 33*(2), 193–196.

McKie, R. (2010, August 15). Male and female ability differences down to socialisation, not genetics. *Guardian.*

MGSM. (2014). MGSM announces major investment into women's management education. Retrieved November 21, 2014, from https://www.mq.edu.au/newsroom/2014/11/21/mgsm-announces-major-investment-into-womens-management-education/

Ozga, J. (1993). *Women in educational management.* Milton Keynes, UK: Open University Press.

Sandberg, S. (2013). *Lean in: Women, work, and the will to lead.* Random House.

Shad, S. (2017, March 15). When female managers are better at kicking you down than helping you up. *Telegraph*. Retrieved from www.dailytelegraph.com.au

Simpson, R. (1995). Is management education on the right track for women? *Women in Management Review, 10*(6), 3–8.

Smith, C., & Hutchinson, J. (1994). Addressing gender issues in management education: An Australian initiative. *Women in Management Review, 9*(7), 29–33.

Taylor, E. W. (2000). Analyzing research on transformative learning theory. In J. Mezirow & Associates (Eds.), *Learning as transformation: Critical perspectives on a theory in progress* (pp. 29–310). San Francisco, CA: Jossey-Bass.

The Globalist. (2014, March 8). 10 facts for International Women's Day. *The Globalist*.

van der Gaag, N. (2014, September 29). Women are better off today, but still far from being equal with men. *Guardian*.

Wan, H. (2014, May 20). The surprising racial bias against Asians. *CNN*.

Wells, R. (2016, March 8). 'What are you planning to do for a job?': How pregnancy changes careers. *News.com.au*.

Wheeling, K. (2015, November 30). The brains of men and women aren't really that different, study finds. *Science*. Retrieved from sciencemag.org

Index

A
Action learning, 176
Administrative environment, 180–181
Anticipatory stress, 98–99, 101, 103–110
Apartheid, 11–14, 17
Asian Institute of Management (AIM), 31–32

B
Business
 of business, 1–8
 education, 11–24, 27–39, 78, 83, 115, 117, 119, 120, 133, 141, 151, 203–205, 223
 ethics, 57, 59, 61, 88, 90, 140, 149–166, 204, 206
 programs, 28, 36, 37, 150
 schools, 6, 7, 11–21, 28, 30–33, 36–39, 52, 53, 116, 117, 119, 141–145, 151, 190, 201, 203–206, 219, 220, 223
 students, 36, 115, 120, 133, 141–143, 205
 traditional business goals, 118

C
Capitalism, 11, 14, 19, 21, 28, 35, 90
Capstone course, 189, 191–199
Chain of command, 52
Chain of events, 50
Classroom, 7, 22, 23, 66, 69, 119–121, 142, 151, 163, 164, 171–185, 199, 228, 232
 classroom as organization (CAO), 173–185
Co-creation, 156, 159–161, 163
Cognitive perspective, 150
 cognitive understanding, 143, 152
Collaboration, 73–79, 223, 228, 230

Conflict, 5, 39, 179, 183, 191, 194, 197–200, 206, 230
Conventional system, 65–71
Corporate
  behaviour, 88, 140
  governance, 5, 86, 140
  objectives, 118
  social responsibility, 2, 5, 19, 27, 28, 31, 32, 36, 38, 84, 86–90, 116, 117, 140–144, 150, 184, 202–204, 211
  values, 5, 8
Corporate social responsibility (CSR), 2, 5, 19, 27, 28, 31, 32, 36, 38, 84, 86–90, 116, 117, 140–144, 150, 184, 202–204, 211
Cultural responsibility, 27–39
Culture, 7, 28, 35, 36, 38, 39, 45, 47, 54, 58, 75, 76, 97, 151, 159, 161, 163, 226
  organizational cultures, 37, 54, 55, 58, 78
Curricula/curriculum, 7, 13, 14, 16, 18–23, 28, 32, 34, 45, 50, 55–57, 59, 60, 66, 69, 70, 84, 89, 115–120, 133, 141–145, 151, 171, 190, 199, 200, 202–207, 210, 212, 213, 224, 225, 228–231

D
Data
  collection, 121, 122, 194, 195
  organization, 150
de Bono, Edward, 228–230

Decision, 5, 50, 55, 56, 60, 70, 77, 79, 152, 153, 158, 166, 194, 204, 211, 212, 228, 230
  decision-making, 76–78, 194, 197, 198, 204, 211–213, 228, 230
Demand and supply, 83, 84, 87, 91
Devil's advocate, 1–8
Dispositional factors, 108
Dissonance, 22, 153, 171–174
Distance learning, 36–37
Distraction, 100
Diversity management, 23

E
Educational system, 29, 35, 67, 180, 181
Educators, 66, 83, 106, 151, 156, 172–175, 178–180, 185, 194, 195, 202, 207, 227
Emotional understanding, 153
Engagement, 16, 19, 22, 28, 69, 97–110, 158–160, 163, 178
Environment
  environmental pressures, 84, 87, 97–110
  environmental sustainability, 4, 117, 139, 144
Ethical challenges, 51, 55, 60
  ethical learning, 23, 201
Ethics
  education, 59, 61, 89, 149–164, 203–206
  training, 49–61
Experiential learning and teaching
  experiential learning activities (ELAs), 76, 150, 153–166
  experiential methods, 59, 143

F

Focus groups, 154–159, 161–163
Friedman, Milton, 1–5, 7, 85, 88
Future, 22, 28, 33, 66, 67, 77–79, 87, 107, 117, 120, 130, 141, 144, 159, 161, 179, 180, 183, 192, 198–203, 206, 209, 211–213, 230
 generations, 65, 66, 116, 140, 142

G

Gender, 7, 28, 57, 122, 125, 129, 131, 143, 218, 219, 221–224, 226, 230, 231
Global, 2, 4, 5, 19–21, 28, 31–33, 68, 74, 77, 121, 141, 142, 164, 166, 202, 205, 206, 222
 global economic systems, 144
Greed, 3, 50, 53, 60, 141

H

Higher education, 13–15, 21–23, 30, 31, 35, 57, 97, 115–134, 151, 153, 171, 173, 174, 178, 225, 227
Historical perspective, 43–47
 historical research, 27–39
Holistic approaches, 173, 202, 206, 207
Honeymoon hangover, 100, 103–105, 108–109
Human resource management (HRM), 23

I

India, 31, 43–47, 49, 50, 52, 54, 57, 58, 60, 61, 65–71, 155
Indian perspective, 49–61
Instructor, 77, 98, 99, 101, 104–110, 116, 119, 133, 191, 192, 194–200, 209–212, 225, 227, 228
Insurance, 87
Integration strategies, 115–134
Interaction, 78, 84, 108, 157, 175, 191, 192
International, 2, 4, 6, 7, 19, 20, 27, 28, 31, 32, 38, 49, 57–59, 68, 69, 90, 108, 121, 143, 149, 151, 154, 155, 157, 158, 160–162, 165–166, 211
 international accreditation agencies, 19
Irresponsible behaviour, 53, 84–86, 90, 201

J

Job motivation, 23
 job satisfaction, 23

K

Kolb's theory of learning styles, 150, 202, 207, 208

L

Language, 17–21, 30, 34, 45, 47, 157–158, 163, 226
Leaders, 2, 6, 18, 19, 28, 33, 37, 50, 67, 69, 75–79, 115–117, 119,

120, 133, 192, 201–203, 205, 206, 212, 222
Leadership, 18, 19, 23, 27, 33, 34, 58, 70, 73–79, 141, 190, 203, 206, 210, 219, 221, 222, 225–228
Learning
  critical action learning (CAL), 150, 153–157, 161–163
  experience, 18, 19, 23, 175, 195
  experiential learning, 18, 20, 24, 153, 162, 189–213
  to love, 101, 103, 104, 109–110

M

Management
  education, v–vii, 8, 13–17, 21–24, 28, 39, 43–47, 55–56, 60, 61, 68, 73–79, 84, 89–91, 97–110, 118, 133, 139–145, 171–173, 184, 201–213, 220–224, 227, 228, 230, 231
  education curricula, v, 55, 59, 84
  education for women, 217–231
  theories, 171–185
  theories in action, 171–185
  triple bottom-line management, 140
Managerial
  action, 50
  behaviour, 16, 55, 83–91
  procedures, 50
MBA
  classrooms, 142
  curriculum, 142, 223
  programs, 14–16, 27, 37, 85, 142, 223
Method, vii, 14, 17, 23, 61, 77, 120, 121, 124, 127–129, 134, 142, 143, 150, 152–154, 157, 173, 190, 191, 199, 202, 205, 208–209, 227–228, 230, 231
Methodology, 31, 56, 59, 126, 152, 174, 204–206, 208, 213
Moral, 3, 5–7, 23, 28, 30, 49, 52, 54, 85, 86, 88, 89, 141–143, 152, 153, 202, 204–206, 212
Motivation
  nepotism, 50
  student, 160, 163, 199
Movie
  Corporate, 53
  Rocket Singh: Salesman of the Year, 53–55

N

Nation building, 31, 33, 37, 49, 73–75
Network, 27, 33, 54, 69, 159, 184, 185, 197, 221–223

O

Occupation, 27–39
Organization, 1, 3, 5, 7, 20, 22, 28, 31, 33, 37, 50, 52, 54, 55, 57, 67, 69, 79, 84, 90, 171–185, 201, 202, 206, 218, 221–223
  in the classroom, 171–185
Organizational hierarchies, 55, 60

P

Paradigm shift, 179, 224, 225, 230, 231
Pedagogical approaches, 20–23, 143, 212

Pedagogy, 16, 18, 19, 21–23, 32, 69, 107, 152
Penance, 86, 87
People's Action Party (PAP), 74
Performance management, 23
Personal dissatisfaction, 56
Philippines, the, vi, 29, 34, 38, 39
Power of personal choice, 61
Prejudice, 50
Principles for responsible management education (PRME), vi, 14, 17–22, 24, 67–68, 141, 142, 144
Private sector, 2, 5, 16, 78
Private universities, 37, 38
Profit, 2, 4–6, 53, 88, 117
Psychotherapy, 59, 61
Public sector, 12, 15, 16, 51, 79, 84, 222
Puerto Rico, 29, 34–36, 38, 39

R

Resource constraints, 54, 56, 60
Responsible behaviour
  responsible for own actions, 2
  responsible management education (RME), vi, 16, 17, 139–145, 203, 212
  responsible managers, vi, 89, 139–145

S

Satisfaction, 53, 118, 159, 163, 183
Scenario, 22, 59, 61, 77, 115, 165–166, 229

Self
  self-discipline, 159, 162, 163
  self-organization, 174
Shareholders, 1–4, 6, 44, 141
Shareholder value, 3, 141
Singapore, vi, 73–79, 155
Six thinking hats, 228, 230
Social expectations
  social factors, 108
  social interaction, 23
  social pressures, 53
  social sciences, 7, 13
  social stereotypes, 230
Sociological imagination, 23
South Africa, vi, 11–24
Spiritual emptiness, 56
Stakeholders, 4, 20, 22, 24, 65, 69, 70, 78, 84–87, 89, 90, 140–144, 150, 152, 164, 173, 180, 184, 185, 192–193, 199, 203, 204, 206, 209
Stereotypes, 218, 219, 224, 226, 230, 231
Striving to win, 53
Structure, 19, 54, 154, 176, 182, 223
Students
  engagement, 160
  satisfaction, 23
Sustainability
  concern, 115–134
  goals, 118
  integration strategies, 115–134
Sustainable development, 66, 68, 69, 116, 184
  sustainable management, 21, 140, 142

T

Teaching
  business ethics, 151–153, 163, 204
  tools, 115–134
Teams, 22, 160, 172, 175, 176, 179–181, 190, 197, 205, 218
Teamwork, 159, 160, 163, 173, 231
Theory, 3, 7, 56, 59, 61, 85, 90, 119, 143, 150, 153, 161, 163, 202, 207–209, 226, 227
  theory and practice, 32, 153, 156, 163, 173, 190, 192, 193
Training for empire, 43–47
Trajectories, 5, 49, 74, 100–101, 103–110
Transformation of business education, vi, 11–24
Transformative, 23, 110, 224–231
Transition, 12, 108, 207, 228
Tri-sector leadership, 73–79

U

Unemployment, 12, 15, 23, 32
Unethical actions, 61
Universities
  university education, 12, 163
  University of Puerto Rico, 36, 37
US occupation, 29–35

W

Whistleblowers, 51, 52
Women, 1, 6, 38, 125, 131, 234
  in management, 224, 228